Mastering the NEW PMI Certified Associate in Project Management (CAPM®) Exam (2023 Version)

Project Management Institute (PMI) is the leading professional association for project management, and the authority for a growing global community of millions of project professionals and individuals who use project management skills. PMI offers several certifications in the areas of project management, risk management, and other related areas.

The Certified Associate in Project Management (CAPM®) is one credential offered by the Project Management Institute (PMI). The CAPM® is an entry-level certification for project practitioners. Designed for those with less project experience, the CAPM® is intended to demonstrate candidates' understanding of the fundamental knowledge, terminology, and processes of effective project management.

This certification is a popular prerequisite that helps employers find the professionals most suited to fulfill specific roles in their organizations. Most study guides just explain the contents of the exam without providing tools to maximize learning. The authors, as authorized training partners with PMI, translate the new 2023 examination content outline into what exam takers need to do and know in preparation for the exam. It also provides them with exercises and prep questions as a quick and easy check to ensure they are on the right path in preparation for the exam, thus maximizing their chance of passing.

T0300472

Mastering the NEW PMI Certified Associate in Project Management (CAPM®) Exam (2023 Version)

By

Klaus Nielsen, Giampaolo Marucci, and Jean-Luc Favrot

A PRODUCTIVITY PRESS BOOK

First published 2024
by Routledge
605 Third Avenue, New York, NY 10158

and by Routledge
4 Park Square, Milton Park, Abingdon, Oxon, OX14 4RN

Routledge is an imprint of the Taylor & Francis Group, an informa business

ISBN: 9781032611785 (hbk)
ISBN: 9781032611778 (pbk)
ISBN: 9781003462378 (ebk)

DOI: 10.4324/9781003462378

Typeset in Garamond
by Deanta Global Publishing Services, Chennai, India

Contents

Preface

Thank you for buying this handbook. **It is our sincere goal with this book that you will be successful at the CAPM® exam, the way leading to the exam has been in your own pace and worth the effort**. We all completed our first PMI certifications more than ten years ago, the PMP exam for all of us. Some passed while others failed it the first time.

Since then, we have worked as a practitioner, at the university, doing consulting and training participants for years and learning the tips and tricks in passing the various PMI certification exams. During these years we have been buying and using a wide range of exam prep books, some better than others but all in all great needed resources for supplementary materials for training courses or when preparing for an exam without taking a course.

As you may know, the CAPM® exam has changed to reflect the needs of the market, which is great as the NEW PMI CAPM® certification will become even more relevant for many practitioners. It is a much better and more relevant product than before. When we run our training courses, we tell our participants to sign up for a PMI membership to get access to the PMI materials and at the same time receive a discount on the exam. Now this advice is more important. As mentioned, we have used various prep books for various certifications; however, most, if not all of them, include the same content already found in the literature, and in this case the *PMBOK® Guide* 7th Edition (2021), *The PMI Guide to Business Analysis* (2017), *Business Analysis for Practitioners: A Practice Guide* (2015), **the** *Agile Practice Guide* (2017), and the *Process Groups: A Practice Guide* (2022) and less emphasis on the *Project Management Answer Book* 2nd Edition and *Effective Project Management: Traditional, Agile, Extreme, Hybrid* 8th Edition.

This handbook is somewhat different. We have aligned it with the PMBOK® and PMI standards, highlighted what we felt was essential, added content to link these different sources, and provided tips. In addition, we have explained what you can read to expand your knowledge on various topics, and where you can find it in these PMI publications. Thanks to all these, this book alone covers everything you need to pass the CAPM® exam and reading all the PMI literature is optional (though, of course, highly recommended for your project management practice beyond the certification matter).

Besides reading, the high value of a prep book is plenty of sample test questions, which all have been written by leading AI technologies, so no extra resources are needed besides this handbook and, if possible, the PMI standards.

Best of luck preparing and passing the CAPM® exam.

We hope you will enjoy being part of this journey and would love to hear from you on LinkedIn.

Best regards, Klaus, Giampaolo, and Jean-Luc

Acknowledgment

Acknowledgment is the recognition or favorable notice of an act or achievement, which is numerous in creating this work. Our only plea is forgiveness from all not mentioned but not by any means forgotten. First, we would like to extend our thanks and gratitude to the people who have helped in making this work a reality. By doing so, we want to acknowledge the work done by the Project Management Institute and the amazing team at Routledge. Thank you Kris Mednansky for believing in us and for making this dream possible and a wonderful experience. This work would not have been made possible without the support of all the people who have taken part in one way or the other in ensuring the content and quality of this work. Thank you, we owe you our greatest gratitude. Also, thank you, Project Management Institute, for bringing us together during the work on the core team for the *PMBOK® Guide* 7th Edition and all the opportunities to cross paths that have fostered this international bond of friendship and knowledge sharing.

Many people have contributed over the years to the evolution of this book as many of the ideas in this book have been formed, sharpened, and aired at meetings, training sessions, debates, and lectures around the world.

Our deepest appreciation also goes to our families and loved ones who have been more supportive than any author or man could ever dream of.

Any errors, of course, are ours.

Klaus, Giampaolo, and Jean-Luc

About the authors

Klaus Nielsen holds a master's degree in E-commerce from the IT University of Copenhagen, which was supplemented with a year in Cambridge (UK) and later dual MBAs (HRM and Technology) from the US. He has worked in Project, Programs, and Portfolio Management, plan-based and agile for more than 25 years, and still does and has been embracing many of the international best practices for years. Author of the books *I am Agile* (2013); *Mastering the Business Case* (2015), *Achieve PMI-PBA® Exam Success* (2015), *Agile Certified Practitioner Exam* (2016), *Agile Portfolio Management* (2019), *Mastering the PMI Risk (PMI-RMP) Management Professional Exam (2021),* and writer of several industry articles published worldwide. He has been Subject Matter Expert (SME) on various publications from PMI and Axelos, and recently PMI core team member on the *PMBOK® Guide* 7th Edition. Mr Nielsen is the co-founder of Global Business Development (gbd.dk), a PMI Authorized Training Partner (ATP) and Scrum/DevOps training company where he trains, e.g., PMI Authorized Training Partner Instructor and consults to businesses ranging from small start-ups to top 500 companies worldwide. Since 2012, Klaus has taught part-time at the IT University of Copenhagen as a faculty lecturer and is a frequent speaker at events, conferences, and tradeshows. Klaus holds a wide range of certifications from various Scrum organizations, PMI, Axelos, DevOps Institute, LeSS, Disciplined Agile, Kanban, SAFe, and others in which many of them he has trained for years.

Giampaolo Marucci is Project Management Professional currently employed at IBM. He works remotely for worldwide distributed and remote teams committed to modernizing clients' legacy software applications to DevOps processes and technologies, Hybrid Cloud architecture, Mainframe modernization, and Artificial Intelligence. He's Authorized Training Partner

– Instructor – from Project Management Institute (PMI ATP Instructor). He teaches Project Management Professional (PMP), Disciplined Agile Senior Scrum Master(DASSM), and Discipline Agile Scrum Master (DASM) certification exam preparation. Past decades of experience in managing, facilitating, supporting projects for software implementation and maintenance, design of software architectures, business analysis, presales engineering, and consulting in the field of public administration and large private companies, working for enterprises in the field of software products and services. Previous years of experience in analysis, programming, and software engineering for Avionics. He holds a master's degree in computer science from the University of L'Aquila. He is one of the co-writers of the book *PMBOK® Guide* 7th Edition edited by Project Management Institute. He's certified in the most important Project Management, Agile, and software engineering certifications, including PMI-PMP, PMI-ACP, and PMI-DASSM.

Jean-Luc Favrot is an executive consultant, coach, trainer, and international speaker. His 30 years of professional experience have allowed him to hold responsibilities in large public and private organizations and to create companies specializing in project management, agility, and innovation in Europe and Oceania. He holds an engineering degree in information technology from Polytech' Montpellier (France), and some major professional certifications, including PMP, PMI-ACP, DASSM, PRINCE2, PRINCE2 Agile, SAFe SPC, CSM, PSM, CSPO, PSPO, Management 3.0, and UXC (UX, Design Thinking, Lean UX). As a trainer, he is an authorized PMI ATP Instructor (PMP, DASM, DASSM). He is also teaching project management and digital strategy at the University of French Polynesia. He is one of the co-authors of the *PMBOK® Guide* 7th Edition (development team) and has been a contributor to the strategy and content of the PMI Standards+ digital platform. He is also Vice President of the PMI France chapter, in charge of the Horizons branch (overseas and international). He currently lives in Tahiti, French Polynesia, but spends time on several continents each year, giving conferences and training courses both locally and remotely. For any service request, he can easily be contacted on his LinkedIn profile: https://www.linkedin.com/in/jlfavrot/.

Chapter 1

Introduction

This book is organized around three core values, these being value, support, and retrieval. Value is the goal alignment and learners' perspective of the CAPM® exam. Preparing and going for the CAPM® exam is an emotional change which is fully supported by this content of the fundamental value found in Chapters 1–3.

The support value focuses on the mastery of the core content for the exam, which is supported by the additional background content. This is done with meaningful tasks and relevant information found in Chapters 4–7, supported by the content found in Appendixes A–F.

The retrieval value emphasizes on reflection and practice tests, which we call passing the exam, which is supported by sample test exams found in Chapters 8 and 9. The full list of content is decomposed in Table 1.1.

Table 1.1 How this book is organized

	Chapter #	Fundamental knowledge	Mastering the content	Passing the exam	Background content
Chapter title	*1–9*	*Value*	*Support*	*Retrieval*	*Support*
Introduction	1				
Pretest knowledge assessment	2	X			
Certification overview	3	X			
Project management fundamentals and core concepts	4		X		
					(Continued)

DOI: 10.4324/9781003462378-1

Table 1.1 (Continued)   How this book is organized

Chapter title	Chapter #	Fund-amental knowledge	Mastering the content	Passing the exam	Back-ground content
	1–9	Value	Support	Retrieval	Support
Predictive, plan-based methodologies	5		X		
Agile frameworks/methodologies	6		X		
Business analysis frameworks	7		X		
Full practice exam one	8			X	
Full practice exam two	9			X	
Appendix A: Introduction to the *PMBOK® Guide* 7th Edition	A				X
Appendix B : Introduction to the Agile Practice Guide	B				X
Appendix C: Introduction to the Business Analysis for Practitioners: A Practice Guide	C				X
Appendix D: Introduction to the PMI Guide to Business Analysis	D				X
Appendix E: Code of Ethics and Professional Conduct	E		X		
Appendix F: PMI Project Management Ready	F				X
Glossary of terms and acronyms				X	
Reference list					X

1.1 Step-by-step study plan – 30 steps for Success

The following is a step-by-step study plan for passing a CAPM® certification:
1. Go to the PMI global website and download
   a. PMI Certified Associate in Project Management (CAPM®) Examination Content Outline 2023 Exam Update
   b. PMI Certifications Handbook
   c. PMI Continuing Certification Requirements (CCR) Handbook
2. Optional – Go to the PMI global website, log-in (requires membership), and download
   a. *PMBOK® Guide* 7th Edition

   b. *The PMI Guide to Business Analysis* (2017)
   c. *Business Analysis for Practitioners: A Practice Guide* (2015)
   d. *Agile Practice Guide* (2017)
   e. *Process Group: A Practice Guide* (2022)
3. Optional – Visit PMIstandards+™
4. Optional – Get hold of
   a. *The Project Management Answer Book* (Second Edition)
   b. *Effective Project Management: Traditional, Agile, Extreme, Hybrid* (8th Edition)
5. Flip through the literature (Step 2) and look at the organization, figures, tables, and such to get familiar with the flow and style
6. Flip through this book, look at the organization, figures, tables, and such to get familiar with the flow and style
7. Read Chapters 1 and 3
8. Start out with the pretest knowledge assessment test – Chapter 2
9. The pretest will help identify your strengths and weakness
10. Signup for the CAPM® exam, so you have a goal/target
11. Read Chapter 4
12. Chapter 4 – Complete all sample test questions
13. Read Chapter 5
14. Chapter 5 –Complete all sample test questions
15. Read Chapter 6
16. Chapter 6 –Complete all sample test questions
17. Read Chapter 7
18. Chapter 7 –Complete all sample test questions
19. Rinse and repeat (step nos. 11–18) for Chapters 4–7
20. Read Appendixes A–E
21. Take one of the full sample practice exams – Chapter 8
22. Ensure that you understand why the answers are right or wrong
23. Repeat selected sections if you have wrong answers on that topic
24. Take one of the full sample practice exams – Chapter 9
25. Ensure that you understand why the answers are right or wrong
26. Repeat selected sections if you have wrong answers on that topic
27. Feel free to join a CAPM® prep course; however, you won't be needing it!
28. If you want flashcards for remembering, find an app or go online
29. Pass the CAPM® exam with success in the first attempt
30. Go out and apply the content, if possible, do this before the actual exam

Chapter 2

Pretest knowledge assessment

The pretest includes 15 CAPM® sample exam questions. Use no more than 20 minutes to complete this pretest. The questions are found in Section 2.1, while Section 2.2 has the answers and explanations. Table 2.1 includes the alignment of the sample exam questions to the four domains found in the PMI Examination Content Outline 2023 Exam Update.

The pretest is a good way to test your knowledge before getting really started and to see which strengths and weaknesses you want to exploit. You may also save the pretest knowledge assessment for later use. The pretest has sample exam questions from each of the four domains. Table 2.1 contains the full pretest knowledge assessment breakdown.

Table 2.1 CAPM® pretest knowledge assessment breakdown

Domain	Split	Questions	Test questions
Project Management Fundamentals and Core Concepts	36%	4	1–4
Predictive, Plan-Based Methodologies	17%	3	5–7
Agile Frameworks/Methodologies	20%	4	8–11
Business Analysis Frameworks	27%	4	12–15
Summary	100%	15	1–15

DOI: 10.4324/9781003462378-2

2.1 Pretest knowledge assessment questions

Question 1

In the context of project management, what best describes the term "constraints"?

  A. The ethical guidelines that all PMI members and certification holders must adhere to
  B. Factors that will limit the project team's options, including available resources and conditions that will affect the execution of the project
  C. A set of projects managed in a coordinated manner to achieve strategic objectives
  D. The act of checking the accuracy and completeness of the project scope

Question 2

Which of the following refers to a methodological approach that is frequently employed in projects where requirements and solutions evolve through the collaborative effort of cross-functional teams?

  A. Predictive approach
  B. Program management
  C. Adaptive approach
  D. PMI code of ethics and professional conduct

Question 3

Which of the following risk response strategies involves taking actions to reduce the probability or impact of a risk to an acceptable level?

  A. Avoidance
  B. Mitigation
  C. Transference
  D. Acceptance

Question 4

Which of the following can be utilized to understand the opinions, beliefs, and feelings of stakeholders regarding a particular topic or challenge?

  A. Pareto analysis
  B. Work breakdown structure (WBS)
  C. Focus group
  D. Gantt chart

Question 5

What is the purpose of a change control board (CCB) in managing change requests in a predictive project?

A. To approve or reject change requests based on their impact and feasibility
B. To immediately accommodate all change requests without evaluation
C. To bypass the change control process and make decisions independently
D. To review change requests informally and make ad hoc decisions

Question 6

Project closure is an important process group in project management that involves formally ending the project and ensuring all project requirements have been met. Which of the following activities is typically performed during the project closure process?

A. Resource allocation and assignment
B. Scope identification and verification
C. Risk identification and mitigation
D. Lessons learned documentation and review

Question 7

Which of the following statements best describes the purpose of conducting a Root Cause Analysis?

A. To assign blame and identify individuals responsible for project issues
B. To develop a comprehensive risk management plan for the project
C. To identify and address the fundamental reasons behind project issues
D. To analyze the impact of changes on project performance

Question 8

Which Agile framework/methodology places a strong emphasis on customer collaboration and early and frequent delivery of working software?

A. Lean Startup
B. Predictive
C. Scrum
D. Six Sigma

Question 9
What is the purpose of the Team Charter in Agile projects?

A. To define the scope and objectives of the project
B. To outline the roles and responsibilities of the project team
C. To establish the project's high-level timeline and milestones
D. To establish the team's values, norms, and working agreements

Question 10
What is the purpose of a Cumulative Flow Diagram (CFD) in Agile project management?

A. To track the progress of user stories throughout an iteration
B. To visualize the flow of work and identify bottlenecks in the process
C. To measure the team's velocity and predict the project's completion date
D. To monitor the team's adherence to the defined WIP limits

Question 11
What is the purpose of the Sprint Retrospective in Scrum?

A. To review and demonstrate the completed work to stakeholders
B. To plan the work to be done during the Sprint and create a Sprint Backlog
C. To reflect on the team's performance and identify areas for improvement
D. To conduct daily meetings to discuss progress and address any issues

Question 12
Acceptance criteria are used to:

A. Define the project scope
B. Evaluate the performance of a team
C. Determine when a deliverable is complete
D. Identify project risks

Question 13
What is the purpose of a business case?

A. To document detailed requirements
B. To analyze the cost and benefits of a proposed solution

C. To define the project timeline and milestones
D. To identify and analyze project risks

Question 14

What is the purpose of a wireframe in the context of business analysis?

A. To create a visual representation of user interfaces
B. To define the business requirements for a project
C. To identify and prioritize project risks
D. To analyze the performance of a system

Question 15

What is the purpose of a stakeholder analysis?

A. To identify and prioritize project risks
B. To create a visual representation of user interfaces
C. To define the business requirements for a project
D. To identify and understand stakeholders and their interests

2.2 Pretest knowledge assessment answers

Answer to Question 1: The correct answer is B.
Constraints in project management refer to factors that limit the project team's options. They can include a variety of aspects, such as time, budget, resources, and scope. Recognizing and managing these constraints is essential for successful project completion.

Answer to Question 2: The correct answer is C.
Adaptive approach, often associated with Agile methodologies, refers to a methodological stance wherein requirements and solutions evolve through the collaborative effort of cross-functional teams. Unlike the predictive approach, which is linear and fixed, the adaptive approach is iterative and allows for flexibility in response to changing requirements or conditions.

Answer to Question 3: The correct answer is B.
Risk Mitigation is a risk response strategy that involves taking actions to reduce the probability or impact of a risk to an acceptable level. It focuses

on proactively addressing the risk to minimize its potential negative effects on the project. Avoidance (answer A) aims to eliminate the risk by taking actions to prevent it from occurring. Transference (answer C) involves shifting the risk to a third party, such as through insurance or outsourcing. Acceptance (answer D) is about acknowledging the risk and deciding not to take any specific actions to address it.

Answer to Question 4: The correct answer is C.
A focus group is a qualitative research technique where a diverse group of people is gathered to participate in a guided discussion about a particular topic or challenge. The main goal is to understand the opinions, beliefs, and feelings of stakeholders on that topic.

Answer to Question 5: The correct answer is A.
The purpose of a change control board (CCB) in managing change requests in a predictive project is to approve or reject change requests based on their impact and feasibility. The CCB is typically composed of key stakeholders, including project sponsors, subject matter experts, and other relevant parties. The CCB evaluates change requests by considering their potential impact on the project's scope, schedule, budget, resources, and other constraints. They assess feasibility, risks, and benefits associated with each change request and make informed decisions on whether to approve, reject, or modify the requested changes.

Answer to Question 6: The correct answer is D.
During the project closure process, one of the typical activities is documenting and reviewing lessons learned from the project. Lessons learned refer to insights and knowledge gained throughout the project's lifecycle, including successes, challenges, and areas for improvement. The lessons learned documentation captures this valuable information and serves as a reference for future projects. On the other hand, Resource allocation and assignment (answer A) typically occur during the project planning and execution process group, rather than during project closure; Scope identification and verification (answer B) is typically performed during the project initiation and planning process group to define and confirm project scope, not during project closure; Risk identification and mitigation (answer C) activities are commonly performed during the project planning and execution process group to proactively manage project risks, not during project closure.

Answer to Question 7: The correct answer is C.

The purpose of conducting a Root Cause Analysis is to identify and address the underlying or fundamental reasons behind project issues or problems. It aims to go beyond addressing the symptoms of the issues and seeks to identify the core causes that led to the problem's occurrence. By addressing the root causes, project managers can implement effective corrective actions to prevent similar issues from recurring in the future.

Answer to Question 8: The correct answer is C.

Scrum is an Agile framework that places a strong emphasis on customer collaboration and early and frequent delivery of working software. Scrum is designed to enable iterative and incremental development, where the product is developed in small increments called "Sprints". Throughout the development process, the Scrum team collaborates closely with the customer or product owner to gather feedback, refine requirements, and deliver working software at the end of each Sprint. Lean Startup (answer A), on the other hand, is a methodology for developing new products and services with a focus on rapid experimentation and validated learning. Predictive (answer B) is not an Agile framework/methodology. Six Sigma (answer D) is a methodology primarily focused on process improvement and reducing defects.

Answer to Question 9: The correct answer is D.

The purpose of the Team Charter in Agile projects is to establish the team's values, norms, and working agreements. The Team Charter is a collaborative document created by the team members themselves to define how they will work together, communicate, and make decisions. The Team Charter outlines the team's shared values, guiding principles, and behavioral norms. It helps establish a common understanding of how team members should interact, collaborate, and address conflicts. The Team Charter also includes agreements on aspects such as meeting protocols, decision-making processes, and communication channels.

Answer to Question 10: The correct answer is B.

A Cumulative Flow Diagram (CFD) is a valuable tool in Agile project management for visualizing the flow of work across different stages over time. It provides a graphical representation of how work items move through the workflow, allowing the team to identify bottlenecks, understand the work distribution, and analyze the overall efficiency of the process. This visual representation enables the team to make data-driven decisions to improve the workflow, optimize resource allocation, and identify opportunities for process improvements.

Answer to Question 11: The correct answer is C.
The purpose of the Sprint Retrospective in Scrum is to provide an opportunity for the Scrum Team to reflect on their performance during the Sprint and identify areas for improvement. It is a time for the team to review their processes, interactions, and outcomes in order to enhance their effectiveness and efficiency. During the Sprint Retrospective, the Scrum Team discusses what went well, what didn't go so well, and what actions can be taken to improve their performance in future Sprints. This includes examining the team's collaboration, communication, and adherence to Scrum practices. The goal is to foster a culture of continuous improvement and to make iterative changes that enhance the team's productivity and delivery.

Answer to Question 12: The correct answer is C.
Determine when a deliverable is complete. Acceptance criteria are specific conditions or criteria that must be met in order for a deliverable to be considered complete and accepted by the stakeholders. They are typically defined in collaboration with the stakeholders and serve as a basis for evaluating whether the deliverable meets the required standards and expectations.

Answer to Question 13: The correct answer is B.
A business case is a document that is prepared to justify the initiation or continuation of a project or initiative. It provides an analysis of the expected costs and benefits of the proposed solution, allowing stakeholders to make informed decisions about whether the project is worth pursuing. The business case typically includes information on financial analysis, return on investment, risks, and other relevant factors.

Answer to Question 14: The correct answer is A.
To create a visual representation of user interfaces. A wireframe is a basic visual representation or blueprint of a user interface or a webpage. It outlines the layout, structure, and placement of various elements on the interface, such as buttons, forms, menus, and content sections. Wireframes are used to visually communicate and understand the design and functionality of a system or application before moving on to detailed design and development.

Answer to Question 15: The correct answer is D.

To identify and understand stakeholders and their interests. Stakeholder analysis is a technique used in business analysis to identify, analyze, and understand the stakeholders involved in a project or initiative. It helps in identifying the individuals, groups, or organizations that have an interest in or may be impacted by the project. Stakeholder analysis helps in understanding their needs, expectations, influence, and potential impact on the project, enabling effective communication, engagement, and management of stakeholders throughout the project lifecycle.

Chapter 3

CAPM® certification overview

3.1 Certification

This chapter will answer the who, what, when, where, why, and how questions, regarding the PMI Certified Associate in Project Management (CAPM®) certification. Some of these answers are derived from the core of Project Management Institute (PMI) publications, which are freely available at the PMI global website.

- PMI Certified Associate in Project Management (CAPM®) Examination Content Outline 2023 Exam Update
- PMI Certifications Handbook
- PMI Continuing Certification Requirements (CCR) Handbook

3.2 Why become certified?

The new CAPM® certification exam (2023) better supports you in your career journey. By going beyond A Guide to the Project Management Body of Knowledge (*PMBOK® Guide*), the new exam integrates content across project management including business analysis and agile principles. It's an asset that will distinguish you in the job market and enhance your credibility and effectiveness working on – or with – project teams.

DOI: 10.4324/9781003462378-3

3.2.1 Why you should become certified now?

We meet a lot of participants completing a CAPM® course and end up not taking the CAPM® exam as they do not think they have the time, do not see the need for the certification or are afraid of not passing the exam. These are all valid reasons for not taking the exam however we would encourage you to go the extra mile and take the CAPM® exam. Completing a decent CAPM® course means most of the content has been covered to some degree, so you are already halfway done. You got your diplomas of attendance; however, the real PMI certificate holds much higher value and recognition. The certification is a great way of documenting your extensive knowledge of project management. If you take a CAPM® course including the opportunity to take an exam, but you do not do it then people may notice and think about the certifications as the extra icing on the cake. You need to know when the certification will come in handy. We do our share of consulting and before a job we need to send our resume including certification to the firm, but we never really know what the customer is looking for, so we rather have or include too much than too little. Klaus used to remove his BA degree in Chinese from his IT resume, but for some reason it is always a great talking point and a way to differentiate. The CAPM® certification can also help build credibility (demonstrate knowledge) that you know something about project management (demonstrate dedication to the profession). For us certifications can result in whether we land the job (advance career potential) or not. For some consulting jobs various certifications are mandatory requirements for consideration for the job. In other organizations, we experience increased competences like certifications as a route to obtain a higher salary. In some industries the project management maturity is high; however, we often see that hybrid project management knowledge is more scarce, so now you can bring something extra to the table. Completing a certification requires an extra effort and by doing so you learn a lot, and the key takeaway is a common vocabulary and toolbox that may come in handy in many projects ahead. Taking one step back, we see project management as one of the key amplifiers for more successful projects (participants may apply the knowledge and skills to a higher degree than non-certified professionals), which is important due to the amount and sheer size of projects changing organizations these days.

Being a certified project management practitioner includes a wide range of benefits as an individual; however, it also results in an increased value for the organization that employs certified project management practitioners.

Some of the key benefits for the organizations are highlighted in the following list:

■ Certifications acknowledge the competency of individuals who perform a role, which is increasingly recognized as a vital component of any successful project.
■ Certifications can demonstrate the ability to transfer knowledge across the organization.
■ Global knowledge of the working methods and standards of the organizations.
■ Certifications can be identified as individuals with an advanced level of knowledge and qualifications.
■ Certifications demonstrate a commitment to quality and may increase the effectiveness of working for the organization.
■ Certifications obtain a relatively high value as the effort to pass the certification or the costs associated are worth the gains from passing.
■ Certifications produce reliable, quality results with increased efficiency and consistency.
■ The value of certifications makes risk management indispensable for business results.

3.3 Who certifies?

Project Management Institute is the world's leading not-for-profit professional membership association for the project, program and portfolio management profession. Founded in 1969, PMI delivers value for more than 2.9 million professionals working in nearly every country in the world through global advocacy, collaboration, education and research.

The Project Management Institute (PMI)® delivers a wide range of certifications listed below, with corresponding frameworks including processes, tools, and techniques to deliver for project as well as program and portfolio management:

■ Certified Associate in Project Management (CAPM®)
■ Project Management Professional (PMP)®
■ PMI Risk Management Professional (PMI-RMP)®

- PMI Agile Certified Professional (PMI-ACP)®
- PMI Scheduling Professional (PMI-SP)®
- PMI Professional in Business Analysis (PMI-PBA)®
- Program Management Professional (PgMP)®
- Portfolio Management Professional (PfMP)®
- PMI Project Management Ready
- Agile Certifications (Disciplined Agile)
- Micro-Credentials (AHPP, CDP, and such)

To fully comprehend the value of a project management certification, it is imperative to examine some questions that many justifiably ask. Before taking on a certification, one should inspect which organization, company, or group that has created the certification. This enables you to know the quality that certification might hold based on the development, material, and use of the certification. The value of certification tends to increase with the amount of people being certified and the demand from the industry.

Currently, more than 60,000 professionals hold CAPM® certifications and numbers are increasing as we speak. This book is closely aligned with the certification from PMI®. PMI® is an entity that is well known and trusted by organizations and their hiring managers for their credential standards. PMI® is a global organization and recognized in more than 217 countries. There are more than 684,000 active individual members globally. This creates a solid foundation for a highly valued certification.

Other companies develop different kinds of certifications in the form of products. In most cases, look for international standards and similar recognitions when judging value. Of course, if the company is a recognized world leader, companies like Microsoft®, Amazon®, and SAP®, the product speaks for itself.

The second and third questions you should ask are *"What is in it?"* and *"What is in it for me?"* A certification is a diploma showing competencies within an area, so it is highly important that the content is of some value. This means that the content of the certification ought to cover best practices from an industry and academic viewpoint.

The more comprehensive and advanced the content is the better. For example, the CAPM® certification is created by specialist project management practitioners and aligned with the ISO standard and the various

PMI publications. As a result, the CAPM® certification is well positioned to become, if it is not already, the new standard of knowledge for project management professionals, with the PMP® certification for more senior project managers. This is enhanced by the recent changes of including predictive, hybrid, and agile approaches, which makes it even more valuable. When content is the best practice, it can provide the certification with an increased value if thought leaders have been part of the development. This is a mark of quality and may create a wide recognition in the industry.

3.4 Who becomes certified?

To some degree, who becomes certified follows the same patterns as adopting project management practices. Predictive project management has had a focus from the larger enterprises running major infrastructure and construction projects. This is a big firm you all know and trade with. This group may be new to agile and hybrid project management as they have firm best practices, data, and years of experience. The software industry knows agile but may be less mature when it comes to predictive project management. They can learn a lot from the predictive content or hybrid as going predictive would be too much for them. Hybrid project management is new to many practitioners as many come from working predictive or agile. Another group comprises all the risk managers or business analysts who need more knowledge of project management to deliver success no matter how the project is specified, planned, and delivered.

3.5 How to become certified

The CAPM® credential process is conducted online at the PMI® website http://www.pmi.org and is highlighted by the timeline of the CAPM® credential process. The PMI Certifications Handbook explains this process, rules and regulations, costs, and all in detail. The process includes steps toward approval for taking the exam and processes for renewable of the certification after obtained as it has a 3-year duration (Table 3.1).

Table 3.1   CAPM® credential process

Processes	Step	Explanation
Application process	1	Application submission (fill in the application)
	2	Application completeness review (5 working days)
	3	Application payment process
	4	Audit process (audit or not)
	5	Multiple-choice examination eligibility (application approved – now you can schedule the exam)
Certification renewable process	1	Certification cycle (certification renewable process)
	2	Certification maintenance
	3	Certification renewal
	4	Certification suspension
	4	Credential expiation

On Your journey toward the CAPM® certification, you need to fulfill the CAPM® eligibility requirements. These are found in Table 3.2 and contain educational background and project management education.

Table 3.2   CAPM® eligibility requirements

	Eligibility requirements
Educational background	Secondary degree, such as a high school diploma, general educational development (GED), or global equivalent
Project management education	23 hours of education (refer to the CAPM® Exam Content Outline document to know which are the methods by which you can get the 23 hours of education)

> **TIPS: Most CAPM® training courses (ATPs) may provide you with the 23 hours of education. Alternative use non-PMI project management education.**

You can satisfy the project management education requirements by demonstrating the successful completion of courses, workshops, and training sessions offered by one or more of the following types of education providers:

A. PMI Authorized Training Partners (ATPs)
B. Employer/company-sponsored programs
C. Training companies or consultants (e.g., training schools)
D. Distance-learning companies, including an end-of-course assessment
E. University/college academic and continuing education programs

3.5.1 Documenting the CAPM® eligibility requirements

The documentation of your educational degree and project management education is fast and you just need to describe it and if you are pulled out for audit, then share a copy of the transcripts.

3.5.2 Continuing certification requirements (CCRs)

Passing the CAPM® eligibility requirements and the actual exam is one thing; another aspect is the continuing certification requirements program. The continuing certification requirements program is an online application created to enhance ongoing professional development and foster learning opportunities and to sustain the global recognition and value of certification. This is managed by collecting 15 professional development units (PDUs) within a 3-year cycle. The continuing certification requirements program includes education activities as well as "giving back to the profession" activities. Tables 3.3 and 3.4 describe the activities and the maximum professional development units obtained within each category.

Table 3.3   Education

Education	Maximum PDU within the category in a 3-year cycle
Ways of working	2
Power Skills	2
Business Acumen	2
Remaining PDUs in any area	3
Maximum is 9 PDUs within a 3-year cycle.	

Table 3.4 Giving back to the profession

Giving back to the profession	Maximum PDU within the category in a 3-year cycle
Creating knowledge	No maximum
Volunteering	No maximum
Work as a professional in project management	2 PDUs
Maximum is 6 PDUs within a 3-year cycle	

Please keep in mind that some categories may have a maximum of 2 professional development units. In general, 1 PDU is awarded for 1 hour.

Question: Which of the following activities are accepted by PMI® as professional development units (PDUs) and what amount of PDU can one expect from these activities?

1. Attending a conference on IT practices?
2. A work meeting on project management?
3. Reading a book on project management practices?
4. Taking part in a free online Webinar?
5. E-learning from IEEE® or ACM®?
6. Traditional project management 2-day course?
7. Doing extra work on a project as a project manager?

Answer: All activities in this exercise are provided as professional development units. However, the amount of professional development units may vary depending on the actual activity. This also stresses the fact that professional development units are not necessarily costly or bound to the PMI®. It's all about ongoing professional development and fostering learning opportunities, to sustain the global recognition and value of the certification.

> **TIPS: Don't worry about PDUs before passing the exam.
> Some renew their certifications others don't.**

3.6 When to become certified

During the CAPM® credential process, when the audit process is completed and you have the multiple-choice examination eligibility, which enables you to schedule your examination online at Pearson Vue, a globally recognized test center near you or schedule an online exam. At this stage you can select an appointment that fits with your training and readiness. Most practitioners schedule a time as early as possible to have a fixed point for completing the certification; however, the actual exam is often a few months out in time. When you are approved for the exam, you have one year to take the actual exam, so plenty of time. The one-year exam approval does count toward the active certification, so in case of Examination Content Outline changes the exam approval does not allow you to take the old exam but the active one. In most cases, any changes to the exams are informed six months in advance, which provides you with time to schedule the exam in case of changes.

3.7 Where to become certified

Pearson Vue, a globally recognized test center, is located throughout the world and found in most capitals and major cities which should limit your travelling, or you can take the exam at home or office online. The online exam has more options for time and dates than the test center where spots may be limited due to limitations or demands.

3.8 What is the CAPM® certification

The PMI Certified Associate in Project Management (CAPM®) certification from the Project Management Institute (PMI®) is described and publicly available in the PMI Certified Associate in Project Management (CAPM®) Examination Content Outline 2023 Exam Update (ECO). Before going into details of the actual certification, let us look at the development of the certification as it demonstrates the magnitude of the content and the approach, which varies from normal practice. The typical PMI® certification, e.g., the Project Management Professional (PMP®), is based upon a large framework, best practice, and academic in its approach to project management. Academics and large US companies like NASA®, GE®, and the Department of Defense® have provided input to the framework.

The CAPM® certification was formulated by a PMI supplier, the Alpine Testing Solution, and to some degree based upon the work by project management specialists throughout the years and exiting PMI publications. However, the CAPM® exam is so much more.

Exam candidates should be aware that the PMI Certified Associate in Project Management (CAPM®) examination is not written according to any single text or singularly supported by any specific reference. PMI does not endorse specific review course resources, references, or other materials for certification preparation. The references listed below are not inclusive of all resources that may be utilized and should not be interpreted as a guaranteed means of passing the exam. As the CAPM® exam is a competency-based credential that assesses the integrated set of knowledge, skills, and abilities as gained from both practical and learned experiences, it should also be noted that the references identified herewith are but one element of a broader set of educational resources and texts that might possibly be utilized for exam study and preparation. All exam questions were written and extensively reviewed by subject matter experts and can be found in a minimum of two references of the following: *PMBOK® Guide* 7th Edition, The *PMI Guide to Business Analysis* (2017), *Business Analysis for Practitioners: A Practice Guide* (2015), *Agile Practice Guide* (2017), *Process Groups: A Practice Guide* (2022), *The Project Management Answer Book* (Second Edition), and *Effective Project Management: Traditional, Agile, Extreme, Hybrid* (8th Edition).

This book has identified what you need to read in the PMI publications which are mostly available as part of your PMI membership which also gives you a discount on the exam. The additional books found in the CAPM® examination reference list are ALL included in this work, which should save you a significant amount of time/money and at the same time present the ideas and concepts in a cohesive manner, which will increase your understanding significantly and the likelihood of passing the CAPM® certification exam with flying colors.

> **TIPS: Consider reading the Agile Practice Guide from the Project Management Institute and Agile Alliance**

3.9 What is a certification blueprint

The CAPM® certification exam consists of 150 questions, in which 135 questions are scored, while 15 questions are unscored. The questions are randomly mixed. The time allocated for the exam is 3 hours and 30 minutes for the online tutorial before the actual exam and for the survey after completing the exam. The details are accumulated in Table 3.5 – This gives you a little more than a minute pr. questions, which may sound like very little; however, after completing this book it will become enough time for you.

Table 3.5 Exam questions and time allocated

No. of scored questions	No. of unscored questions	No. of questions in total	Time allocated
150	15	135	3 hours

The number of correct answers for passing the CAPM® certification exam is not published by the PMI; however, the passing score for all PMI exams is determined by sound psychometric analysis most test takers estimate the needed score in the range of 63–67%. Anyhow, it is not verified by the PMI® or any other sources.

The content of the CAPM® certification is described in the PMI Certified Associate in Project Management 2023 Exam Update (CAPM®) Examination Content Outline (ECO). The CAPM® exam consists of four domains. Each domain includes 3–6 tasks that have enablers. Enablers are illustrative examples of the work associated with the task. Please note that enablers are not meant to be an exhaustive list but rather offer a few examples to help demonstrate what the task encompasses. Chapters 4–7 explain the domains, tasks, and enablers in detail. The overall blueprint is found in Table 3.6, which divides the questions within the domains.

Table 3.6 CAPM® Exam blueprint

Domain	Tasks in the domain	Percentage of items on test
Project Management Fundamentals and Core Concepts	5	36
Predictive, Plan-Based Methodologies	3	17
Agile Frameworks/Methodologies	5	20
Business Analysis Frameworks	6	27

The pretest knowledge assessment chapter 2 and the two full sample exams chapters 8 and 9 follow the CAPM® exam blueprint.

3.10 CAPM® examination information

The CAPM® examination comprises 150 multiple-choice questions; however, the types of multiple-choice questions vary. You may encounter the following types of multiple-choice questions:

- **Multiple-choice questions**: Small text and four options. This is still the most common and predominant type of question.
- **Point and click (hot spot/hot area)**: For these types of items, the candidate will be given a small scenario and an image. Based on what the scenario says, the candidate will be tasked with clicking on a specific area on the image to get the question correct.
- **Drag-and-drop-style**: The candidate drags and drops various items into the right sequence or columns; see enhanced matching.
- **Enhanced matching**: For most enhanced matching (drag and drop) items, candidates will see two columns of boxes where various items need to be placed correctly to get the question correct.
- **Animation video**: For animation video items, candidates will watch the animation video. Candidates can watch the animation multiple times and use the video controls to start, stop, rewind, etc. Based on the scenario, the candidate will be presented with a multiple-choice question to answer.
- **Comic strip**: For comic strip items, the candidate will read the comic strip. The candidate may need to scroll down to see the complete comic strip. Based on the scenario in the comic strip, the candidate will be presented with a multiple-choice question to answer.

Chapter 4

Project management fundamentals and core concepts

4.1 Introduction

Before delving into the fundamentals of project management, we believe it's important to understand the spirit, history, and architecture of the main PMI books on which the new CAPM® exam is based. This is a first overview, which will be the subject of numerous developments and details throughout this book.

The *PMBOK® Guide* actually contains two books: one on the project management standard (ANSI standard) and the other to guide the reader through the application of the project management body of knowledge.

Before its 7th edition, the *PMBOK® Guide* considered the project management standard to be based on processes or more precisely on groups of processes: initiating, planning, executing, monitoring and controlling, and closing. This standard was supplemented by a guide proposing ten knowledge areas (scope management, schedule management, cost management, etc.).

The result of this logic was that project management could be described through 49 project management processes, which were as many crossings between process groups and knowledge areas, for example, plan schedule management, manage communications, control quality, etc.

The exact number of project management processes changed with each successive version of the PMBOK®, but the spirit remained the same. Around the world, hundreds of thousands of project managers, even millions probably, have learned and progressed in their project management practice through this structure.

Historically, project management was based on predictive development approaches (see Chapter 5 – Predictive, Plan-Based Methodologies), and versions of the *PMBOK® Guide* were necessarily inspired by them. However, in the field, project managers adapted pragmatically to their environment and adopted practices that were more or less adaptive, and sometimes even hybrid, before these notions were truly identified as such. For example, the rolling wave planning technique has some similarities with an adaptive approach, and it has been used for decades (you will find further information about this in Chapter 5). Since the 49 project management processes had a possible tailoring dimension, project management experts were able to determine how to reconcile this with the *PMBOK® Guide*, up to version 5.

With the development of agile approaches (see Chapter 6 – Agile Framework/Methodologies) on an ever-increasing scale, *PMBOK® Guide* 6th Edition in 2017 marked the first more explicit consideration of these. Agile-related additions were included in the *PMBOK® Guide*, and another book accompanied it: the Agile Practice Guide (see Appendix B – Introduction to the Agile Practice Guide). In a way, the *PMBOK® Guide* 6th Edition consisted in grafting agility onto a body of knowledge that hadn't been designed for it in the first place.

With the 7th edition of the *PMBOK® Guide* (see Appendix A – Introduction to the *PMBOK® Guide* 7th Edition), PMI has taken an extremely important turn. The book has been completely rewritten so that, by design, it can be applied to whatever the development approach is: predictive, adaptive, or hybrid. This was widely seen as a wonderful and salutary revolution, but it also worried some of the professionals who had based their knowledge and practices on the 49 project management processes, since these seemed to have disappeared from the *PMBOK® Guide*. But they didn't.

The biggest change was to move the project management standard from a process-based to a principle-based logic. You'll find plenty of articles and videos to illustrate this change on the internet, which is also covered in the introduction to the *PMBOK® Guide* 7th Edition.

Since we, the three authors of this book, were also part of the team of 12 experts on the *PMBOK® Guide* 7th Edition development team, we can clarify what our intentions were. Since projects are run by people for people, we felt it was essential to help project participants adopt a mindset and behavior that were as supportive as possible of the production of outcomes and value. This is why the standard associated with the 7th edition is based on 12 principles. These are listed in Table 4.1 because they are essential to the understanding of project management and will facilitate the reading of this study guide and, in particular, this chapter on fundamentals. Details can be found in Appendix A – Introduction to the *PMBOK® Guide* 7th Edition.

Table 4.1 Project management principles

Principle title	Principle label
Stewardship	Be a diligent, respectful, and caring steward
Team	Create a collaborative project team environment
Stakeholders	Effectively engage with stakeholders
Value	Focus on value
Systems thinking	Recognize, evaluate, and respond to system interactions
Leadership	Demonstrate leadership behaviors
Tailoring	Tailor based on context
Quality	Build quality into processes and deliverables
Complexity	Navigate complexity
Risk	Optimize risk responses
Adaptability and resiliency	Embrace adaptability and resiliency
Change	Enable change to achieve the envisioned future state

All that you need to lead projects can be found in the *PMBOK® Guide* 7th Edition but that doesn't mean we'd suddenly wish to throw away the processes and the decades of knowledge accumulated and applied in the field. It's just that process groups are no longer centrally positioned as standards but are now identified as one of the models you can apply if you think it's most effective in the context of your project.

Until recently, only the five process groups were mentioned in the *PMBOK® Guide* 7th Edition, and the 49 project management processes were described in detail in the PMIstandards+ platform (free access for PMI members). In 2022, PMI published the new book *Process Groups: A Practice Guide*, so that they are also available in book form.

In conclusion, today, as shown in Figure 4.1, PMI offers a balanced project management knowledge "ecosystem": *PMBOK® Guide* 7th Edition is at the heart and can be applied to whatever the development approach is (predictive, adaptive, and hybrid). It is complemented by the agile practice guide, dedicated (mainly) to agile approaches, and the process groups practice guide, dedicated (mainly) to predictive approaches. The PMIstandards+ digital content platform includes and extends the content of these books (and other PMI standards and guides). It provides articles, case studies, templates, interactive graphics, and videos.

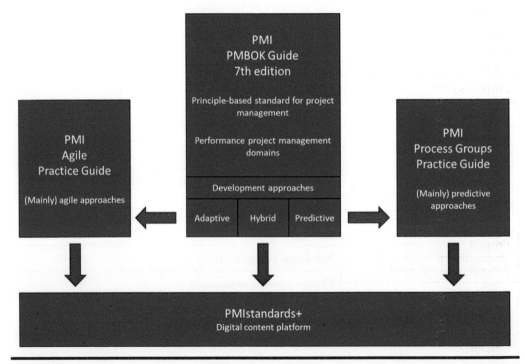

Figure 4.1   *PMBOK® Guide* 7th Edition "ecosystem".

Other practice guides exist (risks, schedule, etc.). You'll find them on the PMI website, but we won't go into them here, as they are not part of the reference list on which the new CAPM® certification is based. In addition to these three books, *The PMI Guide to Business Analysis* and the *Business Analysis for Practitioners,* which are also on this list, will be covered in Chapter 7.

4.2 Terms

Table 4.2 Glossary of some important terms used in this chapter

Terms	Source	Page
Adaptive approach	*PMBOK® Guide* 7th Edition	235
Assumption	*PMBOK® Guide* 7th Edition	235
Constraint	*PMBOK® Guide* 7th Edition	237
Deliverable	*PMBOK® Guide* 7th Edition	239
Hybrid approach	*PMBOK® Guide* 7th Edition	241
Issue	*PMBOK® Guide* 7th Edition	241
Life cycle	*PMBOK® Guide* 7th Edition	242
Milestone	*PMBOK® Guide* 7th Edition	243
Operations	Process Groups: A Practice page 4	4
Outcome	*PMBOK® Guide* 7th Edition	244
Portfolio	*PMBOK® Guide* 7th Edition	244
Predictive Approach	*PMBOK® Guide* 7th Edition	244
Product	*PMBOK® Guide* 7th Edition	244
Product Management	*PMBOK® Guide* 7th Edition	245
Program	*PMBOK® Guide* 7th Edition	245
Project	*PMBOK® Guide* 7th Edition	245
Project management	*PMBOK® Guide* 7th Edition	245
Project manager	*PMBOK® Guide* 7th Edition	246
Project team	*PMBOK® Guide* 7th Edition	246
Resource	Process Groups: a Practice	339
Risk	*PMBOK® Guide* 7th Edition	248
Scope	*PMBOK® Guide* 7th Edition	249
Sponsor	*PMBOK® Guide* 7th Edition	250
Stakeholder	*PMBOK® Guide* 7th Edition	250
Value	*PMBOK® Guide* 7th Edition	252

4.3 Mapping the exam content outline to the readings

Here is Table 4.3 with the list of tasks defined in the CAPM® ECO – Exam Content Outline for the domain "Project Management Fundamentals and Core Concepts" related to some of the referenced books where you can read details about the contents, which we are going to describe in the next

Table 4.3 Mapping the ECO Domain #1 to the PMI reference books

Project Management Fundamentals and Core Concepts – 36%	PMI PMBOK® Guide 7th Edition (2021) Standard	PMI PMBOK® Guide 7th Edition (2021) Guide	PMI Agile Practice Guide (2017)	PMI Process Groups: A Practice Guide (2022)
Task 1: Demonstrate an understanding of the various project life cycles and processes	4, 8–11, 34–36, 44–46	131–134 122–128	17–32	1–9
Task 2: Demonstrate an understanding of project management planning	18–20, 31–34	51–53 63–66, 82–87, 82–91, 170–171 185–186, 188, 217–225		77–129, 195
Task 3: Demonstrate an understanding of project roles and responsibilities	12–16, 21–33, 40–43	16–30, 73–74, 207–210	33–38	51–65
Task 4: Determine how to follow and execute planned strategies or frameworks (e.g., communication, risks, etc.)	34–36, 47–49	8–10, 64, 69–77, 184		69–71, 133–159, 161–192
Task 5: Demonstrate an understanding of common problem-solving tools and techniques	31–33	8–14, 64, 179–180,174–177	53–54	249, 250, 274, 287

chapters of this book. The number of questions in the CAPM® exam related to this domain is the 36% of the total number of questions of the whole CAPM® exam.

The next sections will describe one by one the tasks defined in Table 4.3.

4.4 Task 1 – Demonstrate an understanding of the various project life cycles and processes

4.4.1 *Distinguish between a project, a program, and a portfolio*

To begin your journey into the domain of project management, it is fundamental to understand and distinguish three main concepts: projects, programs, and portfolios.

Suppose you have decided to write a novel. You have a story in mind, a budget for getting it published, and a goal: to see your name on the cover of the book. This endeavor is what we refer to as a **project**. A project is a unique endeavor with a clear objective, a specific beginning and end, and typically, a defined budget.

On a corporate level, consider a manufacturing company aiming to build a new factory. This is a project since it's a one-time task with a specific goal – successfully constructing the factory – within a stipulated time frame.

According to the *PMBOK® Guide* 7th Edition (see Table 4.1), a project is a temporary endeavor undertaken to create a unique product, service, or result. It has a definitive start and end date, a unique goal, and a set of activities designed to achieve that goal.

Now, think about a publishing house planning to release a series of novels under a new genre. Each novel represents a different project, with its unique storyline, timeline, and budget. But they all align with the publishing house's overarching aim – to make a mark in this new genre. This grouping of related projects is known as a **program**. According to the *PMBOK® Guide* 7th Edition (see Table 4.1), a program is a group of related projects managed in a coordinated manner to obtain benefits and control not available from managing them individually.

Going to a higher level, our publishing house might have a portfolio that includes the program of new genre novels, a project for redesigning its website, and another project for conducting nationwide author search events. These endeavors might not be directly interrelated, but they all support the firm's strategic vision of expanding its market presence. According to the

PMBOK® Guide 7th Edition (see Table 4.1), a **portfolio** refers to a collection of projects, programs, subportfolios, and operations managed as a group to achieve strategic objectives. The projects and programs in the portfolio may vary widely but collectively contribute to the company's strategic objectives.

Figure 4.2 illustrates an example of a portfolio structure.

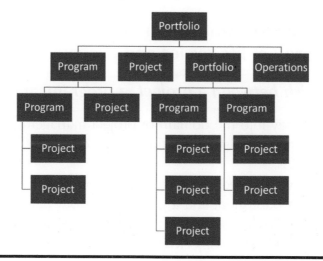

Figure 4.2   Example of a portfolio structure

> **TIPS: Keep in mind that portfolio management includes operations related to the business area considered, which is not the case for program or project management.**

4.4.2 Distinguish between a project and operations

With an understanding of projects, let's delve into how they differ from operations. Imagine running a café. When you first opened the café, everything from finding the location, getting the right equipment, designing the space, and launching it was a **project**. It had a defined beginning and end, with the goal of creating a running café. Once your café is open and functioning daily, that's an **operation**. Operations are the ongoing, repetitive activities that produce goods or provide services. They maintain the business and its outputs over the long term. In our café example, the daily preparation and serving of coffee and pastries, managing inventories, and cleaning up are all operations.

Projects and operations are closely linked. The output of a project often becomes an input to an operation. In the café scenario, the project of opening the café led to the operation of running the café.

Now, think about a company planning to implement a new IT system. The design and setup of the system is a project. But once it's installed, maintaining the system, troubleshooting, and user support become part of the company's daily operations. In a nutshell, while operations keep the lights on and maintain the current business activities, projects aim for improvement, innovation, and achieving specific and unique goals.

Table 4.4 describes the main differences between project management and operations management.

Table 4.4 Main differences between project management and operations management

Aspect	Project management	Operations management
Primary goal	Fulfill objectives and close the project	Maintain business stability and continuity
Duration	Temporary with a defined start and end	Continuous without a specific end
Outcome	Unique product, service, or result	Repetitive services or products
Changes	Managed via change control processes	Continuous improvement focus
Knowledge transfer	Knowledge is handed over at project completion	Knowledge remains within the operation
Resource allocation	Resources allocated for project duration	Resources are generally stable

4.4.3 *Distinguish between predictive and adaptive approaches*

As mentioned in the introduction to this chapter, the *PMBOK® Guide* 7th Edition covers the full spectrum of development approaches (predictive, adaptive, and hybrid). But how do we define and distinguish between these different approaches?

Think about constructing a house. Before starting, a detailed plan is mandatory, including the architectural drawings, the list of materials, the construction stages, and so on. You need to know at the very beginning what the result is supposed to be as precisely as possible, and you will follow sequential phases to get there. The **predictive approach**, also called a traditional or waterfall approach, requires that the details of the project are clear from the beginning, so that the project's scope, time, and cost can be determined early and accurately in the project lifecycle. Once set, these factors are relatively fixed. Changes are not forbidden, but they must be carefully and formally managed. It is sequence-driven. It's very well adapted to projects where the product is well-understood, and changes are minimal or non-existent during the project lifecycle. You will find more details about this in Chapter 5 – Predictive, Plan-Based Methodologies.

Now, consider organizing an improvisational theater show. You know the basic structure of the performance, but the actual content is created all along the show, taking into account new ideas and reactions of the audience. This is an example of the **adaptive approach**, also called agile. Here, the plan is flexible and regularly adjusted based on project experiences and feedback. It is more flexible and collaborative. It is well adapted when the end product is not fully known at the beginning of the project or when the project is likely to encounter significant changes during its lifecycle. The adaptive approach thrives in volatile, uncertain, and complex project environments where creativity, innovation, and flexibility are vital. You will find more details about this in Chapter 6 – Agile Frameworks/Methodologies, including information about how to choose between predictive and adaptive approaches.

Table 4.5 describes the main differences between predictive and adaptive approaches.

Table 4.5   Comparing predictive and adaptive approaches

Aspect	Predictive approach	Adaptive approach
Project scope	Detailed at the beginning	Discovered all along the project
Delivery	End of the project	Incremental and frequent
Customer engagement	Primarily at the beginning and end	Continuous and collaborative
Performance measurement	Based on adherence to plan	Based on delivering customer value
Feedback loops	Longer and infrequent	Short and regular
Flexibility	Limited once scope is defined	High, to adjust to emerging needs

TIPS: There is no absolute best approach: the best is the one that suits the context of your project.

In fact, many projects use a combination of both predictive and adaptive approaches, which is called a **hybrid approach**. Hybrid approaches can take different forms, depending on the degree of mix between predictive and adaptive ways of working. You shouldn't primarily focus on the approach but on the value you want to deliver (see "Value" principle) so tailoring the best way of working is central to the *PMBOK® Guide* 7th Edition (see "Tailoring" principle, "Development approach and life cycle" performance domain, and "Tailoring" chapter).

4.4.4 Distinguish between issues, risks, assumptions, and constraints

As you navigate project management, you may encounter four elements: issues, risks, assumptions, and constraints.

Suppose you have planned a road trip. But when the departure day comes, your car doesn't start. This unexpected event is an **issue**. An issue is a current problem that needs immediate attention and action. In project management, issues are problems that are currently happening and affecting the project. These are obstacles that are actively hindering project progress, causing delays, or obstructing team members' ability to complete their tasks. They require immediate attention because they are real and present problems.

Now, imagine you're aware of an upcoming snowstorm in your road trip direction. The storm might cause delays or even block some roads. This potential problem is a **risk**. In project management, risks are potential future events. They represent uncertainties that could negatively (threats) or positively (opportunities) impact the project.

For your road trip, you've supposed that a sufficient number of gas stations will be open all along your path. This is an **assumption**. In project management, assumptions are beliefs or statements considered as true or certain in the planning phase, without any empirical evidence or proof. They help in decision-making but must be tracked, as incorrect assumptions can affect the project.

You only have a week-long vacation for your road trip. This fixed time limit is a **constraint**. In project management, constraints are factors that limit the team's options. These could be time, budget, resources, or even specific project requirements. Constraints are restrictions or limitations that the project operates within.

Table 4.6 describes the main differences between issues, risks, assumptions, and constraints.

Table 4.6   Comparing issues, risks, assumptions, and constraints

Aspect	Issues	Risks	Assumptions	Constraints
Definition	Current problems that need resolution	Potential future events or conditions	Beliefs taken as truth for planning	Boundaries that limit options
Nature	Present and real	Uncertain and might happen	Generally accepted conditions or truths	Limiting factors or rules
Timing	Already occurred	Future-based	Made at the beginning and during planning	Established at the start
Management	Managed using an issue log	Managed using risk management processes	Continuously verified and validated	Considered during planning and execution
Effect on project	Can cause immediate disruptions	Can affect project's objectives if realized	Can impact project if proven false	Shapes project's course and limits flexibility
Resolution	Requires prompt action	Requires proactive planning and response	Need validation or may become risks	Often accepted and planned around

4.4.5   Review/critique project scope

Suppose you are planning a birthday party for your best friend. The guest list, the place, the menu, and the activities to be done are the details that form the scope of your project, the party. In project management, scope gathers all the activities that are necessary to deliver the project's end product or service. Scope sets the limits of what's included in the project and what's not, in order to avoid any misunderstanding between stakeholders. Reviewing and assessing the scope is like making sure all party preparations align with the goal – a memorable birthday party. You check that the guest list suits your friend's preferences, the venue can accommodate all guests, the food aligns with dietary requirements, and the activities are enjoyable for all. In project management, scope review involves systematically assessing that the project remains on track, aligns with the objectives, and does not encompass tasks that don't contribute to the project goal (scope creep). It's about ensuring the project delivers what it intends to, no more and no less. If you are using a predictive approach, the whole scope is supposed to be comprehensive and detailed at the very beginning of the project. To verify its completeness, you can use a tool as the Work Breakdown Structure (WBS). You will find further information about this in Chapter 5 – Predictive, Plan-Based Methodologies.

If you are using an adaptive approach, the scope is not detailed at the start of the project, but the work to be done is generally described in the Product backlog, which is a living and prioritized list of items. The high-priority items are detailed because they will be soon developed. Conversely, the low-priority items stay as long as possible in a rough state, to avoid spending time in detailing something that may not be developed. You will find further information about this in Chapter 6 – Agile Frameworks/Methodologies.

Regardless of the development approach, reviewing the project scope includes verifying that its content is aligned with the value that the project is expected to deliver and that the stakeholders' perspectives have been taken into consideration.

4.4.6 Apply the project management code of ethics to scenarios (refer to PMI Code of Ethics and Professional Conduct)

The role of a project practitioner includes meeting ethical standards. Ethics shape the way we navigate challenges, interact with team members, and influence project outcomes. The Project Management Institute's Code of Ethics and Professional Conduct serves as our compass, guiding us to make decisions that promote fairness, honesty, and respect. You will find further information about it in Appendix E – PMI Code of Ethics and Professional Conduct. Let's illustrate its application in different scenarios.

Let's say you're planning a community event, and a supplier offers a personal gift to secure a contract. This situation calls for "**Responsibility**", one of the core values of the Code of Ethics. It would be best if you declined the gift, ensuring decisions are made objectively, based on merit.

Or suppose you discover a miscalculation in your project budget halfway through the event planning. You face a dilemma: should you inform the committee, potentially causing delays and reputational damage, or proceed, hoping for the best? The principle of "**Honesty**" guides you to disclose the error promptly and work toward a solution.

Now, imagine you're leading a global project and one of your team members from a different cultural background feels alienated due to certain team practices. This is when the principle of "**Respect**" comes into play. Instead of dismissing their concerns, you'd organize a team meeting, encouraging open dialogue about diverse work cultures and ensuring that everyone feels valued and heard.

Eventually, picture this: Two equally skilled team members compete for a crucial role in the project. One of them is a close friend. Here, "**Fairness**" should be your guiding principle. Making a decision based on personal relations can compromise the project's integrity. Instead, assess both candidates impartially, possibly through a structured evaluation or a panel review, ensuring the best fit for the project.

> **TIPS: The 12 principles of project management are aligned with the 4 values of the PMI Code of Ethics and Professional Conduct (Responsibility, Respect, Fairness, and Honesty).**

4.4.7 Explain how a project can be a vehicle for change

Imagine that your local community is facing the challenge of waste management. You propose a project to introduce recycling initiatives, aiming to educate residents and establish a sustainable waste management system. This project, if successful, will bring about a change in the community's attitude toward waste and improve the local environment. Projects are powerful tools for change. They help organizations' transition from their current state to a desired future state. Think about technological advancements. Companies often implement projects to adopt new technologies, altering the way they operate. The project could involve training staff, upgrading hardware and software, and redesigning business processes. The key to utilizing projects as vehicles for change lies in defining clear objectives, aligning them with the organization's goals and effectively managing all aspects of the project to ensure that the desired change is achieved. Projects are instrumental in driving change within organizations, industries, and societies. That's why one of the 12 project management principles is dedicated to Change: "Enable change to achieve the envisioned future state".

As a project manager, you become a change agent. You can make a difference, whether it's in a corporate setting, a social context, or even at a broader community or societal level.

4.5 Task 2 – Demonstrate an understanding of project management planning

4.5.1 Describe the purpose and importance of cost, quality, risk, schedule, etc.

Suppose you want to organize a road trip across the country with a group of friends. Every detail counts – the itinerary, the schedule, the budget, the quality of accommodation, the car and other resources, communication with your friends, potential roadblocks, outsourcing needs like local guides, and considering everyone's preferences. Each element corresponds with a key aspect of project management:

Planning a road trip involves budgeting for fuel, food, accommodation, and more. This is your project **cost**, the financial plan you need to manage meticulously to keep the project within its budget. Similarly, every project has a defined budget that needs careful management. The challenge is to deliver the project within this financial boundary. Overstepping the budget can put in danger the project and negatively impact the organization's financial health. Effective cost management allows for efficient resource usage and increases the probability of project success.

In a road trip, **quality** might mean a comfortable ride, good food, and great experiences. In a project, quality signifies the project's deliverables meeting the expectations and requirements set by the stakeholders. It's about delivering a product, service, or result that provides the intended value. Ensuring that the project's outputs are fit for purpose is critical as it impacts customer satisfaction, the project's credibility, and the reputation of the organization.

Just like planning when to leave, when to reach each stop, and when to return, the project **schedule** sets out the tasks, milestones, and deadlines, ensuring the timely completion of the project. In a project, the schedule maps out the timeline, milestones, and deadlines for the project tasks. Managing the schedule effectively ensures the project is delivered on time.

The trip's destinations, sightseeing spots, and activities set the **scope**. Similarly, in project management, the scope defines what the project will accomplish, the work involved in delivering the project, and the project's boundaries. Managing the scope prevents "scope creep", ensures all required work is included, and helps align the project with its objectives.

The car, the GPS, the road trip playlist – these are **resources** you need for your road trip. In project management, resources refer to people, materials, equipment, and other essentials required to execute project tasks. Resource management involves planning, organizing, and managing resources to bring about the successful completion of specific project goals and objectives.

Effective **communication** is vital in a road trip – coordinating with your friends, updating them about plans, and listening to their inputs. Similarly, project communications involve disseminating relevant information to the right people at the right time. Good communication ensures all stakeholders are informed, are aligned, and work collaboratively toward project goals.

Potential slowdowns like a flat tire or a closed highway represent **risks** in your road trip. These uncertainties could affect your trip negatively if they occur. Conversely, you may be surprised by a wonderful landscape and want to go on a half-day hiking activity that you didn't plan but that you would really enjoy, improving drastically your experience. Similarly, in project management, risks are uncertain events that could impact the project's objectives. Identifying, analyzing, and responding to risks are vital for the project's success.

Procurement for your road trip might be booking a local tour guide or renting a campervan. In project management, procurement refers to obtaining necessary goods or services from outside the project team. Effective procurement ensures that projects receive the necessary resources at the best possible price.

In your road trip, your friends, your car rental agency, or the hotel staff are stakeholders. In project management, **stakeholder engagement** involves identifying all people or organizations impacted by the project and ensuring their needs and expectations are understood and, where appropriate, managed. Effective stakeholder engagement can lead to better project outcomes and higher stakeholder satisfaction.

As the trip planner, you're the conductor, ensuring all the elements of the journey fit together perfectly. In project management, **integration** means the coordinated management of all the above project elements to ensure they work together effectively. It involves making trade-offs among competing objectives and alternatives to achieve stakeholder satisfaction. While considering all these aspects of project management, don't forget that the ultimate goal of a project is to produce outcomes and deliver value.

TIPS: See Planning project management performance domain for further information in the *PMBOK® Guide* 7th Edition.

4.5.2 *Distinguish between the different deliverables of a project management plan versus a product management plan*

Project management and product management represent two different perspectives, which are nevertheless closely related to each other, as well as to program management and portfolio management. From a project management perspective, a project has a predefined start and end date. The project ends when the associated product or service is completed and delivered. Once their project is finished, project teams transfer deliverables to the teams in charge of operations and maintenance.

The product management perspective, on the other hand, considers the period between the birth of the product idea and the withdrawal of the product – in other words, the product's lifespan. During this period, the product life cycle passes through several phases (introduction, growth, maturity, and decline/retirement).

One or more projects may be launched during this period. Some may correspond to one phase (e.g., product introduction), and sometimes one phase may include several projects (e.g., several product improvement projects during the maturity phase). These projects can be grouped together in one or more programs during the product lifecycle and then combined into a portfolio.

Figure 4.3 illustrates the structure described above.

Product lifecycle	Introduction		Growth				Maturity			Retirement	
Portfolio	Product portfolio P1										
Programs	Program I1		Program G1		Program G2		Program M1			Program R1	
Projects	Project I11	Project I2	Project G11	Project G12	Project G21	Project G22	Project M11	Project M12	Project M13	Project R11	Project R12

Time ➡

Figure 4.3   Example of relations between a product lifecycle, a portfolio, programs, and projects

In a very simplified way, a **project management plan** describes how the project team will work, how it will be possible to verify that this way of working is respected, and what to do if it is not. In other words, it describes how the project will be executed, monitored, and controlled. The project management plan is composed of subsidiary management plans corresponding to each of the aspects we described in 4.5.1 (cost, schedule, quality, etc.). The project management plan also comes with baselines, when applicable: scope baseline, cost baseline, and schedule baseline. It can also include the change management plan, the configuration management plan, the performance measurement baseline, the project lifecycle and the development approach, and the management reviews. You will find further information about this in Chapter 5 – Predictive, Plan-Based Methodologies.

Product management has its own specific activities that are not specifically described by PMI. To illustrate that a **product management plan** is different from a project management plan, it may include a Product roadmap, a Market analysis, a Product requirements document, a Go-to-market strategy, and a Product lifecycle plan. Without going deeper, remember that a product management plan addresses the strategic aspects of the product and how it will be developed, launched, marketed, and maintained throughout its lifecycle.

However, the boundaries between project and product management are not strict, since they require certain common skills and even a common mindset based on value delivery.

> **TIPS: The project management principles defined in the *PMBOK® Guide* 7th Edition could just as easily be applied to product management.**

4.5.3 Distinguish differences between a milestone and a task duration

Consider our cross-country road trip once more. It's a journey encompassing many things from major events like reaching a very famous monument to smaller details like refueling or choosing the perfect road trip playlist. Similarly, the execution of a project also includes both significant accomplishments and smaller tasks that together contribute to the overall success. Let's delve deeper.

In our road trip analogy, reaching a long-awaited destination represents some of the most important moments. They mark significant achievements or turning points in our journey, giving us a sense of progression and accomplishment. In project management, a **milestone** marks a key moment in the project. It may be, for example, the end of a phase, the completion of a major deliverable, or a decision point. A milestone represents an instant, so it has no duration. It is helpful for the team and all stakeholders to visualize the project's overall progress.

During our road trip, we have to achieve a lot of small activities. For example, it may be refueling the car, grabbing meals on the way, or following a specific route. In project management, **tasks** are individual activities that contribute to the accomplishment of the work to be done. A duration of a task is simply the time needed to complete it. Be careful, this is actually time, not to be confused with workload. Thus, its unit is, for example, the hour, the day or the week. This duration may vary depending on several potential parameters, such as the volume of work to be done, the number of people involved, and their skills.

Table 4.7 describes the main differences between milestones and task durations.

Table 4.7 Main differences between milestones and task durations

Aspect	Milestones	Task durations
Definition	Significant events or markers within a project	Time taken to complete specific activities or tasks
Duration	Typically zero duration; a point in time	Have a definable timespan, from hours to days or even months
Examples	– Completion of a phase – Approval of a deliverable	– Designing a website (2 weeks) – Coding a software module (3 days)
Management focus	Monitored for project progress and stakeholder reporting	Managed for resource allocation and scheduling
Impact on schedule	Doesn't consume time but affects the schedule's flow	Directly consumes time and affects project end date

4.5.4 Determine the number and type of resources in a project

Suppose you're a project manager in an advertising agency. Your new project consists in launching a nationwide advertising campaign for a leading smartphone brand. Just like any project, it requires resource planning. Let's see how you can determine the number and type of resources needed for your project.

Breakdown project into tasks

The first move involves breaking down your project into bite-sized tasks using a technique such as the Work Breakdown Structure (WBS). Think of

WBS as a project map, helping you visualize all the necessary steps to turn your advertising campaign from an idea into a reality. WBS is a hierarchical decomposition of the total scope of work to be carried out by the project team to accomplish the project objectives and create the required deliverables. Each descending level represents an increasingly detailed definition of the project work.

Estimate work effort for each task

After listing down your tasks, gauge the work effort needed for each. How many hours will the graphic designer need to create those stunning visuals? How much time will the copywriter require to craft the perfect slogan? Remember to consider the complexity of each task and the proficiency of the assigned team members in your estimates. This estimate involves determining the number of work-hours or work-days it will take to complete each task, considering the complexity of the task and the skill level of the assigned resources.

Categorize the resources required

Once you have the effort estimates, pinpoint the resources needed to complete each task. Typically, resources in project management are divided into two types:

- **Human resources**: These include your team members, like graphic designers, copywriters, market researchers, and more, who have the skills and knowledge to execute the tasks.
- **Physical resources:** These can range from the software required for graphic designing and copywriting to the hardware needed.

Determine resource needs

After categorizing the resources, estimate the quantity of each type needed. How many graphic designers are necessary to meet your creative demands? What volume of software licenses is needed? Remember to consider the skill levels required and the estimated work effort for each task when making these estimations. Regarding physical resources, think about the volume or capacity of materials or equipment necessary.

Evaluate resource availability and constraints

Finally, take into account the availability and constraints of your resources. Check your team members' schedules and commitments, ensuring they have enough bandwidth to handle their assigned tasks. For human resources, look at the availability of your team members considering their other commitments, holidays, etc. For physical resources, check the availability in terms of logistics and time frames.

4.5.5 Use a risk register in a given situation

Suppose you're heading up a project to launch a new software application, and several risks have come to light. In this context, and more generally in every project, a risk register is very useful. A risk register is a living document that provides a comprehensive list of all recognized risks, including their analysis and the management strategies to be employed. Let's delve deeper and see how a risk register comes into play in this context.

Risk register initiation

First, record all identified risks in your risk register. Each risk entry should include several key details, such as:

- **Risk description:** This is a brief statement that explains the risk. For instance, you could write, "There's a chance that coding mistakes could compromise the application's functionality".
- **Risk category:** This helps classify the risk. In this case, coding mistakes could fall under "technical risks".
- **Probability:** This is an estimate of the likelihood of the risk realization. You can express it as low, medium, or high, or use numbers to represent it.
- **Impact:** This represents the potential effect of the risk on the project if it materializes, expressed in the same way as probability.
- **Risk owner:** This is the person appointed to monitor and manage the risk.

This list of items is not exhaustive, and other information can be added depending on the level of attention you wish to pay to risk management on your project.

Risk analysis and prioritization

Next, analyze these risks and rank them based on their probability and potential impact. This step is essential in determining where to focus resources and efforts. High-ranking risks require prompt attention and robust mitigation strategies. We are describing here what is qualitative risk analysis. Quantitative risk analysis is also possible, but note that it is rarely used, because of its costs, which is only justified for very large projects. Quantitative risk analysis requires the use of sophisticated statistical tools, such as Monte Carlo simulation, and specialists who master them.

Risk response strategies

For each identified risk, plan a response strategy. These strategies should consider if the risk is a threat (negative risk) or an opportunity (positive risk). Table 4.8 describes the different possible strategies, with similarities and differences between threats and opportunities.

Table 4.8 Risk response strategies

Threats	Opportunities
Avoid Eliminate the risk entirely, putting to zero the probability and/or the impact	**Exploit** Ensure the opportunity is realized at 100%
Mitigate Decrease the probability or negative impact	**Enhance** Increase the probability or positive impact
Transfer Assign the impact of the risk to a third party	**Share** Leverage the advantage through partnership
Acceptance This can be either passive or active. Passive acceptance is simply acknowledging the risk without preparing anything in advance should it occur. Active acceptance goes further than acknowledgment and includes the creation of a contingency reserve, in order to benefit from time, money, or resources should the risk become a reality.	

TIPS: For both mitigation (threats) and enhancement (opportunities), the risk response strategy consists in doing something in order to modify the probability and/or the impact of the risk.

Examples of risk response strategies:

- Implementing a rigorous quality assurance process could be a mitigation strategy for the risk of coding errors.
- Using an insurance contract is transferring a threat.
- Creating a joint venture is a way of sharing an opportunity.

Risk monitoring and review

The risk register must be checked and revised regularly, as new risks may emerge and old ones may become obsolete as the project progresses. In addition, the probability and impact of risks may evolve as circumstances change. Remember that risk management is much more than an administrative routine you might perform to comply with potential internal corporate processes, it's a critical activity for the success of your project. It is also a powerful way of making all stakeholders continually aware of the situation and potentially conscious that they can take their part of responsibility to increase the project's chances of success, in a more or less uncertain environment.

4.5.6 Use a stakeholder register in a given situation

A project exists through its stakeholders: the people who will benefit from the value it will bring, the members of the project team and, more generally, any person or any organization who has a direct or indirect interest in the project, or who will be affected by its results, or even who may perceive that they will be. So, it's no surprise that the identification of stakeholders is part of the project's initialization. Omitting a stakeholder who could help or impede the project can have major consequences, and it's just as crucial to pay a level of attention proportionate to the importance of each stakeholder. The appropriate document for identifying and monitoring stakeholders is the stakeholder register. To illustrate its use, let's consider a project aiming at the construction of a high-rise building.

Identify stakeholders

The first step is to set a list of stakeholders. For the high-rise building construction, they could be, for example, the construction company, architects, engineers, future residents, city representatives, and suppliers.

Record stakeholder information

Once the stakeholders are identified, the next step is to capture essential details about each in the register. This info generally includes the following:

- **Identification data:** Name, role in the project, contact information, just like in a directory.
- **Assessment:** What the stakeholder's main interests and concerns in the project, their potential influence (either positive or negative), and their expectations from the project are.
- **Classification:** This involves categorizing stakeholders according to their power (influence), urgency (need for immediate attention), and legitimacy (relevance of their involvement).

Analyze stakeholders

Next, an analysis of the stakeholders is conducted, considering their potential impact on the project. Their interest, influence, and authority related to the project are evaluated. Stakeholders with high influence and interest are typically major decision-makers and should be closely managed.

Develop stakeholder management strategies

With a clear understanding of the stakeholders' interests and influence, appropriate management strategies for each stakeholder are designed. High-power, high-interest stakeholders, for instance, may need constant engagement and regular updates about the project's progress, whereas those with less power or interest may be kept informed without engaging in day-to-day decision-making.

Continual updates

As the project progresses, the stakeholder register needs to be regularly updated. Stakeholders might change, their interests or influence may shift, and new issues may arise that affect stakeholders. By keeping the stakeholder register up-to-date, the project manager can ensure efficient stakeholder management throughout the project lifecycle.

> **TIPS: Risk management is a core activity of project management. That's why in the *PMBOK® Guide* 7th Edition, one of the 12 project management principles is dedicated to Risk:**

"Optimize risk response", and corresponding activities are detailed in the "Uncertainty" project management performance domain.

4.5.7 Explain project closure and transitions

Project closure and transitions mark the conclusion of a project's life cycle. These phases officially acknowledge the completion of all project activities and the acceptance of the final product or output. Here, we'll dissect the intricate procedures involved in these pivotal concluding steps.

Project closure

Often known as "closeout", project closure signifies the final phase of the project life cycle. This stage validates that every facet of the project has been adequately finalized and evaluated. The primary steps involved include the following:

■ **Completion of work:** Confirm that all project tasks are finished, and all deliverables have been accepted by the appropriate parties.
■ **Document project performance:** Record the project's performance compared to its initial objectives. This includes evaluating adherence to the project's scope, schedule, and budget, and the degree to which it satisfied stakeholder needs. This performance record can be an insightful learning resource for future projects.
■ **Release resources:** Resources (human, physical, or financial) dedicated to the project should be freed and redirected to their original sources or allocated to new projects.
■ **Project review:** Execute a post-project evaluation or a "lessons learned" discussion. This examination allows the team to consider the project's successes and areas for improvement, valuable for future projects.
■ **Formal project closure:** Officially close the project by communicating its conclusion to all stakeholders. This could be in the form of a project closure report or a closure meeting.

Project transitions

Project transitions involve the transfer of the final project deliverables to the end users or customers. This procedure also encompasses the transfer of project knowledge and resources to those who will oversee the operation and maintenance of the final product. The steps involved include the following:

- **Handover of deliverables:** Transfer the final product, service, or result of the project to the client or end user, ensuring their full comprehension and acceptance.
- **Knowledge transfer:** Share all relevant details and knowledge about the final product, like operation guidelines, maintenance procedures, and troubleshooting processes. This could involve conducting training sessions or preparing comprehensive operation manuals.
- **Ongoing support:** Develop procedures for handling queries, concerns, or issues that may emerge post-project transition. This could involve establishing a support team or a helpdesk.
- **Stakeholder sign-off:** Secure a formal agreement from the stakeholders, indicating their acceptance of the final product and the termination of the project.

4.6 Task 3 – Demonstrate an understanding of project roles and responsibilities

4.6.1 Compare and contrast the roles and responsibilities of project managers and project sponsors

Project manager and sponsor are probably the two more critical roles for a successful project, each one having its own specificities.

According to the *PMBOK® Guide* 7th Edition (p. 4), a **project manager** is the person assigned by the performing organization to lead the project team that is responsible for achieving the project objective.

More generally, depending on the project context, some of the project manager's duties may be performed centrally by one person, decentral by a group, or by a combination of the two.

The overall purpose of a project manager is to ensure that the project meets its expectations in terms of outcomes and delivered value while effectively managing the processes involved, such as those relating to scope, schedule, costs, resources, risks, quality, etc.

The **sponsor** of a project can be an individual or a group and is committed to fostering its success. Project sponsors are usually at a high level in the organization, so they have sufficient power and influence to support the project team and bridge the project to the overall strategy. Their main activities on a project can include the following:

- **Vision and strategy:** Setting the direction, in line with the organization's strategic objectives.
- **Resource support:** Helping to obtain resources, particularly in the case of organizational conflicts.
- **Outcomes monitoring and decision-making:** Continually ensure project alignment with strategy.
- **Advocacy:** Generate team support and maintain stakeholder interest in the project.
- **Solution provider:** Take ownership of problems beyond the project team's reach, and get them solved.

TIPS: The desirable behaviors of a project manager and more widely of any individual taking part in a project and aiming to deliver value are described in the 12 project management principles. An appendix of the *PMBOK® Guide* 7th Edition is dedicated to the sponsor role (Appendix X2 – Sponsor).

4.6.2 Compare and contrast the roles and responsibilities of the project team and the project sponsor

Now that we have seen above the strategic dimension of the project sponsor role, let's consider the operational responsibilities of the project team. The project team is composed of different people who work together on various tasks in order to achieve the project's goals. Their responsibilities can include:

- **Executing tasks:** The main goal of the project team is to complete the tasks defined in the project plan, with each member bringing his or her own skills to contribute to the project's progress.
- **Problem solving:** Throughout the project, the team may be faced with various problems and will need to find and implement solutions.
- **Collaboration:** The more collaborative a project team is, the more effective it will be. This means sharing information, transparency, mutual trust, respect, and a common determination to succeed.

- **Quality control:** Quality needs to be monitored all along the project, so that corrective action can be taken as soon as possible, ensuring that deliverables meet expectations.
- **Communication:** Communication involves informing the project manager and other team members of the progress of tasks and problems encountered. It extends to the effective exchange of any relevant information within the team and with other stakeholders.

TIPS: Dive into the *PMBOK® Guide* 7th Edition to consider the "Team" principle ("Create a collaborative project team environment"), and the "Team" performance domain.

4.6.3 Explain the importance of the role the project manager plays (e.g., initiator, negotiator, listener, coach, working member, and facilitator)

The activities of a project manager are multidimensional and diverse. They can be described through the following roles.

As an **initiator**, the project manager gets things moving. They define the project's scope, develop the project plan, assemble the project team, and consolidate the project's vision. They prepare the stage for the project's work and are often the driving force that turns ideas into reality.

Project managers often act as **negotiators**. They negotiate resource allocations, schedules, changes to the project scope, and other key project elements. They have continuously to evaluate, negotiate, and communicate about what different stakeholders may ask for and what can realistically be achieved.

The project manager must be able to **listen** to ideas, feedback, and concerns from the project team and other stakeholders. This role helps the project manager understand differing viewpoints, identify potential issues before they become problems, and build stronger relationships with the team and stakeholders.

Project managers provide guidance, support, and motivation, helping team members learn and improve. As a **coach**, the project manager enhances team spirit, assists in resolving conflicts, and nurtures a positive workspace conducive to high productivity and high-quality work.

In smaller projects or particular situations and provided it doesn't impede one to effectively manage the project, the project manager may also be a

working member of the team, performing some of the project tasks. This role can help project managers understand better the reality that some team members may face in their work or the technical difficulty of some tasks.

As a **facilitator**, the project manager demonstrates servant leadership abilities, ensuring that all team members benefit from the best possible environment in which to carry out their work, both materially and psychologically. The project manager supports team members, working to eliminate obstacles and foster the effectiveness and efficiency of the team as a whole.

> **TIPS: Consider reading the functions associated with projects in the *PMBOK® Guide* 7th Edition to understand what is expected to be covered regardless of the development approach.**

4.6.4 Explain the differences between leadership and management

Management and leadership are two ways of heading a team. Some people caricaturally oppose them, with leadership being the best and only way, and management being confused with "micromanagement", which represents a form of excessive control over individuals. The reality is that every project manager should combine leadership and management, depending on the context, so that the team performs at its best in a secure and motivating environment. Let's now consider these two concepts:

Leadership is about defining a clear vision that inspires team members to follow it, in their common interest while feeling personally valued. Key aspects of leadership include:

- **Vision:** Leaders provide a clear path for their groups, explaining where the group intends to go and the rationale behind it.
- **Inspiration:** They inspire their teams to embrace the vision and give their best effort.
- **Influence:** Rather than just leveraging their titles, leaders use their qualities and abilities to win people's trust and guide them.
- **Change:** They are always open to new methods and solutions. They're comfortable with uncertainty and recognize that taking chances can lead to growth.

Management is more about organizing and monitoring resources to achieve specific goals efficiently and effectively. Key aspects of management include:

- **Planning:** Managers define what needs to be done, the strategy, and the timeline to achieve the objectives.
- **Organizing:** They coordinate tasks, resources, and people, ensuring the plans are implemented effectively.
- **Control:** Managers monitor the progress of activities, and they make adjustments as necessary to keep all things aligned.
- **Stability:** Managers focus on producing predictable outcomes, using plans and processes as much as possible. They strive for efficiency and order.

TIPS: Leadership is key for the project manager but it is as well applicable to any stakeholder (see "Leadership" project management principle).

4.6.5 *Explain emotional intelligence (EQ) and its impact on project management*

Emotional intelligence, often denoted as EQ (emotional quotient) is sometimes seen as the ability to understand the emotions of others, but this is limiting because it also includes identifying and mastering our own emotions. Given the importance of human relations to the success of a project, it's easy to see how a good command of emotional intelligence can have a highly beneficial effect on project performance.

Emotional Intelligence consists of four main components:

- **Self-awareness:** This is the ability to recognize your own emotions, strengths, weaknesses, values, and motivators. In project management, a leader with this capability can perceive how their emotions and actions resonate with others, thereby enabling effective leadership.
- **Self-management:** This refers to controlling your emotions, especially in stressful situations, and adapting to changing circumstances. A project leader proficient in emotion regulation remains level-headed, thinks rationally, and makes judicious decisions even amid unforeseen challenges.
- **Social awareness:** Also known as empathy, this is the ability to understand the emotions, needs, and concerns of others. In a project environment, a leader with empathetic awareness is positioned to comprehend the aspirations and potential challenges of their team, fostering improved interactions and team dynamics

■ **Relationship management:** This is about building and maintaining good relationships with others. Within projects, effective relationship management can promote teamwork, address conflicts constructively, and satisfy the involved parties.

The main impacts of EQ on project management are as follows:

■ **Improved team performance:** A project manager can create an environment where team members feel valued and understood, fostering an environment of trust, open communication, and mutual respect. This leads to heightened team cohesion and motivation.

■ **Effective conflict resolution:** Project leaders can handle conflicts in a way that respects everyone's feelings and perspectives, leading to a more harmonious and productive environment.

■ **Enhanced communication:** Leaders can communicate more effectively by paying attention to the emotional states and needs of the team members. They can tailor their communication style considering the situation and the individual, resulting in clearer, more effective communication.

■ **Stronger stakeholder relationships:** Project managers can build and maintain strong relationships with stakeholders. They can empathize with stakeholders' needs and concerns, anticipate their reactions, and communicate effectively to manage their expectations.

TIPS: Emotional intelligence and other interpersonal skills such as conflict management are to be found in the Team project performance domain of the *PMBOK® Guide* 7th Edition.

4.7 Task 4 – Determine how to follow and execute planned strategies or frameworks (e.g., communication, risks, etc.)

4.7.1 Give examples of how it is appropriate to respond to a planned strategy or framework (e.g., communication, risk, etc.)

The effective execution of planned strategies or frameworks is a fundamental aspect of good project management. The correct response to these strategies can greatly affect the project's successful completion, for example, within the context of communication, risks, scope, or procurement. Let's review how to aptly respond in each of these areas:

A communication strategy outlines how, when, and what information should be exchanged among the project stakeholders. It can be part of a formal communication management plan. For instance, should the communication strategy outline that stakeholders receive weekly email updates regarding the project's progress, the project manager ensures these updates are sent out consistently and on time. In cases where unexpected situations arise, the project manager follows the set communication protocol for such events – including determining who needs to be informed, the method of communication, and the timeframe.

The **risk management strategy** provides a roadmap for identifying, evaluating, and dealing with potential project risks. It is generally included in a risk management plan. For instance, if the risk management strategy requires that a risk register be maintained and regularly updated, the project manager ensures that this is done, using the register as a guiding tool for decision-making. When a new risk that wasn't initially considered arises, the project manager follows the established process for assessing and addressing this risk, which might involve estimating its potential impact and probability, determining suitable responses, and conveying it to the relevant stakeholders.

Scope management strategy involves defining and controlling what is and is not included in a project. For example, if the scope management plan outlines a change control process for any changes to the project scope, the project manager ensures to follow this process when such changes occur. This could involve submitting a change request, reviewing the impact of the change, and getting approval before implementing it.

The **procurement management strategy** involves obtaining and managing the necessary resources for the project. For instance, if the procurement management strategy specifies a particular process for selecting and managing vendors, such as a competitive bidding process, the project manager follows this process. This could involve preparing requests for proposals (RFPs), evaluating bids, and managing the selected vendors according to the established terms and conditions.

4.7.2 Explain project initiation and benefit planning

Before initiating a project, the sponsor, or the person he or she has appointed to do so, usually writes a business case. This can be based on documents sometimes written earlier, the needs assessment, and the project benefit management plan. The needs assessment summarizes the business objectives and risks of the envisaged project. According to the Process Groups Practice Guide (p. 28), the benefits management plan describes how and when the benefits of the project will be delivered, and how they will be measured. It may include sections such as Target benefits, Strategic alignment, Time frame for realizing benefits, Benefits owner, Metrics, and Risks. The business case studies the project's economic feasibility and is often used to decide whether to authorize the project. All these documents potentially written before the project initiation are called business documents. They are not part of the project management documents, but they contain information that will be used later by some of them should the project be authorized. The main example is the first project management document developed to initialize the project after its authorization – the project charter. Further information on this can be found in Chapter 5 – Predictive, Plan-Based Methodologies.

4.8 Task 5 – Demonstrate an understanding of common problem-solving tools and techniques

4.8.1 Evaluate the effectiveness of a meeting

In all projects, meetings are essential for discussing information, making choices, addressing issues, and monitoring progress. To ensure these meetings benefit your project, it's key to assess their quality. Here's how you can do that.

Define clear objectives

Before the meeting, set clear, measurable objectives. What should the meeting achieve? What decisions should be made? What problems should be solved? After the meeting, evaluate whether these objectives were met. If they weren't, it's an indication that the meeting might not have been effective.

Monitor participation

An effective meeting encourages active participation from all attendees. Did everyone contribute to the discussion? Or were some people silent? If participation was limited, it might be a sign that the meeting was not inclusive or engaging enough.

Assess decision-making

An important function of many meetings is to make decisions. After the meeting, evaluate the quality and timeliness of these decisions. Were decisions made based on sound reasoning and sufficient information? Were they made efficiently, without unnecessary delays?

Review action items

At the end of the meeting, all participants should agree with a set of action items to be done later. Evaluate whether these action items are compliant with the SMART acronym: specific, measurable, achievable, relevant, and time-bound.

Gather feedback

Finally, you can ask attendees if they found the meeting useful and what could have been improved. This direct feedback will enhance the effectiveness of future meetings.

4.8.2 Explain the purpose of focus groups, stand-up meetings, brainstorming, etc.

Effective project management relies on the right use of various meeting types, each designed to meet certain objectives. This section provides insight into the roles of focus groups, stand-up meetings, and brainstorming sessions, illustrating their importance within a project environment.

Focus groups are organized discussions led by an expert facilitator, usually involving a select group of six to ten participants. They act as a method to obtain detailed information and perspectives on a specific topic. Within a project setting, focus groups fulfill the following roles.

- **Collecting Varied Opinions**: Focus groups offer a platform for obtaining diverse viewpoints from different stakeholders. For example, when introducing a new digital tool, a focus group can be assembled with potential users to gather their insights and expectations.

- **Evaluating preliminary versions**: They allow for immediate feedback on project outputs. If launching a new online platform, a focus group with potential users can provide essential feedback about its design, user-friendliness, and functionalities.
- **Determining user desires**: Through focus groups, you can directly understand what users are looking for and their hopes for a product or service. This knowledge is crucial during a project's initial stages to shape its goals and direction.

Often referred to as daily scrums in the Scrum framework, **stand-up meetings** are brief, typically not exceeding 15 minutes, and consistently take place at a predetermined time and spot. Attendees usually stand, ensuring the session remains short and focused. The primary goals of stand-up meetings include:

- **Sharing accomplishments:** Each member succinctly updates on their recent achievements. For instance, a software engineer might mention finalizing a particular software component.
- **Identifying challenges:** Team members mention any issues they're facing in completing tasks. These might include technical problems, needing support from peers, or the need for additional information or tools.
- **Maintaining consistency:** Regular stand-up gatherings ensure everyone remains informed about the project's status, promoting synchronized efforts and mutual understanding.

Brainstorming sessions are structured to enhance creative thought, aiming to produce a range of ideas related to a specific topic or challenge. These sessions encourage unrestricted thinking and open dialogue. The main functions of brainstorming sessions consist of as follows:

- **Generating ideas:** These sessions promote the flow of creative thoughts. In a promotional project, such a session might be utilized to brainstorm concepts for a new advertising approach.
- **Encouraging innovation:** These gatherings stimulate fresh thinking and can lead to unique solutions. They're especially valuable when a project needs creative problem-solving.
- **Promoting teamwork:** Brainstorming fosters collaboration, as participants contribute and expand on each other's ideas. This collaborative environment can enhance team unity and uplift morale.

TIPS: The "Models, Methods, and Artifacts" chapter of the *PMBOK® Guide* 7th Edition provides numerous problem-solving tools and techniques. Most of them are detailed and documented with case studies in the PMIstandards+ platform, so we strongly encourage you to dive into it to support your preparation for the exam, and more widely to broaden your project management toolbox.

4.9 Sample test questions on project management fundamentals and core concepts

Question 1

Which of the following best describes the purpose of a portfolio in project management?

A. It is a temporary endeavor undertaken to create a unique product, service, or result

B. It refers to the coordinated management of multiple projects and programs to achieve strategic objectives

C. It is a group of related projects, subprograms, and program activities managed in a coordinated way to obtain benefits not available from managing them individually

D. It involves managing the day-to-day activities of the organization

Question 2

Which of the following is an example of a risk response strategy that involves accepting the potential risk without taking any specific action?

A. Avoidance

B. Mitigation

C. Transference

D. Acceptance

Question 3

Which of the following best describes the role of a project sponsor within a project?

A. The project sponsor is responsible for managing the daily tasks and the project team

B. The project sponsor is primarily responsible for gathering requirements from stakeholders

C. The project sponsor provides resources and support for the project and champions the project within the organization

D. The project sponsor is tasked with creating the project plan and ensuring its execution

Question 4
What is the purpose of a project charter in project initiation?

A. To create a detailed project schedule

B. To allocate resources and define project roles and responsibilities

C. To document the project objectives, scope, and stakeholders

D. To assess and mitigate potential project risks

Question 5
During a stand-up meeting in an Agile project, what is the primary purpose?

A. To provide a status update to the project manager

B. To identify and address any obstacles or issues

C. To discuss detailed technical implementation plans

D. To assign tasks to team members

Answer to Question 1: The correct answer is B.
A portfolio in project management refers to the coordinated management of multiple projects and programs to achieve strategic objectives. Option A is a description of a project, not a portfolio. Option C describes a program, and option D pertains to operations management, which is routine work that keeps an organization running but does not involve changes or improvements. Portfolios allow organizations to manage multiple projects and programs in a coordinated way to achieve strategic objectives. The purpose of portfolio management is to ensure that projects are aligned with organizational strategies and to optimize the use of resources across projects (Project Management Institute, 2017).

Answer to Question 2: The correct answer is D.
Acceptance is a risk response strategy that involves acknowledging the potential risk but choosing not to take any specific action to address it. This

strategy is typically used when the potential impact of the risk is low, the cost of mitigation outweighs the benefit, or when there are limited resources available to address the risk. Avoidance (option A) involves eliminating the risk by taking actions to prevent it from occurring. Mitigation (option B) involves taking proactive measures to reduce the probability or impact of the risk. Transference (option C) involves transferring the risk to a third party, such as through insurance or outsourcing.

Answer to Question 3: The correct answer is C.
The project sponsor provides resources and support for the project and champions the project within the organization. In essence, they act as a bridge between the project team and the upper management and stakeholders. They make critical business decisions and help overcome obstacles that might hinder the project's progress. The role of a project sponsor is often misunderstood or underestimated. According to the *PMBOK® Guide* (Project Management Body of Knowledge) from PMI® (Project Management Institute), the project sponsor plays an important role, assisting with project charter development and participating in project management plan development. They also use their influence within the organization to garner support and resources for the project.

Answer to Question 4: The correct answer is C.
A project charter is a key document created during project initiation, and its purpose is to document the project objectives, scope, and stakeholders. It serves as a formal authorization for the project, providing a clear understanding of what the project aims to achieve and the boundaries within which it will operate. The project charter typically includes information such as the project's purpose, objectives, high-level requirements, deliverables, stakeholders, and initial high-level timeline. It sets the foundation for the project by providing clarity and alignment among project stakeholders regarding the project's goals and boundaries. While resource allocation, defining project roles and responsibilities and assessing and mitigating potential project risks are important aspects of project initiation, they are not the primary purpose of a project charter.

Answer to Question 5: The correct answer is B.
The primary purpose of a stand-up meeting in an Agile project is to identify and address any obstacles or issues that may be hindering the progress of

the team. It is a short daily meeting where team members come together to provide brief updates on their work, discuss any challenges they are facing, and collaborate on finding solutions. The focus is on problem-solving, coordination, and removing any impediments that may impact the team's progress. Providing a status update to the project manager (option A) can be a secondary outcome of the stand-up meeting but is not its primary purpose. Detailed technical implementation plans (option C) are typically discussed in separate meetings or planning sessions. Assigning tasks to team members (option D) is not the main objective of a stand-up meeting; it is more focused on coordination and issue resolution.

4.10 Summary of project management fundamentals and core concepts

You have completed the Project Management Fundamentals and Core Concepts domain. This should have provided you with an understanding of the various project life cycles and processes including being able to distinguish between a range of common concepts such as project, program, portfolio, project and operations, predictive and adaptive approaches, issues, risks, assumptions, project scope, and constraints. As it was illustrated, project management is more and more led by principles that help guide behavior. Supporting principles is the PMI Code of Ethics and Professional Conduct which highlights right and wrong.

This section should also have provided you with an understanding of project management planning. This entails various constraints such as cost, quality, risk, time, etc. Also, it is important to be able to distinguish between the different deliverables of a project management plan and those of a product management plan. In most organizations products might be on the market for many years while projects are kept short. When planning the actual schedule, it's important to know about activities, dependencies, milestones, estimation, type of resources, and a task effort/duration. Supporting the planning is the use of the risk register and the stakeholder. Project management and scheduling requires clear roles and responsibilities, and an understanding of the various roles and their importance such as the project managers, sponsor, and such. This is supported by knowledge on the differences between leadership and management which both are highly applied, and the soft skills supporting this, being emotional intelligence (EQ) and similar. The last part of the domain had an emphasis on how to follow and execute planned strategies or frameworks and some of the common problem-solving tools and techniques. If you feel uncertain about part of this summary, consider going back and refreshing your knowledge of one or more of the topics highlighted in this domain. By doing so it would help you master the following domains that build upon these core concepts.

Chapter 5

Predictive, plan-based methodologies

5.1 Introduction

In Chapter 4 of this book ("Domain #1 – *Project Management Fundamentals and Core Concepts*"), we introduced the different approaches, including the Predictive one, that is, a development approach (ref. *PMBOK® Guide* 7th Edition – section 2.3.3 – "Development approaches", ref. Agile Practice Guide – section 3.1.1 – "Characteristics of Predictive life cycles") used within projects, where project planning and execution are based on a pre-defined and detailed plan. This approach relies on the assumption that the project requirements, scope, time, and budget are fixed, and they can be clearly defined upfront, allowing for accurate planning and estimation of resources, timeframes, and costs.

Some of the key elements and characteristics of Predictive approach in project management are as follows:

Planning in advance: A Predictive approach emphasizes extensive upfront planning to define project objectives, scope, deliverables, milestones, and dependencies. It involves creating a comprehensive project

DOI: 10.4324/9781003462378-5

plan that outlines all the activities, their sequence, and estimated durations.

Low uncertainty, stable scope: Predictive approach assumes that project requirements can be determined and documented early in the project life cycle. The scope of the work is typically defined at the beginning; any changes to the requirements are expected to be minimal and monitored through a Managing Change Request Process. Project managers usually identify potential risks and develop risk mitigation strategies during the planning process group. This includes analyzing risks, assigning responsibilities for risk management, and creating contingency plans to address potential issues that may arise during project execution.

Sequential execution: In Predictive approach, projects are often executed sequentially. A Predictive project is usually divided in sequential *Phases* (ref. *Process Groups: A Practice Guide* – section 1.7.2. – "Project Phase"), each phase of the project is completed before moving on to the next one. This means that project activities in one phase are dependent on the successful completion of previous ones. A common process model to use in Predictive projects is the "Process Group" model (ref. *PMBOK® Guide* 7th Edition – section 4.2.7.4. – "Process Groups", ref. *Process Groups: A Practice Guide* – chapters 4–8) that defines five groups of project management processes: *Initiating, Planning, Executing, Monitoring and Controlling, Closing*. All the five Process Groups are executed within each phase. So, it's important not to confuse Phases with Process Groups. Process Groups are not phases of a project, and a phase of project is characterized by the execution of the process groups within it (ref. *Process Groups: A Practice Guide* – Figure 1.4 – "Interrelationship of key components in projects"). Example of phases within a construction project could be Design, Build, Test, Release. At the end of each phase (closure of the phase), usually there is a *Check Gate* or *Phase Gate* (ref. *Process Groups: A Practice Guide* – section 1.7.3. – "Phase Gate") where the project management team execute a verification and validation of the outcomes of the phase, to get the go/no go to the next phase.

Single delivery cadence: A predictive project has one single product delivery at the end of the project, also if it's divided in sequential phases (ref. *PMBOK® Guide* 7th Edition – section 2.3.2. "Delivery cadence").

Cost and time estimation: Predictive projects heavily relies on accurate estimation of project costs in advance (ref. Process Groups: A Practice Guide – section 5.12. – "Estimate costs") and time frames (ref. *Process Groups: A Practice Guide* – section 5.9. – "Estimate activity duration"). Detailed planning enables project managers to estimate the resources required, including human resources, equipment, and materials (ref. *Process Groups: A Practice Guide* – section 5.16. – "Estimate activity resources"). These estimates are used to develop a budget (ref. *Process Groups: A Practice Guide* – section 5.13. – "Determine budget") and create a project schedule with defined start and end dates (ref. *Process Groups: A Practice Guide* – section 5.10. – "Develop Schedule").

Change control: Any changes to project requirements or scope of the work during the execution of the project must go through a formal change control procedure (ref. *Process Groups: A Practice Guide* – section 7.2. – "Perform integrated change control"), involving thorough impact analysis, evaluation of cost and schedule implications, and approval from relevant stakeholders.

Progress tracking: Predictive approach relies on periodic progress tracking to ensure that the project is on track. This involves monitoring key performance indicators, comparing actual progress against the planned schedule, and identifying any deviations (ref. *Process Groups: A Practice Guide* – Chapter 7 – "monitoring and controlling process group"). Any variations from the plan are analyzed, and appropriate actions are taken to bring the project back on track.

Documentation: Documentation is vital in Predictive approach. It includes detailed project plans, requirements specifications, progress reports, change requests, and other relevant project artifacts. Documentation helps ensure clarity, accountability, and transparency throughout the project life cycle (ref. *Process Groups: A Practice Guide* – sections 6.2 and 6.3. – "Manage project knowledge", and "Manage quality"). In the context of predictive project management, we must distinguish between three different and interrelated concepts about the outcomes of project management processes; they are the following: artifacts, documents, and deliverables:

- **Artifact**: An artifact refers to any tangible or intangible item produced during the project's life cycle. It can include physical items, digital files, software components, or any other output that is created as part of the project. Artifacts can be intermediate products, such as design mock-ups or prototypes, or final products, such as a completed software module or a user manual.
- **Document**: A document is a written or recorded representation of information, instructions, or data relevant to the project. It can take various forms, such as text documents, spreadsheets, diagrams, presentations, or audiovisual materials. Documents capture and communicate project-related information, including project plans, requirements, specifications, meeting minutes, reports, and other project-related contents.
- **Deliverable**: A deliverable is a specific output or result that is expected to be produced and delivered as part of a project. It is a tangible or intangible item that satisfies a specific project requirement and is typically provided to the project's stakeholders. Deliverables can be physical products, documents, software components, services, or any other measurable outcomes. Examples of deliverables include a completed software application, a project plan document, a training manual, or a project status report.
- In summary, artifacts are the products created during the project; documents capture project-related information; and deliverables are the specific outputs or results that satisfy project requirements. Documents can serve as artifacts, and deliverables can encompass both artifacts and documents. Together they form an essential part of project management and help document and communicate the work and outcomes of the project.

While Predictive approach is structured with clear planning and control mechanisms, it may face challenges when project requirements evolve, or uncertainties arise. More Adaptive Approaches, such as Agile, Lean, or Hybrid have emerged as alternatives to Predictive approach to address these challenges by emphasizing adaptability, flexibility, and incremental development (see Chapter 6 of this book – "Domain #3 – Adaptive frameworks/ methodologies"). Table 5.1.

5.2 Terms

Table 5.1 Glossary of some important terms used in this chapter

Terms	Source	Page
Artifact	*PMBOK® Guide* 7th Edition	184
Cadence	*PMBOK® Guide* 7th Edition	33
Change Control	*PMBOK® Guide* 7th Edition	66
Deliverable	*PMBOK® Guide* 7th Edition	82
Milestone	*PMBOK® Guide* 7th Edition	243
Phase Gate	*PMBOK® Guide* 7th Edition	244
Phase, Life cycle	*PMBOK® Guide* 7th Edition	42
Planning	*PMBOK® Guide* 7th Edition	52
Predictive approach	*PMBOK® Guide* 7th Edition	35
Process Groups	*PMBOK® Guide* 7th Edition	170
Single delivery	*PMBOK® Guide* 7th Edition	34

5.3 Mapping the exam content outline to the readings

Here is a table with the list of Tasks defined in the CAPM® ECO – Exam Content Outline for the domain Predictive, plan-based methodologies related with some of the referenced books where you can read details about the contents, we are going to describe in the next chapters of this book. (Table 5.2) The number of questions in the CAPM® exam related to the Predictive, Plan-Based Methodologies are 17% of the total number of questions of the whole CAPM® exam.

Table 5.2 Mapping the ECO Domain #2 to the PMI reference books' chapters

Domain 2: Predictive, plan-based methodologies (17%)	The Standard for Project Management 7th edition	PMBOK® Guide 7th Edition	Process Groups: A Practice Guide	Agile Practice Guide
Task/items		Chapters		
Introduction		2.3.3; 4.2.7.4; 2.3.2	1.7.2; 4; 5; 6; 7; 8; 1.7.3; 5.2; 5.9; 5.16; 5.10; 7.2; 6.2; 6.3;	3.1.1
Task 1 – Explain when it is appropriate to use a predictive, plan-based approach	3.7	3	2.1; 2.2	
• Identify the suitability of a predictive, plan-based approach for the organizational structure (e.g., virtual, co-location, matrix structure, hierarchical, etc.)			2.5.1	
• Determine the activities within each process		3	Table 1-4; 1.9	
• Give examples of typical activities within each process		3	1.7.4; 1.9; 5.6; 1.11; 5.8; 5.9; 5.10; Fig. 10.6; 10; 5.11; 5.12; 5.13	
• Distinguish the differences between various project components			1.7	
Task 2 – Demonstrate an understanding of a project management plan schedule		Fig. 2-24; 4.6.6	5.14	

(Continued)

Table 5.2 (Continued)   Mapping the ECO Domain #2 to the PMI reference books' chapters

Domain 2: Predictive, plan-based methodologies (17%)	The Standard for Project Management 7th edition	PMBOK® Guide *7th Edition*	Process Groups: A Practice Guide	Agile Practice Guide
Task/items		*Chapters*		
• Apply critical path methods		4.6.6		
• Calculate schedule variance		Fig. 2-24; 2.7.2.3	Table 10-1; 7.1; 7.5; 7.6; 7.11	
• Explain work breakdown structures (WBS)		2.6	5.5; 5.2	
• Explain work packages			9	
• Apply a quality management plan	3.8	2.6.6.	5.14; 6.3; 7.7	
• Apply an integration management plan	3.9	4.2.7.4	3.4; 5.1	
Task 3 Determine how to document project controls of predictive, plan-based projects.		2.7.2.3; 2.7.2.7; 2.7.2.5; 2.7.1; 2.7.2; 2.7.2.4; 2.7.2.8; 4.41	Table 10.1	
• Identify artifacts that are used in predictive, plan-based projects		4		
• Calculate cost and schedule variances		Fig. 2-24; 2.7.2.3	Table 10-1	

5.4 Task 1 – Explain when it is appropriate to use a predictive, plan-based approach

The tailoring of the approaches within projects is the most important concept in Project Management.

"*Tailor based on context*" is one of the twelve principles of Project Management described in the *Standard for Project Management* (ref. "The Standard for Project Management" in *PMBOK® Guide* 7th Edition – section 3.7 – "Tailor Based on context"), and a full chapter of the *PMBOK® Guide* 7th Edition is dedicated to describing the workflows to tailor the approaches to project (ref. *PMBOK® Guide* 7th Edition – Chapter 3 – "Tailoring").

The "context" of the project (also known as "environment") is the set of variable or factors, external to the project perimeter, affecting the project outcomes or that are affected by the project outcomes. Context of a project is composed by **Enterprise Environmental Factors** (EEFs – ref. Process Groups: A Practice Guide – section 2.1 "Enterprise environmental Factors") and **Organizational Process Assets** (OPAs – ref. Process Group: A Practice Guide – section 2.2 – "Organizational Process Assets).

EEFs are conditions (internal or external to the performing organization hosting the project) not under control of the project team, that influence, constraint, or direct the project at organization, portfolio, program, or project level.

OPAs are artifacts, for example plans, processes, policies, procedures. OPAs are based on the specific knowledges internal to the performing organization, and they are used by the performing organization to give guidelines to projects or operations. These assets influence the management of the projects.

Examples of **External EEFs** are Marketplace conditions; Social and cultural influences and issues; Legal restrictions; Commercial databases; Academic research; Government or industry standards; Financial considerations; Physical environmental elements.

Examples of **Internal EEFs** are Organizational culture; Structure and governance; Geographic distribution of facilities and resources; Infrastructure; Resource availability; Employee capability.

Examples of **OPAs** *are* Processes, policies, and procedures not updated as part of the project work and established by the Project Management Office (PMO) or another function outside of the project; Templates, life cycle, and checklists that can be tailored within the project; Organizational knowledge bases that are updated through the project with project information, for example, updated financial performance information, lessons learned, performance metrics and issues, and defects.

Most of the above-listed factors are sources of uncertainty and complexity affecting the projects within the performing organization. Having awareness of the Context, assessing and analyzing it in terms of EEFs, OPAs, and the level of uncertainty and complexity they cause, is the first step to take before starting tailoring of the approaches to any project. And, several factors can contribute in stabilizing the requirements of the product to realize in large advance, so that a Predictive, plan-based approach can be selected as the appropriate approach for the project. Example of the stabilizing EEFs and OPAs could be the following.

Legal restrictions, government, or industry standard are usually considered as constraints. They give mandatory requirements to projects and/or products to realize by the project, decreasing the measure of uncertainty of the project. The stronger the mandatory requirements or constraints, the lower is the need to adopt an Adaptive approach to projects, preferring a more hybrid or Predictive approach. We always must pay attention to possible changes to legal restrictions, government, or industry standard during the execution of the project, to try and adapt the project to new mandatory requirements or decide to terminate the project, but legal restrictions are commonly changed with lower probability and frequency, compared to common product requirements.

Resource availability, such as infrastructure, technology, and people, at the time of execution of the project, is the most important enabler for the correct execution. A predictive approach requires to plan in advance the resource availability and allocation of time during the execution of the project, so that stakeholders such as functional managers or sponsors are informed of the project needs in advance, to move people, infrastructure, and technologies into the project, to execute the planned work at the planned time.

Organizational Process Assets (OPAs) such as processes, procedures, templates, and checklists, available within the organization and imposed to the project teams, are constraints for the project. The heavier the bureaucracy within the organization, the lesser degree of agility the project has. The more the constraints from the organization the project team must comply with, the less adaptability to project-changing requirements, coming from the project stakeholders, the project has.

In Chapter 6 "Domain #3 – Adaptive frameworks/methodologies", we'll describe in more detail some of the tools in the "Complexity models" field that are useful to understand the scale of complexity of the projects on the basis of the context. The two most important parameters in the complexity field we must consider tailoring the right approach are the degree of uncertainty of project Requirements and the degree of uncertainty of knowledges the project team has on the technologies they have to use or provide within the project.

In this chapter, we just want to know that Predictive approach is mainly applicable within an environment with low degree of uncertainty requirement and high degree of knowledges, by the project team, of the technologies and processes to use or provide within the project.

5.4.1 Identify the suitability of a predictive, plan-based approach for the organizational structure (e.g., virtual, co-location, matrix structure, hierarchical, etc.)

Following are some of the **organizational structures** we find in the current enterprises (ref. Process Groups: A Practice Guide – section 2.5.1 – "Organizational Structure Types")

Functional organizations: A functional organizational structure is the one where employees are grouped into different departments based on areas of expertise. This type of structure is one of the most common types in business, especially in larger companies. Usually, in a functional organizational structure, the project teams are created on the demand when projects start building the project team, with people coming from different functions and releasing them from the project, to return to their functions, at the end of the project. Usually, the project management in charge of the project is one of the functional managers, and usually he/she is the functional manager of the function, where most of the work in scope to the project is in charge.

Matrix organizations: A matrix organization is a type of organizational structure that combines functional and skills-based structures. In a matrix organization, employees are grouped both by function (such as marketing, finance, or engineering) and by "competence centers". This creates a dual reporting system, where employees report to both a functional manager and a "competence center" manager. As in a functional organization, in a matrix organization, employees are assigned to a specific project on demand at the start of the project and released at the end. Usually, the project manager assigned to a project comes from one of the competence centers, or there could be a Project Management competence center where all the project managers are staffed. Its role within the project is mainly a "facilitator" between the needs of the project and the needs of the functions.

Project-oriented organizations: A project-oriented organization is a type of organizational structure that is focused on projects, where projects are complex and require specialized skills and resources. This structure allows the company to be more responsive and flexible to changes in the market and to customer demands. In a project-oriented organization, the project manager has complete authority and control over the project team, including the allocation of resources, the decision-making process, and the overall direction of the project. The project team members are dedicated to the project and work full-time until it is completed.

Product-oriented organizations: The product-oriented organization is often used in industries such as technology, software development, and consumer goods, where the focus is on product innovation and customer satisfaction. This structure allows the company to be more responsive to changes in the market and to customer demands, as product teams are fully dedicated to understanding and meeting customer needs. In a product-oriented organization, the product manager has complete authority and control over the product team, including the allocation of resources, the decision-making process, and the overall direction of the product. The product team members are dedicated to the product and work together to ensure its success.

Procurement-heavy organization: A procurement-heavy organization is a type of organizational structure where a significant emphasis is placed on procurement activities. Procurement refers to the process of acquiring goods, services, or resources from external suppliers or vendors. In a procurement-heavy organization, the procurement function plays a central role in the company's operations. The organization recognizes the importance of efficient and strategic procurement to support its overall goals and objectives. This structure is commonly found in industries, where the procurement of raw materials, components, or specialized services is critical to the organization's success. A procurement-heavy organization prioritizes building and managing relationships with suppliers. This includes identifying and evaluating potential suppliers, negotiating contracts, monitoring supplier performance, and ensuring compliance with agreed-upon terms and conditions.

Also, we consider **geographically distributed organizations** like international companies or big knowledge-based companies. When distribution is high, such kind of organizations can become virtual. **Virtual organizations** are composed of worldwide distributed teams, working on the same product, project, or service, in different time-zones. Independent by the organizational structure, if it's functional, matrix, project-oriented, product-oriented, or procurement-heavy, in any case the employees of a virtual organization work remotely using high effective communication technologies and tools, for example, video conference, chat, email, productivity, shared repositories of documents, artifacts, knowledges, and so on, and all their working processes run on such technologies. In many cases, the communication technologies in virtual organizations are so effective that a highly distributed team can emulate virtually a kind of co-location.

Table 5.3 relates the possible organizational structures with the **level of enablement to Predictive, plan-based projects**.

Table 5.3 Predictive approaches enablement by organizational structure types

Organizational structure	Team members are loyal to	Team members report to	Team members' engagement	Project manager's role	Predictive approach enablement level
Functional	Functional dept	Functional manager	Part-time	Part-time. Facilitator not responsible	**Low.** Resources can have frequent task switching under functional managers' demands, causing deviations from the project plans
Matrix	Conflicted loyalty	Both functional manager and project manager	Part-time	Full-time. Facilitator, not Responsible	**Moderate.** Resources still can have task-switching but less than in functional organizations if resources come from "Competence centers"
Project-oriented	Project	Project manager	Full-time	Full-time. Responsible for any project performance domain	**High.** Teams are formed mainly around projects, programs, or initiatives
Product-oriented	Project	Both project manager and product manager	Full-time	Full time. Responsible mainly for projects in product implementations	**High.** Enablement of dedicated, stable, and long-term teams that can work together on several projects of the same product.
Procurement-heavy	Supplier	Supplier	**Not applicable.** Suppliers' project teams	**Part-time.** Suppliers' proxy, mainly contract management	**High.** High predictability due to contract constraints usually in fixed price, time, and scope.

5.4.2 *Determine the activities within each process*

Each Process Group defines several Project Management processes (ref. *Process Groups: A Practice Guide* – Table 1-4 – "Process Group and Project Management Processes") that could be applied to a Predictive Project, whenever is effective, that is, the processes are tailored on the basis of the dynamic of Enterprise Environmental Factors, Organizational Process Assets, and uncertainty (ref. Process Groups: A Practice Guide – section 1.9 – "Tailoring", ref. *PMBOK® Guide* 7th Edition – Chapter 3 – "Tailoring"). There are 49 processes mapped to the 5 Process Groups as follows.

At the start of the project or at the start of one Project Phase, project managers run the "Develop Project Charter" and "Identify Stakeholders" processes within the **Initiating Process Group**. The Project Charter artifact is described in Section 6.5.4 "Determine input for scope" of this book. The "Identify Stakeholder" process produces as output the "Stakeholder registry" described in Chapter 4 "Use the Stakeholder registry in a given situation" of this book.

The **Planning Process Group** is the Process Group with higher number of Processes. In Planning, the project team could run the following *Management Plans* processes: Plan Scope Management, Plan Schedule Management, Plan Cost Management, Plan Quality Management, Plan Resources Management, Plan Risk Management, Plan Communication Management, Plan Procurement Management, Plan Stakeholder Engagement. Each management plan produces an artifact, that is, a plan that describes how the process will be managed during the execution of the project. In addition to the Management Plan processes, the Planning Process Group contains the following processes:

- Collect Requirements, Define Scope, Create WBS; they all are processes dependent on the process Plan Scope Management
- Define Activities, Sequence Activities, Estimate Activity durations, Develop Schedule, Estimate Activity resources; they all are processes dependent on the process Plan Schedule Management
- Estimate Costs, Determine Budget; they all are processes dependent on the process Plan Cost Management
- Identify Risks, Perform Quality Risk Analysis, Perform Quantity Risk Analysis, Plan Risk Responses; they all are processes dependent on the process Plan Risk Management

In Planning Process Group, also the ***develop project management plan*** process is executed. It produces the Project Management Plan as an artifact, that is, the integration of all the above-defined plans.

The **executing process group** contains the processes of predictive project management that the project management team executes during the realization of the work by the project team within the project. Those processes are as follows: Direct and Manage Project Work, Manage Project Knowledges, Manage Quality, Acquire Resources, Develop Team, Manage Team, Manage Communications, Implement Risk Responses, Conduct Procurements, Manage Stakeholder Engagement. All these processes take input from the artifacts generated by the processes in the Planning Process Group. For instance, the Manage Quality process takes inputs from the Quality Management Plan artifact produced by the Plan Quality Management process, or the Manage Communications takes input from the Communication Plan artifact produced by the Plan Communication Management process.

The **monitoring and controlling** process group contains the processes of predictive project management that the project management team execute to verify that the work executed by the project team aligns with what is planned in the Planning Process Group, and possibly give corrective actions where the work is going to misalign from the plans. Also, adaptation or updates of plans could be done during the monitoring and controlling process group if the project needs to be aligned with changing external or internal EEFs, or changing requirements approved by the Change Control Process. The monitoring and controlling process group is composed of the following processes: Monitoring and Control Project Work, Perform Integrated Change Control, Validate Scope, Control Scope, Control Schedule, Control Costs, Control Quality, Control Resources, Monitor Communications, Monitor Risks, Control Procurements, and Monitor Stakeholder Engagement.

The **closing process group** is only composed of the Close Project or Phase process that describes how the closure of the project will be and what are the triggering conditions that terminate the project. The Close Project or Phase process defines all the artifacts to produce to close the project or phase, for instance, signature by the client of the Acceptance procedure, or closure of all the pending invoices, or archival and distributions of the lessons learned, etc.

5.4.3 Give examples of typical activities within each process

Processes within Process Groups are defined as the execution of activities that transform input artifacts into output artifacts using some techniques and tools (ref. Process Groups: A Practice Guide – section 1.7.4 – "Project Management Processes"). Processes can execute in overlap within a project; not all processes are required or mandatory to execute within a predictive project, because they can be configured on the basis of the tailoring (ref. Process Groups: A Practice Guide – section 1.9 – "Tailoring", ref. *PMBOK® Guide* 7th Edition – Chapter 3 – "Tailoring"). The output artifacts of one process can be the input to some other processes, or they can be deliverables of the project.

Below you will find the description of some of the most important processes in predictive projects that are useful to know for the purpose of this book. We will focus our attention on the integrated processes of the Planning Process Group that takes the project team to have a Project Schedule and Costs Estimates.

The three most important constraints/resources in predictive projects are Scope, Time (Schedule), and Costs. These three variables are known as the "Iron triangle". To estimate the Cost and Time needed to execute a predictive project, we must first define the Scope of the work, so Costs and Time (Schedule) are function of the Scope.

The processes integrated to the Schedule Management are: Plan Schedule Management, Define Activities, Sequence Activities, Estimate Activity durations, Develop Schedule They are executed in the order here provided to get to the Project Schedule artifact.

The processes integrated to the Cost Management are Plan Costs Management, Estimate Costs, Determine Budget. They are executed in the order here provided to get to the Budget estimation.

5.4.3.1 Plan schedule management process

The Plan Schedule Management process is the process with the objective to create the output document called Schedule Management Plan, where the activities to do during the project is described, to create and maintain the Project Schedule (ref. Process Groups: A Practice Guide – section 5.6 – "Plan Schedule Management").

The input artifacts to the project are the Project Charter, the Project Management Plan, including the Scope Management Plan, and the

Development Approach, the Enterprise Environmental Factors, and Organizational Process Assets impacting the project.

Several techniques and tools can be used to create the Schedule Management Plan, for example, the Expert Judgment to get advises and consultancy from experts already experienced in similar projects, as the one we are facing, the Data Analysis including Alternative Analysis, to analyze the input documentation to understand the better approach to describe within the Schedule Management Plan, and conduct meetings with several stakeholders and project teams to agree on the Schedule Management Plan rationales and criteria.

5.4.3.2 Define activities process

The main objective of the Define Activities process is to provide the project Activity List as output of the process. It's the list of all the activities that the project team will execute during the project. The Activities listed within the list could be enriched with some attributes to do a better work. The Activity list can include or can refer a milestone list. A milestone is defined as a particular activity that has zero duration and it remarks the completion of some related activities. Other outputs from the Define Activity process could be some Change Requests to modify some documents or artifacts of the project, because the Activity list created is impacting such artifacts. Also, an update to Project Management Plan could be an output of the Define Activity process because the Activity List will be part of the Schedule Baseline and Cost Baseline.

- The **schedule baseline** is a formal approved version of the Project Schedule.
- The **cost baseline** is a formally approved version of the time-phased project Budget, excluding any Management Reserve and including the Contingency Reserve.
- The **scope baseline** is an approved version of the Scope Statement, plus the Work Breakdown Structure (WBS) and its WBS dictionary.
- The three baselines such as Scope, Schedule, and Costs are the **project baseline** (ref. Process Group: A Practice Guide – section 1.11 – "Project Charter, Project Management Plan, and Project Document" – Baselines). The baselines, if needed, are updated using the Managing Change Requests process with a formal approval process.

The input to the Define Activities process is the Project Management Plan, including Schedule Management Plan and Scope Baseline, EEFs, and OPAs.

In addition to the Expert Judgment, the tools and techniques used within the Define Activities process could be the Decomposition to decompose Activities in sub-Activities or define milestones, meeting to agree on the Activity List with the project team and, if needed, the Rolling Wave Planning technique.

Rolling wave planning is a project management technique that involves planning a project in "waves" or iterations (see Chapter 6 of this book "Adaptive approaches/frameworks"), with detailed planning only being done for the immediate future, while allowing for flexibility and adaptation as the project progresses.

The project is divided into smaller, manageable "waves" of time, with detailed planning and execution being done for each wave separately at the start of each wave and a high-level plan (masterplan or roadmap) defined at the start of the project, mainly to provide a rough estimation of how many waves the project will have.

The length of each wave may vary, and at the end of each wave, the project team reviews the progress made, reassesses the situation, and adjusts the plan for the next wave accordingly. This allows the team to take into consideration new information and lessons learned, which may trigger processes for updating the project scope, timeline, and budget.

Rolling wave planning emphasizes flexibility and adaptability, allowing adjustments to the plan as new information arises. The Rolling wave method is an incremental method, that is, an increment of potential usable product is delivered at the end of each wave. This is the main difference with the Project Phases, that is, at the end of one phase, there is no increment of product, but only release of deliverables needed by the subsequent phase. Also, the main difference between Rolling Wave and Adaptive Agile approach is that a wave has no fixed time-box similar to that is used in Adaptive Agile approaches.

5.4.3.3 Sequence activities process

After having defined the Activity list in the Define Activity Process, the next process to be done to get to the Project Schedule is the Sequence Activities process (ref. Process Group: A Practice Guide – section 5.8 – "Sequence Activities"). The main objective of the Sequence Activities is to have in output the Project Schedule Network Diagram and the updates of the impacted project documents; they are Activity list and Attributes, Assumption logs, and Milestones.

A **project schedule network diagram** is a visual representation of the logical relationships between project Activities (see "Figure 5.2 - Portion of the sample Project Schedule Network Diagram" in this book to get to an example of Project Schedule Network Diagram). It depicts the project activities as nodes and the ***dependencies*** between them as arrows (or links). The diagram provides a clear overview of the sequence and interdependencies of activities in a project.

After having created the Activity List, creating a Project Schedule Network Diagram typically involves the following steps:

- Determine activity dependencies: Identify the dependencies between activities. Dependencies can be of four types:
  - **Finish-to-Start (FS)**: Successor activity cannot start until the predecessor activity finishes.
  - **Finish-to-Finish (FF)**: Successor activity cannot finish until the predecessor activity finishes.
  - **Start-to-Start (SS)**: Successor activity cannot start until the predecessor activity starts.
  - **Start-to-Finish (SF)**: Successor activity cannot finish until the predecessor activity starts.
- Define the sequence of activities: Determine the order in which activities should be performed based on their dependencies. This step establishes the logical relationships between activities.
- Determine if Leads or Lags are needed as attribute of the dependencies.
  - A **Lead** is the amount of time a successor activity can start in advance against the completion of the predecessor activity.
  - A **Lag** is the opposite of a Lead. A Lag is the amount of time delay a successor activity can have after the completion of the predecessor activity. Usually, a Lead time is expressed by a negative number, while a Lag time is a positive number.
- Draw the network diagram: Start by drawing the nodes for each activity and arrange them in the order of their sequence. Connect the nodes with arrows to represent the dependencies between activities. Arrows can be labeled with the type of dependency (FS, FF, SS, or SF) to provide further clarity.

Creating a project schedule network diagram can be done manually using pen and paper or using specialized project management software that offers diagramming capabilities, also automating the generation from a tabular representation of the Activity List and Sequences.

The input to the Sequence Activities process is the Project Management Plan including the Schedule Management Plan and Scope Baseline, the Activity List and Attributes, the Milestone list, the Assumption log, EEFs, and OPAs.

The techniques and tools to use within this process are those needed to design the Project Schedule Network Diagram; they are Precedence diagram method, dependencies determination and integration, Lead and Lags, and possibly a Project Management Information System to help to manage the activities, the sequences, and their drawings.

5.4.3.4 Estimate activity durations process

The Estimate Activity Durations process (ref. Process Groups: A Practice Guide – section 5.9 – "Estimate Activity Durations") has the main objective to produce as output the Duration Estimates of the activities, the Basis of Estimates that are the rationales at the base of the estimations, and the updates to the documents impacted by the estimates. The most important artifact impacted by the estimates is the Activity Attributes (produced during the process Define Activities); indeed, the activity Durations Estimates are attributes of the Activities. Other documents to update, impacted by the Duration Estimates, are the Assumption logs, because the Basis of Estimations became Assumptions, to consider and to monitor during the project execution, so that the Duration Estimates remain consistent over time, and the Lesson Learned registry, because during the estimation process, often we learn how to solve optimization problems.

The input artifacts to the Estimate Activity Durations are Project Management Plan, including Schedule Management Plan and Scope baseline, to know what way of working to adopt in the process, and for which work packages of the WBS (from the Scope baseline) we must estimate the durations of the related activities. The input to the process also includes all the artifacts produced by the integrated scheduling process we have executed until now, such as Activity List with Attributes, Milestone list, Assumption log, Lessons Learned registry, Risk register, EEFs, and OPAs, as usual.

But the most important information we need in input to the Estimate Activity Duration process is that which is related to the Resources, both Human Resources and Physical Resources. Indeed, the Duration Estimates of the activities depend on the available resources, their calendars, and, for the Human Resources, their skills, that must fit with the work required to do. So, we need to get in input also Project Team Assignment, Resource Breakdown Structure (for the physical resources); Resource Calendars, and Resource Requirements (especially for Human resources, where the required skills are described).

Tools and techniques useful within the Estimate Activity Durations process, in addition to the usual Expert Judgment, Data analysis, and of course meetings, are the Estimation Techniques:

- **Analogous estimating** is a technique used to estimate the duration or cost of a project activity by drawing comparisons to similar activities or projects that have been completed in the past. It relies on historical data and expert judgment to make the estimates. This technique is quick and less detailed compared to other methods, making it useful in the early stages of a project, when limited information is available.

- **Parametric estimating** is a technique that uses mathematical models and historical data to estimate project parameters such as cost, duration, or resource requirements. It involves identifying variables that influence the parameter being estimated, establishing mathematical relationships between these variables and the parameter, and applying the models to calculate the estimates. Parametric estimating is useful when historical data is available, and the relationships between variables and the parameter are well defined. For instance, having as parameter that one person has done the work in two weeks, probably the same person can do double the work in four weeks or two people, with the same skills, probably can do the work in one week.

- **Three points estimating** involves estimating project durations or costs by considering three estimates: the optimistic estimate, the most likely estimate, and the pessimistic estimate. These three estimates are used to calculate a weighted average, known as the expected estimate, which provides a more accurate estimate than a single-point estimate. Three-point estimating considers the uncertainties and risks associated with the project.

- **Bottom-up estimating** is a detailed estimation technique that involves estimating the durations or costs of individual project activities or work packages and then rolling them up to obtain the overall project estimate. It requires breaking down the project into smaller components, estimating each component, and then aggregating the estimates. Bottom-up estimating provides a high level of accuracy, but it can be time-consuming, making it suitable for projects that require a detailed and accurate estimation.

■ **Decision-making with voting** is a technique used when estimating project parameters, such as durations or costs, by involving a group of experts or stakeholders. Everyone provides their estimate, and these estimates are collected and aggregated. Various voting methods, such as majority vote, average value, or range analysis, can be used to arrive at a final estimate. This technique leverages collective expertise and reduces biases or errors that can occur with individual estimates. Several types of workshops or meetings are usable for voting, for example, Wide Band Delphi, or Planning Poker

■ Also, in Adaptive projects, the **relative estimating techniques and affinity estimating** (a kind of relative estimating techniques) are used (see Chapter 6 Domain #3 – Adaptive framework/Methodologies – for Relative estimations with Story Points).

5.4.3.5 Develop schedule process

The Develop Schedule process (ref. *Process Groups: A Practice Guide* – section 5.10 – "Develop Schedule") is the last process integrated to the integrated Schedule Management processes. At this stage, we have all the information to produce a Project Schedule, that is, the most important output artifact of the process. Those input information are the Project Management Plan, including Scope Management Plan and Scope baseline, all the project documents we produced during the previous Schedule processes (Activity list and attributes, Milestone list, Duration estimates, Basis of estimates, Project schedule network diagram, Resource calendars, Resource requirements, Project team assignments, Assumption log, Lessons learned registry, Risk registry), the Agreements, and, as usual, EEFs and OPAs.

The Project Schedule is composed of Schedule Data and Project Calendars that are also output of the Develop Schedule process. The Develop Schedule is an interactive process where several reviews can take place by different stakeholders to get to an approved version of the Project Schedule. As we have seen in the previous chapter, a formally approved version of a Project Schedule is a Schedule Baseline, that is also an output of the Develop Schedule process.

We can use several tools and techniques to produce the Project Schedule such as Schedule network analysis, Resource optimization, Data analysis especially What-if scenario analysis and Simulations like the Monte Carlo simulation, Lead and Lags , Agile release planning, if we are in an Hybrid or Adaptive project (see Chapter 6 Domain #3 – Adaptive framework/methodologies of this book), possibly a Project Management Information system, to help us automate some Scheduling tasks, but the most important tools that we need to use are the Critical Path Method (CPM) and the Schedule Compression.

Critical path method (ref. Process Group – A Practice Guide – Figure 10.6 – "Example of Critical Path Method") is a project management technique that is used to schedule and manage activities in a project. It helps identify the critical path. The **critical path** in a Project Schedule Network Diagram is the sequence of activities of the Network that determines the shortest possible duration to complete the project. The activities in a critical path are called **critical activities**. There could be several critical paths in a Project Schedule Network, because the sequences of activities of the network that determines the shortest possible duration to complete the project, could be more than one and all of such sequences have the same total duration. The total duration of the critical path is the sum of the durations of all its critical activities. The characteristic of the critical activities is to have a float equal to zero. The **float** or **slack** of an activity is the amount of time the activity can be delayed from its *early start date,* without delaying the project finish date or consecutives activities. Any delay to a Critical Activity will delay the project finish date because the Critical Path is the sequence of activities that determines the shortest possible duration to complete the project. Of course, all the non-critical activities have a float greater than zero, that is: delaying a non critical activity will not impact the project finish if such delay is less than the Float of the same non critical activity.

Having the Project Schedule Network Diagram available in input to the Develop Schedule process, the workflow of the Critical Path Method, to get to the Project Schedule, is the following:

■ *Critical path determination*: Calculate the duration of each path through the network diagram. The critical path is the longest path in terms of duration and represents the minimum time required to complete the project.

■ *Project schedule development:* Use the critical path and activity durations to create a project schedule. This schedule will outline the start and end dates for each activity and the overall project completion date.

The Critical Path Method helps project managers identify the activities that are most critical to the project's timeline and enables them to allocate resources and manage dependencies effectively. By focusing on the critical path, project managers can prioritize activities and ensure timely completion of the project.

We'll run through an example of using the Critical Path Method in the next chapter of this book.

Schedule compression techniques (ref. Process Groups: A Practice Guide – chapter 10 – "Tools and techniques") are project management techniques used to shorten the project schedule without compromising the project's objectives or quality. These techniques are employed when there is a need to expedite the project or meet a tight deadline. The following are the two commonly used schedule compression techniques:

■ **Crashing**: Crashing involves allocating additional resources to critical path activities to reduce their duration and accelerate the project schedule. By adding more resources or working overtime, the activities can be completed in a shorter time. However, crashing typically incurs additional costs due to the increased resource usage. Project managers analyze the cost-time trade-offs to determine the optimal crashing strategy that minimizes schedule duration while considering cost constraints.

■ **Fast tracking**: Fast-tracking involves overlapping sequential project activities that would typically be performed sequentially. Instead of waiting for one activity to complete before starting the next, activities are partially or fully overlapped to shorten the overall project duration. Fast-tracking involves a higher level of risk since dependencies are not entirely resolved before proceeding. It requires close coordination and communication to manage any potential issues or conflicts that may arise due to the overlapping activities.

These techniques can be used individually or in combination, depending on the project requirements and constraints. It's important to note that schedule compression techniques may introduce additional risks, resource constraints, or quality concerns. Project managers should carefully evaluate the impact and trade-offs associated with these techniques before implementing them, ensuring that the project's overall objectives and quality are not compromised.

5.4.3.6 *Plan cost management process*

The plan cost management process (ref. *Process Groups: A Practice Guide* – section 5.11 – "Plan Cost Management") is the one where it is described how the costs of the project are estimated to determine the budget, how those costs are allocated over the timeline of the project, and how they are monitored and controlled during the execution of the project. The objective of the Plan Cost Management process is to produce in output the Cost Management Plan artifact.

The inputs artifacts to the Plan Cost Management process are the Project Charter, the Project Management Plan, including the Schedule Management Plan and Risk Management Plan, and, as usual, the EEFs, and OPAs.

The tools and techniques used to produce the Cost Management Plan Meetings with stakeholders to agree on the Cost Management Plan, Data Analysis like Alternative Analysis, to find the best way of working to estimate and manage costs, and the Expert Judgment to get consultancy and reviews from people who have worked in managing costs in similar projects.

5.4.3.7 *Estimate costs process*

The Estimate Costs process (ref. Process Groups: A Practice Guide – section 5.12 – "Estimate Costs") produce in output the Costs Estimates of activities and Work Packages, the Basis of Estimates, and the updated documents impacted by the estimates; they are Assumptions logs to receive the Basis of Estimates, The Risk Register, and the Lessons Learned.

The artifacts to consider in input to the process are the Project Management Plan, including the Cost Management Plan, where the way of working for the Estimate Costs process is described, the Quality Management Plan to adhere to some possible quality polices related to the Costs Estimates, and the Scope baseline to have full understanding of the work to estimate for costs. Also, in input to the process, we need the Project Schedule to know when to allocate (spend) costs during the project, the Resource Requirements to know the costs of the Resources, Risk Register, and Lessons Learned Registry to get some possible additional knowledges to use within the process of estimation, in addition to the EEFs and OPAs.

The tools and techniques used in Estimate Costs process are the same when compared to those in the Estimates Durations process, except for the additional tool Cost of Quality to be aware of in the Estimates Costs process.

To determine the budget the Costs Estimates are usually produced using the **bottom-up estimating** technique. Cost estimates using the bottom-up technique involve a detailed breakdown Work Packages in the WBS available in input to the Estimates Costs process, because we have the Scope baseline. Indeed, as we described in the previous chapter of this book, the **scope baseline** is an approved version of the Scope Statement, plus the WBS, and its WBS dictionary. Each leaf Work Package in the WBS refer to its own Schedule Network of activities, and estimating the cost for each individual Work Package means estimating the costs of the activities in the Schedule Network of such Work Package and aggregate the costs of the activities to the referred Work Package. The costs estimate with bottom-up techniques is a methodical and granular approach to cost estimation that provides a comprehensive understanding of the project's cost structure. Here's how it works in detail:

- Take the WBS from the Scope Baseline; it breaks down the project into smaller, manageable work components. The WBS organizes the project into a hierarchical structure, starting with the major deliverables and progressively breaking them down into smaller packages.
- Activity and Work Packages Cost Estimation: Assign cost estimates to each activity in the Schedule Network referred by the Work Packages in the WBS, and assign the costs estimates also to those that do not refer a Schedule Network, because they are possibly in charge of an external supplier in a turnkey contract. The estimates of such last type of Work Packages can be based on historical data, vendor quotes, market research, or expert judgment. The more detailed the WBS, the more accurate the cost estimation will be.
- Resource Estimation: Identify the resources required for each activity in the Schedule Network or Work Package in the WBS. This includes considering the labor hours, materials, equipment, sub-contractors, and any other resources needed to complete the tasks. Estimate the cost associated with each resource, based on market rates, supplier quotes, or internal cost data.

- Cost Calculation: Multiply the estimated resource quantities by their respective rates to calculate the cost for each activity or work package. For example, if an activity requires 20 hours of labor at a rate of $50 per hour, the cost estimate for that activity would be $1,000.
- Aggregation and Contingencies: Sum up the costs of all the activities or work packages to calculate the total project cost. It is also common to include **contingency reserves** to account for potential risks or unforeseen circumstances. The contingency amount can be a percentage of the total cost, determined based on the project's complexity and risk assessment.
- Documentation and Review: Document the detailed cost estimates, including the breakdown of costs for each activity or work package, assumptions made during estimation, and any supporting documentation. Conduct a thorough review of the estimates to ensure accuracy and consistency.

The bottom-up technique provides a more accurate and detailed cost estimate compared with the other estimation techniques, as it accounts for specific requirements of each activity. However, it can be time-consuming and requires a comprehensive understanding of the project's scope and activities. Additionally, changes to the project scope or activities may necessitate revisiting and updating the cost estimates throughout the project life cycle.

5.4.3.8 Determine budget

The last process of the integrated Costs Management is the Determine Budget process (ref. *Process Groups: A Practice Guide* – section 5.13 "Determine Budget"). It produces in output the Cost Baseline (that is the budget plus possible contingency reserve, excluding any management reserves), and the project funding requirements on the basis of the Costs Estimations done in the process Estimates Costs. Also, in output are the updates to the existing documents impacted by the Cost Baseline; they are Costs Estimate, the Project Schedule, and the Risk Register, indeed they can be reviewed during the Determine Budget process.

In input, the Determine Budget process gets the Project Management Plan including the Cost Management Plan, Resource Management Plan, Scope Baseline, the Cost Estimates with their Basic of Estimates, the Project

Schedule, the Risk Registry, additional business documents like Business Case and Benefits Management Plan, Agreements, EFFs, and OPAs.

The Determine the Budget process produces the Cost Baseline using the **Cost Aggregation** technique. The costs of the activities and Work Packages estimated in the Estimated Costs process are here aggregated, summed-up in the hierarchy of the WBS to get to the total cost estimation of the project, that is, the Budget of the project. Having estimated in detail the costs of the activities starting from the Schedule Networks referred to by the Work Packages of the WBS, we also know when these costs will be spent because the activities are scheduled. So, the Budget has also the information about the time frame where the costs will be spent, that is, the Budget Allocation in time.

One important tools and techniques we can use in the Determine Budget, in addition to Cost Aggregation, Expert Judgment as usual, Data Analysis especially about the Reserve Analysis, to set possible Contingency Reserve, Historical Information, especially about costs spent in the past, for instance, using some supplier we have worked with in other projects, Financing tools like forecasting costs, is the Funding Limit Reconciliation. The **Funding Limit Reconciliation** (ref. Process Groups: A Practice Guide – chapter 10 – "Tools and Techniques") is the process of comparing the planned expenditure of project funds against any limits on the commitment of funds for the project to identify any variances between the funding limits and the planned expenditures. We always must have in mind that most budgets assume steady incoming and outgoing flows. Large, sporadic expenditures are usually incompatible with organizational operations. So, funding limits help regulate the outgoing capital flow to protect against overspending.

5.4.4 Distinguish the differences between various project components

Until now, we have used and explained several terms about Project Management and some of them are the **key components of a predictive project** (ref. *Process Groups: A Practice Guide* – section 1.7 – "Project Components and considerations"). Those are Project Lifecycle, Project Phase, Phase Gate, Project Management Processes, Project Management Process Group. To recap those key components, here is a summary of the definitions:

■ **Project lifecycle** is the series of Phases or Stages that a project goes through from its start to its completion. A project can have one or more Phases. Each phase represents a distinct period and has specific objectives and deliverables. A predictive project lifecycle is a sequence of one or more phases planned mostly in advance of the whole project.

■ **Project phase** is a set of related activities within the project to realize results or deliverables useful for the next phase of the project. Each Phase in a project typically include the execution of all the Process Groups: initiation, planning, execution, monitoring and control, and closure.

■ **Phase gate**: A phase gate is a decision point; it is a review and evaluation point at the end of each phase. It acts as a checkpoint to assess the project's progress and determine whether it is ready to move on to the next phase. Key stakeholders review the results and deliverables, evaluate risks, and make informed decisions regarding project continuation.

■ **Project management process** is a set of interrelated activities that are carried out to achieve project objectives. Processes cover various aspects such as defining project scope, developing a schedule, managing resources, controlling quality, and communicating with stakeholders. In the book *Process Groups: A Practice Guide* 49 different Project Management Processes are defined.

■ **Project management process group** is a classification of the project management processes based on their primary focus and purpose. The five Process Groups defined in the *Process Groups: A Practice Guide* are:
  – Initiating: This group includes processes that define the project's objectives, identify stakeholders, and obtain project authorization.
  – Planning: The planning group involves processes that establish project plans, for example, defining project scope, create project schedules, estimate costs, etc.
  – Executing: The executing group focuses on implementing the project plan, managing resources, and performing project activities.
  – Monitoring and Controlling: This group comprise processes for tracking project performance, monitoring progress, and managing changes to ensure the project stays on track.
  – Closing: The closing group involves processes for finalizing and completing the project, including formal project acceptance, documentation, and lessons learned.

It's important to note that while the predictive lifecycle provides a structured approach, it may not be suitable for projects with a high degree of uncertainty or rapidly changing requirements. In such cases, an Adaptive or Hybrid project lifecycle may be more appropriate.

5.5 Task 2 – Demonstrate an understanding of a project management plan schedule

Let's go through an example of a predictive project to apply the knowledges we acquired until now and to learn something new. We will run the integrated Schedule Management Processes to explain the Critical Path Method, using a project management software to support us in the math and dependencies. We'll see how to monitor the project health using the Earned Value Method (EVM) (ref. *PMBOK® Guide* 7th Edition – Figure 2-24 – "Earned Value Analysis showing schedule and cost variance") to calculate the Schedule Variance (SV). We'll give a description with examples of a WBS, and we'll describe in more details the Quality Management Plan in the Plan Quality Management Process (ref. Process Groups: A Practice Guide – section 5.14 – "Plan Quality Management") and the Project Management Plan (Process Groups: A Practice Guide – section 5.1 – "Develop Project Management Plan").

5.5.1 Apply critical path method

We assume that in the Schedule Management Process of our example project we produced a Schedule Management Plan that describe the Schedule Process we are going to explain in the following pages to get to a Project Schedule using the Critical Path Method. Inside our fictional Schedule Management Plan is also written to use the Project Management software MS-Project 2013 to help us to get to the result. Let's execute the integrated Schedule Processes we described in the previous chapters applied to a sample project.

In Figure 5.1, you see the result of the execution of the integrated Schedule process applied to a sample, common, simple project, assuming a start date of 14 June 2023.

4: Develop Schedule process
3: Estimate Activity Duration process
2: Sequence Activity process
1: Define Activity process

ID	Task Name	Predecessors	Duration	Resource Names	Start	Finish
1	**Project**		**37 days**		**14/06/2023**	**03/08/2023**
2	Requirements Analysis		2 days	Analyst	14/06/2023	15/06/2023
3	Design and architecture	2	3 days	Architect	16/06/2023	20/06/2023
4	**Component 1 (C1)**		**15 days**		**21/06/2023**	**11/07/2023**
5	C1: Detailed design	3	5 days	Designer1	21/06/2023	27/06/2023
6	C1: Development, and Component Test	5	10 days	Dev1;Dev2	28/06/2023	11/07/2023
7	C1: Completion milestone	6	0 days		11/07/2023	11/07/2023
8	**Component 2 (C2)**		**9 days**		**27/06/2023**	**07/07/2023**
9	C2: Detailed design	5SS+4 days	3 days	Designer2	27/06/2023	29/06/2023
10	C2: Development and Component Test	9	6 days	Dev3;Dev4	30/06/2023	07/07/2023
11	C2: Completion milestone	10	0 days		07/07/2023	07/07/2023
12	**Integration (I)**		**8 days**		**12/07/2023**	**21/07/2023**
13	(I) Integration Development, Test, Documentation	7;11	8 days	Dev1;Dev2;Dev3;Dev4	12/07/2023	21/07/2023
14	(I) Completion milestone	13	0 days		21/07/2023	21/07/2023
15	Delivery	14	1 day	Architect;Dev1	24/07/2023	24/07/2023
16	Users training	15	5 days	Trainer	25/07/2023	31/07/2023
17	Acceptance Test	16	3 days	Client	01/08/2023	03/08/2023
18	Project completion milestone	17	0 days		03/08/2023	03/08/2023

Figure 5.1   Sample project schedule in tabular format

We first define the Activity List (1: *Define Activity process*). In MS-Project, the Activities are called Tasks, so, for the purpose of this chapter, we'll write Activity/Activities or Task/Tasks with the same meanings. We'll see in the next figures some tables and drawings representing the Activity List (Task List) enriched with additional "Activity Attributes" (Tasks Attributes), like Predecessors, Durations, Resources Names, Start and Finish Dates.

Then, we'll sequence the Tasks (2: *Sequence Activity process*) to get to the Sequence Activity artifact. To sequence the Tasks, we'll refer the Task ID of the "Successor" Task in the "Predecessor" value of the Task. By default, in MS-Project, the Dependencies in the Predecessor column are created of type FS (Finish-to-Start). In the case of Task ID 9 – "C2 Detailed Design", you can see that the dependency with Task ID 5 "C1: Detailed Design" is of type SS (Start-to-Start) with a Lag time of four days, and that's why you read the value "5SS+4 days".

Then, we assign Resources to the Tasks, and we estimate duration of the Tasks (3: *Estimate Activity Duration process*) to get to the Duration Estimates artifact.

Then we execute the *Develop Schedule process* to get the Project Schedule artifact, with Start and Finish dates for both the whole Project and the single Tasks/Activities. In MS-Project, when the Tasks are set in "Auto-Scheduled"

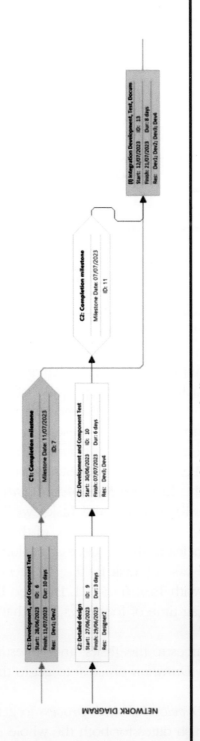

Figure 5.2 Portion of the sample project schedule network diagram

mode, the Project Schedule comes for free from the Tasks durations estimations and Predecessors settings.

In the sample Project Schedule above, you can see also some milestones; they are those activities with zero duration estimates, with no resources assigned; they are point in time to verify and validate the scope of the work if it's a per Scope and Quality plans.

A portion of the Project Schedule Network Diagram view of the above Project Schedule tabular view is in Figure 5.2. You can see in pink colors some *Critical Activities* (those that are in the *Critical Path*), and one milestone pictured in a different format than the Activities.

The Diagram in Figure 5.2 is only a portion of the whole Project Schedule Network Diagram, because if we would printout the whole Project Schedule Network diagram in this page, it would be not readable. The readability of relatively large Project Schedule Network Diagram is the most common problem of such representation of a Project Schedule, that's why, sometimes, it is preferable to have a different view of the Project Schedule that is the Gantt Chart.

A **Gantt Chart** (ref. *PMBOK® Guide* 7th Edition – section 4.6.6 – "Visual data and information") is a visual project management tool that illustrates the Project Schedule in a horizontal bar chart format. It displays project activities as bars, with their lengths representing the duration of each activity. The chart also shows the dependencies between activities and provides a timeline view of the project's start and end dates. Gantt charts help project managers and project teams to visualize the project timeline, track progress, and identify critical paths and potential scheduling conflicts.

The Gantt Chart of our sample project is in Figure 5.3.

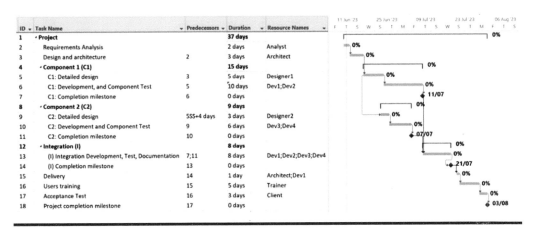

Figure 5.3   Gantt chart of the sample project

In Figure 5.3 in pink color are the Critical Activities; they are those with Task IDs: 2, 3, 5, 6, 7, 13, 14, 15, 16, 17, 18, each one with respectively estimated duration in days: 2, 3, 5, 10, 0, 8, 0, 1, 5, 3, 0. The sum of the Critical Activities estimated duration takes the Critical Path to have the duration of 37 days, that is, the project estimated duration.

Now, let's apply some *Compression techniques* to decrease the project schedule, that is, we have the objective to anticipate the scheduled finish date of the project. Let's apply the *Crashing* technique.

If the assignment of one additional person (Resource), with the right skills, to "C1: Development and component test" (Task ID 5) will allow us to decrease the Estimate Duration of the task, then we can allocate an additional Developer (Dev5) to the Task ID 5, because this is a Critical Activity, and compressing it will decrease the whole project scheduled time, that is, the Critical Path change.

In Figure 5.4, you find the updated Gantt Chart, where the modification of the values is highlighted in green color; we've set for crashing the schedule to modify the critical path.

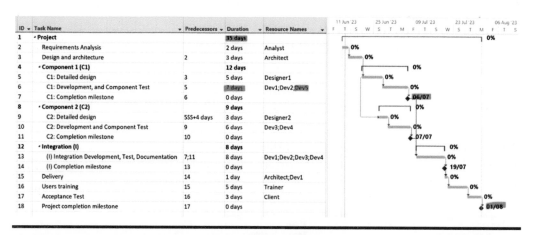

Figure 5.4   Critical path change after crashing technique

With the additional Dev5, in Task ID 5, we estimate that the Task ID 5 will take seven days instead on the initial estimated ten days, landing to a finish date for the "C1; completion milestone" Task ID 7 on 6 July 2023, instead of the date 11 July 2023, that was before the crashing. The crashing of Task ID 5 has taken the full project estimated duration to 35 days, instead of the initial 37 days, landing to a finish date of 1 August 2023 for the "Project completion milestone" Task ID 18, instead of the finish date of

3 August 2023, that was before crashing. Now the activity Task ID 6 "C1: Development, and component test", the one where we applied the Crashing technique, is no more critical, while the Activities Task ID 9 "C2: Detailed design" and Task ID 10 "C2: Development, and component test" have become critical.

5.5.2 Calculate schedule variance

The Schedule Variance (SV) is one of the variables used during the Earned Value Analysis of the Earned Value Method - EVM (ref. *PMBOK® Guide* 7th Edition – Figure 2-24 – "Earned Value Analysis showing Schedule and Cost variance", ref. *PMBOK® Guide* 7th Edition – section 2.7.2.3 – "Baseline Performance", ref. *Process Groups: A Practice Guide* – Table 10-1 – Earned Value calculation summary table").

The Earned Value Analysis is a technique used in most of the Monitoring and Controlling process group. This is a technique especially used in the following processes: Monitoring and control project work (ref. Process Groups: A Practice Guide – section 7.1), Control Schedule (ref. Process Groups: A Practice Guide – section 7.5), Control Costs (ref. Process Groups: A Practice Guide – section 7.6), Control Procurements (ref. Process Groups: A Practice Guide – section 7.11).

EVM is used to track SV, Schedule Performance Index (SPI), Cost Variance (CV), and Cost Performance Index (CPI), during the progress of the project, starting from four monetary base variables, they are Budget At Completion (BAC), Planned Value (PV), Actual Cost (AC), and Earned Value (EV). Also, the EVM allows to calculate the estimation of additional forecasting variable like Estimated To Complete (ETC), and Estimate At Completion (EAC).

Budget At Completion (BAC) is the total approved budget for the entire project, indicating the estimated total cost to complete all project work. BAC provides a baseline for comparison and is used to assess whether the project is within budget or over budget.

Planned Value (PV) is the authorized budget allocated to complete the planned work up to a specific point in time. PV is determined by the project schedule and indicates the value of work that was planned to be completed at a given stage of the project. At the Start date of the project, the PV at the Finish Date of the project is the BAC, while the PV at a date before the project Finish Date is usually less than the BAC.

Actual Cost (AC) represents the total cost incurred in completing the work performed up to a specific point in time. It includes all the costs, such as labor, materials, equipment, and other resources that have been expended on the project.

Earned Value (EV) represents the value of work that has been completed up to a specific point in time. EV is determined based on the project's performance and is typically measured in monetary terms. *EV is directly proportional to the % of Completed work at the point in time where the Earned Value Analysis is conducted.* We can calculate **EV = %Completion * BAC**, where BAC is the Budget At Completion of the project at the point in time of the Earned Value Analysis.

Schedule Variance (SV) is the EVM metric used to assess the schedule performance of a project. It measures the difference between the Earned Value (EV) and the Planned Value (PV) of the project at a given point in time. **SV = EV − PV**. A positive SV indicates in monetary terms how much the project is ahead of schedule, while a negative SV indicates in monetary terms how much the project is behind schedule.

Schedule Performance Index (SPI) is the EVM metric that provides insight into the project's schedule efficiency. It is calculated by dividing the Earned Value (EV) by the Planned Value (PV). **SPI = EV/PV**. An SPI value greater than 1 indicates that the project is ahead of schedule, SPI value equal to 1 indicates that the project is on time, while an SPI value less than 1 signifies a schedule delay (behind schedule).

Cost Variance (CV) is the EVM metric used to evaluate the cost performance of a project. It measures the difference between the Earned Value (EV) and the Actual Cost (AC) of the project at a specific point in time. **CV = EV − AC**. A positive CV indicates in monetary terms how much the project is under budget, while a negative CV indicates how much the project is over budget.

Cost Performance Index (CPI) is the EVM metric that assesses the efficiency of cost utilization in a project. CPI is calculated by dividing the Earned Value (EV) by the Actual Cost (AC). **CPI = EV/AC**. A CPI value greater than 1 indicates that the project is performing under budget, while a CPI value less than 1 indicates that the project is performing over budget.

Let's do an example of how to calculate the SV using the sample project that we created in the previous chapter. We assumed the sample project started on 14 June 2023. Now, let's assume today is 30 June 2023 and we want to run the Control Schedule process to measure the SV, and the SPI today, using the Earned Value Method, to see if we are on time, and if not how much in monetary terms.

In Figure 5.5, you see the Status Report of the sample project at the "Status Date" = 30 June 2023, showing all the calculated variables: SV, and SPI, and the base variables: BAC, PV, EV, %Complete.

ID	Task Name	BAC	PV	EV	% Complete	SV	SPI	Start	Finish		
1	**Project**	35.200,00 €	9.600,00 €	7.600,00 €	31%	-2.000,00 €	0,79	14/06/2023	01/08/2023		31%
2	Requirements Analysis	800,00 €	800,00 €	800,00 €	100%	0,00 €	1	14/06/2023	15/06/2023	100%	
3	Design and architecture	1.200,00 €	1.200,00 €	1.200,00 €	100%	0,00 €	1	16/06/2023	20/06/2023	100%	
4	**Component 1 (C1)**	10.400,00 €	5.600,00 €	5.360,00 €	65%	-240,00 €	0,96	21/06/2023	06/07/2023		65%
5	C1: Detailed design	2.000,00 €	2.000,00 €	2.000,00 €	100%	0,00 €	1	21/06/2023	27/06/2023	100%	
6	C1: Development, and Component Test	8.400,00 €	3.600,00 €	3.360,00 €	40%	-240,00 €	0,93	28/06/2023	06/07/2023	40%	
7	C1: Completion milestone	0,00 €	0,00 €	0,00 €	0%	0,00 €	0	06/07/2023	06/07/2023	06/07	
8	**Component 2 (C2)**	6.000,00 €	2.000,00 €	240,00 €	7%	-1.760,00 €	0,12	27/06/2023	07/07/2023	7%	
9	C2: Detailed design	1.200,00 €	1.200,00 €	240,00 €	20%	-960,00 €	0,2	27/06/2023	29/06/2023	20%	
10	C2: Development and Component Test	4.800,00 €	800,00 €	0,00 €	0%	-800,00 €	0	30/06/2023	07/07/2023	0%	
11	C2: Completion milestone	0,00 €	0,00 €	0,00 €	0%	0,00 €	0	07/07/2023	07/07/2023	07/07	
12	**Integration (I)**	12.800,00 €	0,00 €	0,00 €	0%	0,00 €	0	10/07/2023	19/07/2023	0%	
13	(I) Integration Development, Test, Documentation	12.800,00 €	0,00 €	0,00 €	0%	0,00 €	0	10/07/2023	19/07/2023	0%	
14	(I) Completion milestone	0,00 €	0,00 €	0,00 €	0%	0,00 €	0	19/07/2023	19/07/2023	19/07	
15	Delivery	800,00 €	0,00 €	0,00 €	0%	0,00 €	0	20/07/2023	20/07/2023	0%	
16	Users training	2.000,00 €	0,00 €	0,00 €	0%	0,00 €	0	21/07/2023	27/07/2023	0%	
17	Acceptance Test	1.200,00 €	0,00 €	0,00 €	0%	0,00 €	0	28/07/2023	01/08/2023	0%	
18	Project completion milestone	0,00 €	0,00 €	0,00 €	0%	0,00 €	0	01/08/2023	01/08/2023	01/08	

Figure 5.5   Schedule variance of the sample project

Each value is distributed on each Activity (Task). The Summary Tasks are the one in bold and their monetary values (BAC, PV, EV, SV, SPI) are the sum of the value of the Leaf Tasks correspondent values. The BAC of the whole Project has been set at 35.200,00 Euro at the project Start Date 14 June 2023, this is the "Cost Baseline". The Planned Value (PV) of the whole project at the Status Date 30 June 2023 is 9.600,00 Euro. The Earned Value (EV) of the whole project at the Status Date 30 June 2023 is 7.600,00 Euro. So, the SV (Schedule Variance = Earned Value – Planned Value) of the whole project at the Status Date 20 June 2023 is –2.000,00 Euro, that is, the project is behind schedule, and the monetary value of such delay is 2.000,00 Euro. The same information comes from the SPI (Schedule Performance Index = Earned Value / Planned Value) of the whole project; it is 0.79, a value less than 1, indicating it is behind schedule.

What are the activities causing the delay?

Looking at the values of the SV of each Leaf Task of the Status Report, we see the Activities Task ID 6 "C1: Development, Component Test", Task ID

9 "C2: detailed design", and Task ID 10 "C2: Development, and Component Test", all of them having negative values, respectively –240,00 Euro, –960,00 Euro, and –800,00 Euro. So, they are the Activities that are on delay and causing the project delay.

Are the delayed activities all at the same urgence for applying corrective actions?

No, they are not. The most urgent Activity to analyze to search for work-arounds and possible re-schedules are the Critical Activities that are on delay. Of all the three above Activities only one is Critical and on delay, it is the Task ID 9 "C2: Detailed Design" highlighted in yellow color. The Activity Task ID 6 "C1: development, and Component Test" is on delay but is not a Critical Activity, and the Activity 10 "C2: Development, and Component Test" is on delay, it is also a Critical Activity, but its Start Date correspond with the Status Date, so we can consider the delay a "false positive" case, that is, the delay is not really a delay because the start date of the Activity is equal to the Status Date 30 June 2023. Also, the Task ID 9 is the one with the lowest SPI = 0,2, and looking at the Gantt Chart, you'll see that the Task ID 9 is colored in red in the first part of the bar, it is the highlight in the Gantt Chart of the real Activities we must take care of for further analysis.

Note, the Critical Path at the Status Date is shorter than the initial Critical Path at the Start Date. The Critical Activities at the Status date are only those that must start. The Activities that have already been completed (100% Completion) at the Status Date, if they were Critical Activities at the project Start Date, then they are no more Critical because all the work to do on them has been completed.

How many days of delay is the critical activity on delay?

The Critical Activity Task ID 9 "C2: Detailed Design" at the Status Date 30 June 2023 should have completed 100%, because its Finish Date is 29 June 2023. Of the three days of Duration planned for the Activity Task ID 9 (Start Date 27 June 2023 – Finish Date 29 June 2023), only 0.6 days have been completed because its %Complete is equal to 20%, so the Duration of the work to complete is still 2.4 Days (it is the remaining 80% of duration work to complete). That is, the Task ID 9 is on delay of 2.4 days at least. Indeed, the Task ID 9 is on delay of 3.4 days because the Status Date is 30 June

2023 and the Task ID 9 Finish Date is 29 June 2023, adding one more day of delay to the 2.4 days of delay.

What corrective actions we can do to fix the delay of the project caused by the critical activity on delay?

We can adopt some of the following techniques:

- Try to compress the Project Schedule, adopting one of the Crashing or Fast-Tracking techniques we described in the previous chapters, of the activities that must be started or not yet 100% completed.
- If no compression is feasible, then communicate the project delay to the stakeholders, with a possible project re-schedule (that is, re-baseline of the project schedule) to agree with them.

To summarize, at the Status Date 30 June 2023, using the SV of the Critical Path Method on our sample predictive project, we understood the sample project is behind schedule because the Task IDs 6, 9, 10 are on delay and the most urgent Activity to focus on for further analysis is the Task ID 9.

Warning to better understand the above Status Report: The %Complete assigned to the Summary Tasks is calculated automatically, doing some math, by the software MS-Project on the base of the %Complete manually entered on the Leaf Tasks. The calculation of the EV on each Summary Task done by the software is equal to the sum of the EVs of their Leaf Task. That is, the formula of the EV = %Complete*BAC, in MS-Project, is applicable only to the Leaf Tasks while the EV of the Summary Tasks is the sum of the EV of the Leaf Tasks. So, if you verify the EV of the Summary Tasks using the formula EV = %Complete*BAC, you will find discrepancies against the correct EV calculated using the sum of the EV of the Leaf Tasks.

Note that the %Complete used in the above example is the %Complete of Duration also called %Duration Completed. The %Complete could also be related to the Work that is the Effort; in such case, the %Complete is called %Work Completion or %Work Completed. The %Complete could also be related to the physical completion of the deliverables; in such case, we talk about Physical %Complete. By default, in the MS-Project software system, the type of %Complete set for the base data calculations of the Earned Value Method variables is the %Duration Completed, and this is the one used in the sample project Status Report you see in the above picture. The differences between the three percentages type are the following:

■ **%Complete** (or **%Duration Completed**) refers to the progress made in terms of the time duration or schedule of an activity or task. It represents the percentage of the planned duration that has been completed. It focuses on the time aspect of the activity and provides insights into whether the activity is ahead of schedule, on schedule, or behind schedule.

■ **%Work Completed** (or **%Effort Completed**) measures the progress made in terms of the actual work performed or accomplished for a specific activity. It represents the percentage of the total work that has been completed.

■ **Physical %Completion** is a measure of progress that is commonly used in industries where the physical aspect of the work is significant, such as construction or manufacturing. It quantifies the percentage of physical work or tangible components that have been completed. This can include physical units produced, infrastructure built, or tangible assets installed. Sometime it could be useful to measure the Physical %Completion as ON/OFF, or Done/Not Done, or [0–100%], that is, the progress of the deliverable is measured ON, or Done, only when it's fully completed at 100%, while remain OFF, or Not Done, or 0% completed for the whole time frame of its working until its full completion.

The **Effort** (or **Work**) of an Activity is the time in duration of the Activity multiplied by the number of Resources (people) assigned to the Activity. So, for instance, an Activity with three days of duration, executed by three people has an Effort (or Work) of 9 days = 3 days duration*3 people.

5.5.3 Explain work breakdown structure (WBS)

The WBS (ref. *PMBOK® Guide* 7th Edition – section 2.6 – "Delivery Performance Domain") of a predictive project is created in the Process "Create WBS" (ref. *Process Groups: A Practice Guide* – section 5.5 – "Create WBS"). The Create WBS process is one of the integrated processes for the management of the Scope of a predictive project. The integrated processes for Scope Management are Plan Scope Management (ref. Process Groups: A Practice Guide – section 5.2), Collect Requirements (Process Groups: A Practice Guide – section 5.3), Define Scope (*Process Groups: A Practice Guide* – section 5.4), Create WBS (*Process Groups: A Practice Guide* – section 5.5).

The main objective of the Create WBS Process is to provide in output the Scope Baseline and possibly updates to Assumptions logs and Requirements documentation. As we described previously in this book, the Scope Baseline is an approved version of the Scope Statement, plus the WBS, and its WBS dictionary. So, the Create WBS process, as output, add the WBS and the WBS Dictionary at the Scope Baseline initially composed by the Scope Statement created during the process Define Scope.

In input to Create WBS process we need the Project Management Plan including the Scope Management Plan to know how the WBS should be created, the Project Scope Statement to know what the scope of the work is, what are the product requirements to realize, and as usual EEFs and OPAs.

The most important tool to use, in addition to the Expert Judgment, is the Decomposition. Indeed, the WBS is a hierarchical decomposition of the project scope into smaller, more manageable components called Work Packages.

The ***WBS provides a visual representation of the project's scope of work, in a tree view that is a hierarchical view***. Here are the key characteristics and benefits of a WBS:

- The WBS is a hierarchical decomposition of a project's total scope of work to accomplish project objectives and create the required deliverables (ref. *Process Groups: A Practice Guide* – chapter 9 – "Input and Outputs", section "Scope Baseline", "WBS"). The top level representing the project's major deliverables, and each subsequent level breaking down those deliverables into more detailed components. This decomposition continues until the Work Packages become manageable and assignable to individuals or teams.
- The WBS helps in planning and controlling the project scope. By decomposing the project into smaller components, it becomes easier to identify and capture all the necessary work. Any changes or additions to the project scope can be more effectively managed and controlled by assessing their impact on the WBS.
- The WBS provides a common language and structure for the project team, stakeholders, and other project participants to communicate and understand the project's scope and work breakdown.
- Time and Cost Estimation: The WBS serves as a foundation for estimating the time and cost required to complete each work package. By breaking down the project into smaller components, it becomes easier to assign resources, estimate durations, and develop more accurate project schedules and budgets. Indeed, each Work Package of the WBS refer to its own Schedule and Costs.

The **WBS Dictionary is a companion document to the WBS** that provides detailed information and descriptions for each component or work package included in the WBS (ref. *Process Groups: A Practice Guide* – chapter 9 – "Input and Outputs", section "WBS Dictionary"). While the WBS is a visual view or a diagram, the WBS Dictionary is a document that serves as a reference guide that complements the hierarchical structure of the WBS by providing additional details and clarifications. For each element of the WBS, the WBS Dictionary usually includes the following information: Code of account identifier, that is the unique identification number of the WBS element, description of work, assumptions and constraints, responsible organization, schedule milestones, associated schedule activities, resources required to complete the work, cost estimations, quality requirements, acceptance criteria, technical references, agreement information. Several information in the WBS Dictionary, instead to be written directly inside the document, they can refer or link external projects documents and artifacts, such as schedules, cost estimates, and risk assessments. This integration ensures consistency and alignment between the WBS and other project management processes.

The WBS Dictionary plays a crucial role in change control and baseline management. Any changes or updates to the WBS components can be documented in the WBS Dictionary, including the reasons for the change, impact analysis, and approval status. This helps maintain the integrity of the WBS and facilitates effective change management.

5.5.4 Explain work packages

Several types of WBS can be used within projects, in any type the WBS is a tree where the root node in the upper part of the tree is the Project reference, and the leaf nodes in the bottom part of the tree are the "Work Packages". The structure of the WBS is a decomposition of the scope of the work in the following three layers of nodes of the tree (from the higher layer just below the project reference to the lower layer of the tree): Control Accounts, Planning Packages, Work Packages (ref. *Process Groups: A Practice Guide* – chapter 9 – "Inputs and Outputs", section "Scope Baseline", "WBS").

- **Control accounts**: They are management control points (nodes) where scope, budget, actual cost, and schedule are integrated and compared to earned value for performance measurement.

- **Planning packages (optional layer)**: They are nodes below the control account layer, with known work content but without detailed schedule activities.
- **Work packages**: The work defined at the lowest level of the WBS for which costs and durations are estimated and managed. Work Packages can be linked to Control Account or Planning Packages nodes

Each node in the WBS has an Identifier number that provide a structure for hierarchical summation of costs, schedule, and resource information and form a **code of accounts**.

In figure 5.6 is an example of WBS created for the sample project we started in the previous chapter. (Figure 5.6)

Code Account Id	Name	Package Type	Scope Statement chapter reference	Accountable organization	Team Lead	BAC	Finish
1	Project	Root node		Delivery	Bob	35.200,00 €	01/08/2023
1.1	Phase 1: Design and Development	Control Account		Sponsor	John	18.400,00 €	07/07/2023
1.1.1	Design	Work Package	"Design"	Designers	Frank	2.000,00 €	20/06/2023
1.1.2	Development	Planning Package	"Development"	Developers	John	16.400,00 €	07/07/2023
1.1.2.1	Component 1 (C1)	Work Package		Supplier 1	Rob	10.400,00 €	06/07/2023
1.1.2.2	Component 2 (C2)	Work Package		Supplier 2	Tom	6.000,00 €	07/07/2023
1.2	Phase 2: Integration, and delivery	Control Account		Sponsor	Jim	16.800,00 €	01/08/2023
1.2.1	Integration (I)	Work Package	"Integration"	Integrators	Marc	12.800,00 €	19/07/2023
1.2.2	Delivery	Work Package	"Delivery"	Testers	Jim	4.000,00 €	01/08/2023

Figure 5.6 Example of WBS for the sample project

Looking at the indentation of the Package Names (column Name), you can see the tree or hierarchy of the packages of the WBS. The Code Account ID is in the standard format used to identify univocally the Packages within the WBS, such format gives immediately the understanding of the depth of the packages within the WBS tree. In the sample WBS, not all the Work Packages are linked to a parent Planning Package, indeed the Planning Packages are optional. We have divided the sample project in two phases and the two Control Accounts of the WBS are to control the two Phases. So, in such sample case, the Control Accounts are correspondent to the Phase Gates of the sample project. For each package there is reference to the chapter of the project document "Scope Statement" where the scope of the work is described in detail. Also, for each package we have information on the Accountable organizations, the Team Leader, the Budget (BAC), and the estimated Finish date of the work.

Some of the information in the above WBS could be part of the WBS Dictionary; that is, the attributes in addition to Code Account ID and Name of the Packages could be information described in detail within the WBS

Dictionary. The mandatory information for each package in the WBS is the Code Account ID and the Name of the package.

For each package of type "Work Package" there is the referenced schedule with cost estimations. They are what we created for the sample project in the previous chapter. Using the software MS-Project to create the WBS, as we have done in such sample projects, it's easy to drill down the Work Packages to their schedule and costs estimations.

5.5.5 Apply a quality management plan

Quality in projects is driven by one important principle of the 12 project management principles:

■ Build quality into processes and deliverables (ref. "The Standard for Project Management" in *PMBOK® Guide* 7th Edition – section 3.8 – "Build quality into processes and deliverable")

The principles want to highlight that we need to maintain focus on quality that produce deliverables that meet project objectives and align to the needs, uses, and acceptance requirements set forth by relevant stakeholders. Quality in project is about fulfilling both project and product requirements. It is about to guarantee efficiency of the project via the "Build quality into processes" part of the principle, and efficacy (or value) in realizing the product services or results of the project, via the "Build quality into […] deliverables" part of the principle.

In projects we plan for quality, and we guarantee processes and deliverable are executed and realized with the planned quality, that is, they fit with the scope and quality requirements of the project (ref. *PMBOK® Guide* 7th Edition – section 2.6.6 – "Quality" in "Delivery Performance Domain" chapter).

In the book *Process Groups: A Practice Guide*, there are several integrated processes about Quality; they are Plan Quality Management (ref. *Process Groups: A Practice Guide* – section 5.14) within the Planning Process Group, Manage Quality (ref. *Process Groups: A Practice Guide* – section 6.3) within the Execution Process Group, and Control Quality (ref. *Process Groups: A Practice Guide* – section 7.7) within the Monitoring and control Process Group.

Applying a quality management plan is about Executing the Manage Quality process during the Execution Process Group of the project, and Control Quality process during the Monitoring and Control Process Group of the project, after having planned the quality during the Plan Quality Management process.

You could feel tricky to understand the differences between Manage Quality and Control quality processes. In short, you need to think that Manage Quality is about project processes quality verification, while Control Quality is about project products/deliverables/outputs verifications.

The **Manage Quality** *process is about executing quality processes that has been defined in the Quality Management Plan to identify poor project quality processes and take possible corrective actions to re-align them with the process quality objectives.* The main objective of Manage Quality is to produce the following several outputs: Quality Report, Test and evaluation documents, possibly Change Requests if we must align the quality of some processes or deliverables to the Quality Plan output from the Quality Management Plan process or to improve those processes that are trending to poor quality, possible updates to the Project Management Plan including Quality Management Plan, Scope Baseline, Schedule Baseline, and Cost Baseline, possible documents updates to Issue Logs, Lessons Learned Registry, and Risk Register.

Inputs to the Manage Quality process are the Project Management Plan including the Quality Management Plan, project documents such as Quality Control measurements, Quality metrics, Risk Report, Lessons Learned Registry, and OPAs. The Quality Control measurements and reports coming from the Control Quality process of the project are very important inputs to the Manage Quality process because they give the data to base the decision for further audits, verifications, inspections, or corrective actions to take. Also, the OPAs in Manage Quality are very important inputs because they give the information of what organizational procedure assets such as quality policies, quality procedures, quality requirements, templates, checklists, quality process definitions, metrics measurements, within the project we must comply to.

To Manage Quality we can refer the following several tools and techniques: Checklists for Data Gathering during Audits, Data Analysis techniques such as Alternative Analysis, Document Analysis, Process Analysis, and Root Cause Analysis, Multicriteria decision-making analysis, several data representation like Affinity Diagrams, Cause-and-effects diagrams, Flow charts, Histograms, Matrix diagrams, Scatter diagrams, Audits, Design for X, Problem Solving, and Quality improvement methods like Continuous Improvements.

The **Control Quality** *process is about executing Audits, Inspections and Tests of the project outputs, and deliverables that have been defined in the*

Quality Management Plan to identify poor quality or not completed deliverables, suggests possible corrective actions to re-align them with the product quality objectives, and with the customer expectations.

The output of the Control Quality process are Quality Control measurements that go in input to the Manage Quality process, Verified Deliverables, Work Performance Information, possible Change Requests to take corrective actions or fix defects, possible updates to the Project Management Plan especially to the Quality Management Plan if something in Manage Quality or Control Quality process need to be reviewed, possible updates to project documents such as Issue log to track defects, Risk Registry, Test and evaluation documents to track test results of deliverables, Lessons Learned Registry

The inputs to the Control Quality process are: the Project Management Plan integrating the Quality Management Plan, important to know the way of working in Inspections and the way to execute the tests of deliverables; the Quality Metrics to apply to measurements during inspections and tests; the Test Plans and templates to track the Tests execution activity; the Lesson Learned Registry to know common workarounds to apply in Tests and Inspections; the Approved Change Requests to consider in Tests and Inspections, especially when there was no time to align the Scope documents to the Change Requests after their approvals; the Deliverables because they are the objects to Inspect, to test and to verify for quality; the Work Performance Data, because we can have a better understanding of the processes that have taken to the release of the Deliverables; and EEFs, and OPAs.

The most important tools and techniques used in Control Quality are Inspections and Test/product evaluations. Inspection and Tests requires Meeting with the project team. Some of the tools and techniques used in Manage Quality for processes are also used in Control Quality; they are about Data representation like Cause-and-effect diagrams, Control Charts, Histogram, Scatter Diagram. Other tools and techniques are for Data Gathering such as Checklists, Check sheets, Statistical sampling, Questionnaires and Surveys, Data Analysis with Performance Reviews, and Root Cause Analysis.

5.5.6 Apply an integration management plan

Integrating is the main activity of the project manager within the project. A tailored communication, adapted to context, is the most important tool project manager use for integrating stakeholders, processes, people in teams, and environment (ref. *Process Groups: A Practice Guide* – section

3.4 – "Performing integration"). A project can be a Complex System composed of several components that interacts one with others often having relations and dynamics not predictable, creating an uncertain environment that requires appropriate skills to be navigated (ref. "The Standard for Project Management" in *PMBOK® Guide* 7th Edition – section 3.9 – "Navigate Complexity" principle of project management). Project Managers should be aware of the different source of complexity: Human behavior, System behavior, Uncertainty and Ambiguity, Technological innovation, to try to navigate them in their role of Integrators within the project.

The *PMBOK® Guide* 7th Edition defines and describes eight Project Performance Domains (*PMBOK® Guide* 7th Edition – chapter 2); they are groups of related activities that are critical for the effective delivery of project outcomes. The eight Project Performance domain are: Stakeholder, Team, Development approach and lifecycle, Planning, Project Work, Delivery, Measurement, Uncertainty. The Processes of the Process Groups model we referred until now as a model for managing Predictive projects, described in detail in the book *Process Groups: A Practice Guide*, and referred by the *PMBOK® Guide* 7th Edition as a possible model for managing projects (ref. *PMBOK® Guide* 7th Edition – section 4.2.7.4 – "Process Groups") could be related to some of the Project Performance Domains. For instance, most the Processes in the Planning Process Group, like planning Scope, Costs, and Schedule can be related to the Planning Performance Domain; most the Processes in the Monitoring and Controlling Process Group can be related to the Measurement Performance Domain; the Processes about identify, plan, manage, and monitor Stakeholder Engagement can be related to the Stakeholder Performance Domain; the Process Developing Team can be related to the Team Performance Domain, the Process about Physical Resources management, Communication, Procurement can be related to the Project Work Performance Domain; the processes about Quality management and some of the processes about Scope management can be related to the Delivery Performance Domain; the Processes about Risk Management can be related to the Uncertainty Performance Domain, and the main Components of a predictive project like Phases, Lifecycles, Phase Gates can be related to the Development approach and lifecycle Performance Domain.

So, a Project Manager must be aware of all the above Project Performance Domains and Processes to integrate them effectively within a Predictive Project.

The way project manager integrate things within the project is described in the Project Management Plan. The **Project Management Plan** comes out from the **Develop Project Management Plan** process (ref. *Process Groups: A Practice Guide* – section 5.1) within the Planning Process Group, and it could be updated during the project as many times required by the dynamics and complexity of the evolving project environment. The Project Management Plan itself is the integration of several plans produced within a project. The Project Management Plan could be a compound document having all the other Plans as annexes or attachments. The Project Management Plan is the only output from the Develop Project Management Plan process.

In input to the Develop Project Management Plan process, we need the Project Charter to know what we must realize within the project and with what resources, the EEFs and OPA to be aware of the complexity of the environment, and all the possible outputs coming from the other project management processes available at the time of the development of the project management plan. The Project Management Plan is not always the first document created during planning, it could be the last one in the Planning Performance Domain, integrating all the others plans, or it could be the unique plan within the project, if, for instance, we are facing a simple project, where the project management plan could be comprehensive of all the information to manage and integrate all the aspects of the project.

The tools and techniques to use in developing the Project Management Plan are mostly about personal and social integration skills, also known as ***soft skills*** like Conflict Management, Facilitation, Meeting Management, etc., and Data gathering from Brainstorming, Focus group, or Interviews with stakeholder. Also, having Checklists to follow could be useful to remind the things to verify or manage during the integration process we follow as project managers.

5.6 Task 3 – Determine how to document project controls of predictive, plan-based projects

In the previous chapter, we described some of the most important variables used within the EVM – Earned Value Method. EVM is the most used method to control predictive project variables. To recap, the EVM base variables we described in the previous chapter are BAC – Budget at Completion, PV – Planned Value, AC – Actual Cost, EV – Earned Value. Using some calculations on the EVM base variables we derive the **Baseline Performance** variables (ref. *PMBOK® Guide* 7th Edition – section 2.7.2.3 – "Baseline Performance") commonly used to control the baseline performance of predictive projects in terms of Schedule and Costs; they are: SV – Schedule

Variance, SPI – Schedule Performance Index, CV – Cost Variance, CPI – Cost Performance Index.

In EVM, additional variables can be used for **forecasting** costs at the end of project (ref. *PMBOK® Guide* 7th Edition – section 2.7.2.7 – "Forecasts"), like the Estimate At Completion – EAC, and the Estimate To Complete.

- ▪ **ETC – Estimate To Complete** – is the estimated costs the project needs to spend from the moment of the last Earned Value Analysis to the estimated Finish date of the project. If we do not need to forecast based on past performances usually, we calculate the ETC = BAC – EV; otherwise, we can base the forecast on past performances considering the CPI index; in such case, the formula is ETC = (BAC – EV)/CPI
- ▪ **EAC – Estimate At Completion** – is the total cost the project will have spent since the start of the project to the finish date, estimated at the time of the last Earned Value analysis. Considering past performances to forecasts, if we expect the same performance CPI for the remaining part of the project, then the formula is EAC = BAC/CPI; otherwise if we don't want to use past performance of CPI to forecast, then we can use the formula EAC = AC + BAC – EV. The last one formula can be also expressed as EAC = AC + ETC; in such case, if the ETC was based on performance of CPI then also EAC is, otherwise not.

EVM has several other formulas that can be used to control and forecast project variables (ref. *Process Groups: A Practice Guide* – Table 10.1 – "Earned Value Calculations Summary Table"). Also, a very comprehensive description of the EVM is in the PMI book *The Standard For Earned Value Management*; you can look at that for further details, take in consideration that is outside the purpose of this book.

Additional variables we can control, not strictly related to EVM, and useful when we don't want to use EVM are Effort variance and Duration Variance. Effort variance is the difference between the Effort estimated before the time of evaluation against the Effort consumed at the time of evaluation. Duration variance is the difference between the Duration estimated before the time of evaluation against the Duration consumed at the time of evaluation. Or we could do the same comparing the estimated Finish Date of the project or activities in different points in time of the project.

Additional important variables to measure and verify during the project are those related to the **Business Value metrics**; they are ROI – Return On Investment, NPV – Net Present Value, Cost-benefit ratio, and generally speaking Planned Benefits delivery compared to actual benefits delivery (ref. *PMBOK® Guide* 7th Edition – section 2.7.2.5 – "Business Value"). We'll describe the ROI, NPV, IRR (Internal Rate Return), and Cash flow in the chapter of this book "Agile framework/methodologies".

We can measure and verify **Deliverable metrics** (ref. *PMBOK® Guide* 7th Edition – section 2.7.1 – "Deliverable metrics") like number of defects of deliverables, or measure of some product nonfunctional requirements like reliability, efficiency, or measure the coverage of functional requirements implemented in the product.

We can measure and verify some **Delivery metrics** (ref. *PMBOK® Guide* 7th Edition – section 2.7.2 – "Delivery") like Work In Progress, Lead Time, Cycle Time, mostly used in Hybrid and Adaptive projects. We'll talk extensively about these variables in the chapter "Agile framework/methodologies" of this book.

We can measure and verify the **Resources Utilization** (ref. *PMBOK® Guide* 7th Edition – section 2.7.2.4 – "Resources") comparing the Planned Resources utilization against the actual resource utilization, or the Planned resource costs against the actual resource costs (in such last case, we could use the EVM for costs variance).

And **Stakeholder satisfaction** using Net Promoter Score boards, Mood charts (ref. *PMBOK® Guide* 7th Edition section 2.7.2.8 – "Stakeholders"), Morale of the team, or Turnover of the project team members.

All the above metrics are to do a "**Variance Analysis**" to verify that the actual work we are doing in the project is aligned to what we planned in the past, and if we found misalignments or gaps, then we take *corrective actions* to re-align the performance of the project with what was planned. Also, we could use the "**Trend Analysis**" practice during measures (ref. *PMBOK® Guide* – section 4.4.1 – "Data gathering and analyses"). The trend analysis is to discover if the trend of the variables we are measuring is going to some control limits we can set as *boundaries* (they are usually called *upper control limit and lower control limit* of the variable we are measuring). The difference between the Variance and the Trend Analysis is that the first looks at the past data to discover past overruns of the boundaries with the objective to take possible corrective actions, while the second looks at the past data to discover the trend of the variables (usually in the timeline) with the objective to take *preventive actions (or improvement actions)* to avoid the variables overrun the boundaries in the next future. One of the graphical tool helpful in doing Variance and Trend Analysis is **Control Chart**. Those practices are also related to practices of *Continuous Improvement,* which we'll talk about in the chapter "Agile frameworks/methodologies" of this book.

5.6.1 Identify artifacts that are used in predictive, plan-based projects

The input and output of the processes of project management used within the Process Group model we described until now in this book, in the *PMBOK® Guide* 7th Edition are defined as "Artifacts" as we defined in the past pages of this book. In *PMBOK® Guide* 7th Edition, there is a very important chapter titled "Model, Methods, and Artifact" (ref. *PMBOK® Guide* 7th Edition – chapter 4 – "Models, Methods, and Artifacts" where most of the project management models, methods, and artifacts commonly used in projects are defined. For instance, Situational Leadership Models, Communication Models, Complexity Models, Methods for data gathering and analysis, methods for estimating, and so on, Artifacts (or templates) for planning, Artifacts (or templates) for reporting, etc.

The Process Groups we used to describe the approach to predictive projects inside this book is a Model, most of the tools or techniques in the processes of the Process Groups we described in this book are Methods, and several of the input, output to process of the Process Groups, for example a Project Management Plan, are Artifacts.

Several of the Artifact are used especially to document project control of predictive, plan-based project. We used some of them in the sample project we described in this book in the previous chapter, for example the Gantt Chart, the Project Schedule Network Diagram, Control Charts, etc.

The most important activity to do in a project about measuring and evaluate performance is to Visualize Data and information (*PMBOK® Guide* 7th Edition – section 4.6.6 "Visualizing data and information"), and Reports (*PMBOK® Guide* 7th Edition – section 4.6.7 – "Reports"). They all are Artifacts.

One of the most used Report to visualize information about the current status of the project, to the stakeholders of the project, in predictive projects is the **Status Report**. It may include information on progress since the last report and forecasts for cost and schedule performance.

The variables used in a Status Report to visualize the status of the project are basically those about the Earned Value Method we described in previous chapter. The figures you have seen in the Chapter "Calculate schedule variance" of this book are good examples of information that can be showed in a common Status Report: SV, additional EVM variables, Gantt Chart with %completion, and so on..

In a Status Report for a predictive project, we could also use several additional visualizations, like Cause-and-Effect diagrams (or Ishikawa diagram) to highlight issues and possible root causes, S-Curve types of diagrams to visualize the graphical representation in a timeline of the EVM variables, Quality Report with Control Charts, Risks Report with the status of the Risks in a Probability/Impact matrix, etc.

5.6.2 *Calculate cost and schedule variances*

In the chapter "Calculate schedule variance" of this book, we described how to calculate the SV using the Earned Value Method and we visualized a Status Report of the sample project started on 14 June 2023, at the Status Date of 30 Jun 2023. Now we will visualize the same report enriched with data Actual Cost (AC), Cost Variance (CV), Cost Performance Index (CPI), and the Estimate At Completion (EAC) as additional columns to the Status Report (ref. *PMBOK® Guide* 7th Edition – Figure 2-24 – "Earned Value Analysis showing Schedule and Cost variance", ref. *PMBOK® Guide* 7th Edition – section 2.7.2.3 – "Baseline Performance", ref. Process Group-s: A Practice Guide – Table 10-1 – Earned Value calculation summary table"). You can see the report in the Figure 5.7 Cost variance of the sample project.

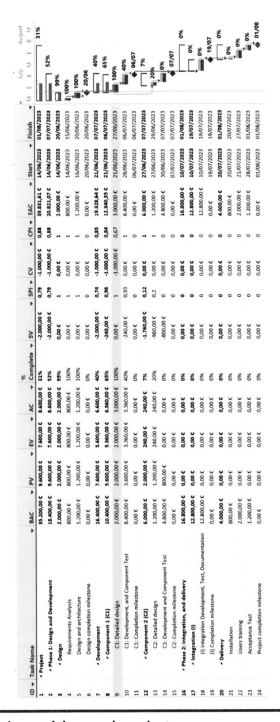

Figure 5.7   Cost variance of the sample project

In the Status Report, you see the CV of the whole project with the negative value at −1.000,00 Euro. The formula is CV = EV − AC = 7.600,00−8.600,00. That is the sample project costs spent at the Status Date is over budget −1.000,00 Euro; the same information is confirmed by the CPI of the whole project, that is, 0,88 (CPI = EV/AC, we remind that CPI<1 means the project is over budget, CPI = 1 means project is on-budget, CPI>1 means the project is under budget)

What is the cause of the project under budget?

Searching in the Status Report for any activity with CV<0 or with CPI<1, we find only one activity, that is the one highlighted in yellow Task ID 9 "C1: Detailed Design"; indeed, such activity has AC=3.000,00 Euro and EV=2.000,00 Euro, that is, CV= −1.000,00 Euro, the same amount of over budget than the whole Projects. All the other Leaf Activities that has not been started yet at the Status Date in the sample project are with CV greater than or equal to 0 and CPI greater than or equal to 1.

The Activity Task ID 9 has spent more money than the money earned as value at the Status Date. There could be many reasons of that (***root-causes***), and the next step of the Analysis is to find the root cause of the over budget of Activity Task ID 9, to try to find a corrective action. Due to the SV for the Activity Task ID 9 is 0 Euro, that is SVI = 1, the activity has been completed (100%) on-time, so the cause of the over budget is not a Duration higher than what was Baselined (initially planned), that is, the Effort at completion of the activity task ID 9 is what was initially planned. In such case, the only possible root cause of the over-budget is a higher cost of some material or tool used to execute the activity.

What is the EAC?

The EAC of the project at the Status Date 30 June 2023 is 39.831,61 Euro. The formula used by MS-Project to calculate the EAC is EAC = AC + (BAC − EV)/CPI, that is the EAC considering the CPI applied to the ETC = (BAC − EV)/CPI. So, the project at the Finish Date is estimated to spend more than what has been baselined (BAC = 35.200,00 Euro).

What corrective actions can we apply?

We have three choices to correct the above issue (EAC greater than baseline BAC) and we could apply the second two only if we fail in finding solution via the first:

1. Try to re-plan the costs (costs re-baseline) using less resources (less costs of resources) for the remaining activities of the project, probably causing delays on the Finish Date to agree with stakeholders (schedule re-baseline), to re-align the EAC to the BAC
2. If 1 fails and there is a contingency reserve outside the baseline BAC to use, then try to cover the over-budget with some *contingency reserve.*
3. If 2 fails, then inform Project Sponsor and stakeholder of the over-budget, describing the root-causes, and the attempts you have done to cover it, then ask for additional budget to re-baseline the BAC (probably there could be some *management reserve,* that is an external to project fund, managed by executives for organizational risk management).

5.7 Sample test questions on predictive, plan-based methodologies

Question 1
In the Earned Value Method (EVM), what does a positive Schedule Variance (SV) indicate?

A. The project is ahead of schedule
B. The project is behind schedule
C. The project is within the planned schedule
D. The project's schedule is indeterminable

Question 2
In the Critical Path Method (CPM), what is the Float of an activity?

A. The maximum duration an activity can be delayed without delaying the project
B. The Lag time of an activity
C. The Lead time of an activity
D. The total number of activities in the project

Question 3

In the Earned Value Method (EVM), if the Actual Cost (AC) is $10,000 and the Earned Value (EV) is $8,000, what is the Cost Performance Index (CPI)?

A. 0.8
B. 1.2
C. 1.25
D. 1.5

Question 4

In a Project Schedule Network Diagram, what kind of dependency relationship means that the successor activity cannot start until the predecessor activity finishes?

A. Start-to-Start (SS)
B. Start-to-Finish (SF)
C. Finish-to-Start (FS)
D. Finish-to-Finish (FF)

Question 5

Which of the following is NOT one of the five Project Management Process Groups?

A. Initiating
B. Planning
C. Executing
D. Closing
E. Analyzing

Answer to Question 1: The correct answer is A.
A positive Schedule Variance (SV) in the Earned Value Method (EVM) indicates that the project is ahead of schedule. It means that the earned value (EV) exceeds the planned value (PV), indicating that the project has accomplished more work than originally planned at a specific point in time. (ref. *Process Groups: A Practice Guide* – Table 10-1 – "Earned Value calculation summary method")

Answer to Question 2: The correct answer is A.
Float, also known as Slack, in the Critical Path Method (CPM) represents the maximum duration an activity can be delayed without delaying the project's

overall completion. It is calculated as the difference between the late start and early start times (LS – ES) or between the late finish and early finish times (LF – EF). Activities with zero Float are Critical and must be closely monitored, as any delay in them would impact the project's schedule. (ref. *Process Groups: A Practice Guide* – "Glossary")

Answer to Question 3: The correct answer is A.
The Cost Performance Index (CPI) is calculated by dividing the Earned Value (EV) by the Actual Cost (AC). In this case, CPI = EV / AC = 8,000 / 10,000 = 0.8 (ref. *Process Groups: A Practice Guide* – Table 10-1 – "Earned Value calculation summary method")

Answer to Question 4: The correct answer is C.
(ref. Process Groups: A Practice Guide – chapter 10 – "Tools and Techniques")

Answer to Question 5: The correct answer is E.
The five Project Management Process Groups are Initiating, Planning, Executing, Monitoring and Controlling, and Closing. "Analyzing" is not one of the recognized Process Groups (ref. *Process Groups: A Practice Guide* – section 1.7.5 – "Project Management Process Group").

5.8 Summary of predictive, plan-based methodologies

In Chapter 5 of this book, we described the knowledges required to attend the Domain #2 questions of the CAPM® exam defined in the CAPM® – ECO – Exam Content Outline.

The Introduction section contains the description of the common characteristics of the Predictive, plan-based projects.

In the Terms section we have definitions of the words coming from the Adaptive domain most used within this chapter of the book.

"The Mapping the Exam Content Outline" section maps the tasks of the CAPM® ECO with reference books useful to read to better prepare to the CAPM® exam.

The Task 1 section describes when it's appropriate to use the Predictive, plan-based approach, identify the suitability of a Predictive, plan-based approach for the organization structure, determine the activity in each process, giving example of typical activities within the integrated Schedule

Management Processes and Costs Management processes, distinguish the differences between the main components of a Predictive project: Lifecycle, Process Groups, Phases, Phase Gate, Processes.

The Task 2 section is the description of project management plan schedule with detailed descriptions of the Critical Path Method, the Earned Value Method, example of applications using a sample project to explain how to apply the Critical Path Method, Calculate the SV, explain the WBS, explain the Quality Management processes, and Integration Management Plan.

The Task 3 section is about determining how to document project control of Predictive, plan-based project, identify artifacts for measurements used in monitoring and control, referring the sample project created in Task 2 to explain how to calculate the CV using the Earned Value Method.

Chapter 6

Agile frameworks/ methodologies

6.1 Introduction

The "Manifesto for Agile Software Development" ("Agile Manifesto" or simply "Manifesto" for short) is the base document from where the Agile movement was born in 2001. You can read the Agile Manifesto on the internet at agile-manifesto.org or in the Agile Practice Guide by PMI. The Agile Manifesto was signed by a group of software engineers, coming from several different experiences. The document starts with the definition of its purpose and value:

> We are uncovering better ways of developing software by doing it and helping others do it. Through this work we have come to value:

- Individual and interactions over processes and tools
- Working software over comprehensive documentation
- Customer collaboration over contract negotiation
- Responding to change over following a plan"

to finish with the definition of the twelve Agile principles:

- "Our highest priority is to satisfy the customer through early and continuous delivery of valuable software.
- Welcome changing requirements, even late in development. Agile processes harness change for the customer's competitive advantage.

DOI: 10.4324/9781003462378-6

- Deliver working software frequently, from a couple of weeks to a couple of months, with a preference to the shorter timescale.
- Business people and developers must work together daily throughout the project.
- Build projects around motivated individuals. Give them the environment and support they need, and trust them to get the job done.
- The most efficient and effective method of conveying information to and within a development team is face-to-face conversation.
- Working software is the primary measure of progress.
- Agile processes promote sustainable development. The sponsors, developers, and users should be able to maintain a constant pace indefinitely.
- Continuous attention to technical excellence and good design enhances agility.
- Simplicity—the art of maximizing the amount of work not done – is essential.
- The best architectures, requirements, and designs emerge from self-organizing teams.
- At regular intervals, the team reflects on how to become more effective, then tunes and adjusts its behavior accordingly.

Purpose, value, and principles of the Agile Manifesto are the agreed synthesis of the experiences in the field of software engineering by the signers of the Manifesto at that time. In 1990, some of the signers of the manifesto created several frameworks/methodologies that were at the base for the Agile Manifesto values and principles. Some of those framework/methodologies have been maintained and evolved by their creators until nowadays, like, for instance: Scrum, eXtreme Programming (XP), Dynamic System Development Method (DSDM), Feature-Driven Development (FDD), Crystal, Agile Unified Process (AUP), ScrumBan. Also, other methodologies/frameworks have been created during the years starting from 2001 until nowadays, most of them are the results of evolution and innovation of technologies, like for instance DevOps, Disciplined Agile, SAFe (Scaled Agile Framework). And, several framework/methodologies have been created outside the field of software engineer, applicable to several domains, after the Agile Manifesto, or before like for instance "Design Thinking" that is applicable to projects where the outcomes are new ideas to implement.

The twelve Agile principles drive to hundreds of "practices" that are described in the framework/methodologies that are the base of the Agile Manifesto or born after the Agile Manifesto creation. The set of four values, twelve principles of the Agile Manifesto, and hundreds of practices derived from them define the "Agile Mindset" (ref. Agile Practice Guide – Fig. 2.3 – "The relationship between the Agile Manifesto Values, Principles, and common Practices").

Most of the Agile principles come from a previous framework of knowledges, born in Production environments, knows as "Lean", or "Lean Manufacturing", or "Lean Production", or "Lean thinking". One of the most known Lean framework/methodologies is "Kanban".

Lean is based on five principles described in Table 6.1:

Table 6.1   Lean principles

Lean – Principle statement	Brief explanation
Map the value stream	A Value stream in Lean is sequence of production' processes (or enterprise functions). A Value Stream starts from a customer' order to activate the set of processes to create, at the end of the Value Stream, deliverables that gives Business Value (benefits) to the customer. The "Value Stream Mapping" is the most important practice in a Lean system to reduce the wastes within the value stream. Value stream mapping consists in analyzing the execution time of each process in the Value Stream and the waste time (for instance, waiting time, goods transport time, etc.), and to minimize the wasted time.
Create flow	The Value Stream is a workflow, so the first thing to do in Lean is to design and visualize all the workflows.
Establish a pull system	A pull system is a system where the items of the work to realize are queued in a Backlog (or Product Backlog) and the workflow of the Value Stream starts from pulling the items from the Backlog to put them in "Work in Progress". The items in the Backlog are usually pulled on the base of their priority, that is, on the base of their relative ordering in the queue.
Pursue Perfection	The searching of efficiency using the value stream mapping, reducing wastes, and working in a flow is repeated cyclic using a continuous improvement mindset ("Kaizen")

One of the Agile framework/methodologies that directly derives from Lean principles is "Lean Software Development" (ref. "Lean Software Development: An Agile toolkit" by Tom and Mary Poppendieck, ref. *Choose Your WoW!* – chapter 2 – "Lean Software Development" in "Being disciplined"). As for the application of any other Lean framework/methodology, when we apply Lean Software Development to Agile projects, we want to maximize the efficiency and minimize the wastage. Indeed, Lean Software Development defines seven principles described in Table 6.2:

Table 6.2 Lean software development' principles

Lean software development – Principle' statement	Brief explanation
Eliminate wastes	Wastes of any type in processes have to be minimized
Empower the team	Give the team who execute the work the right accountability and autonomy to take decisions on how to do the work
Deliver fast	At the end of each iteration a usable and valuable increment of product should be delivered, the "time-box" of each iteration should be the shortest possible
Optimize the whole	Do not optimize only the details of the system architecture because local optimization does not guarantee global optimization, instead start with the objective to optimize globally the whole system to get also to possible local optimizations.
Build quality in	Quality should be embedded within the product the project realize, that is, quality is not only linked to the efficiency of the processes to realize the product but also linked to the efficacy and business value the realized product gives to the stakeholders and users.
Defer decisions	Defer decisions at the last responsible time, that is, take all the time to gather as much information possible to take informed decisions
Amplify learning	Learn from the processes, products and people subject of the project, that is, continuously learn from the errors done and from the feed-back of the people

Also, Lean Software Developments defines the seven wastes of software development, described in Table 6.3, to articulate the "Eliminate wastes" principle of Lean Software Development:

The Agile frameworks/methodologies are a sub-set of the Lean frameworks/methodologies (ref. Agile Practice Guide, Fig. 2.4 – "Agile is a blanket term for many Approaches").

In the project management terminology of *PMBOK® Guide* 7th Edition, the Lean framework/methodologies including the Agile framework/methodologies are all defined as **Adaptive approaches** (ref. *PMBOK® Guide* 7th Edition,

Table 6.3 Lean software development' wastes

Lean software development – Wastes	Brief explanation
Partially done work	We always need to complete what we have started; starting something else before the work is completed is a waste
Motion	The higher the physical distance between coworkers in a team, the higher is the time to get to face-to-face discussions. Co-location is the preferable way of working in a Lean/Agile environment. In a full Lean production system, the "Motion" waste is the "Transport" of goods waste
Waiting	Waiting time, of any time, are wastes; they must be minimized.
Extra processes	We should avoid heavy processes of any type
Extra features	We should avoid embellishment of the product, that is, the product must have only the most valuable features
Defects	We should improve the quality of the product reducing defects of it, that is, we must go through a development process that includes "refactoring"
Task switching	If we are working on a task, we have to avoid switching to other tasks to avoid losing focus (so waste of time) due to change of the work environment

section 2.3.3 - "Development Approaches"). An Adaptive approach is the one useful when requirements at the start of the project are uncertain, volatile, or ambiguous, so they will be refined during the project using iterative approach for refining requirements and/or incremental approach for delivery of product increments potentially usable by the users at the end of each iteration.

The development approaches for projects form a continuum from Predictive to Adaptive, including Hybrid approaches. Agile methods have short iterations (one week to a few months), Lean approaches have even shorter iterations (<1 week) or continuous delivery for incremental work. (ref. *PMBOK® Guide* 7th Edition, section 2.3). Agile frameworks/methodologies are iteratively and incrementally time-boxed, with predefined time-box to work on a product increment. Lean frameworks like Kanban are not time-boxed but still incremental, also falling under Continuous Delivery (ref. *PMBOK® Guide* 7th Edition, section 2.3.2 - "Delivery Cadence")

Table 6.4 relates the main characteristics of some of the project life cycle we talk in this book (ref. Agile Practice Guide – section 3.1 – "Characteristics of project Life cycles")

Table 6.4   The project life cycles in the *Agile Practice Guide*

Project lifecycle	Require-ments	Activities	Delivery	Goal
Predictive	Fixed	Performed once for the entire project	Single delivery	Manage cost
Iterative	Dynamic	Repeated until correct	Single delivery	Correctness of solution
Incremental	Dynamic	Performed once for a given increment	Frequent smaller deliveries	Velocity
Agile (that is Iterative and Incremental)	Dynamic	Repeated until correct	Frequent small deliveries	Customer value via frequent deliveries and feedback

The Discipline Agile Delivery (DAD) toolkit define the six types of Adaptive life cycles you read in Table 6.5 (ref. *Choose Your WoW!* 2nd edition – chapter 6 - "Choice is good: DAD's life cycles"):

Table 6.5   The DAD' adaptive project life cycles

DAD's life cycle	Characteristics
Agile	Mainly based on Scrum, short iterations planned, from one week to one month, to release a potentially usable increment of product
Continuous Delivery: Agile	Short iterations planned, one week time-box or less than one week, to release a potentially usable increment of product
Lean	Mainly based on Kanban to have continuous flow of working, no iteration planning, delivery incremental to release increments of product frequently, typically several times per month
Continuous Delivery: Lean	Continuous flow of working, no iteration planning, release of increments of product several times per day
Exploratory	Mainly based on Lean Startup and Design thinking to explore ideas and prove them, with the goal to have a Minimum Viable Product to present for demonstration to the stakeholders
Program	It's not really a life cycle per se, it could be one of the above life cycles but appliable to multiple teams (Program) that collaborate to realize a product, having dependencies to solve by them. The Program life cycle describe an effective organization by the multiple teams.

Table 6.6 illustrates a simplistic classification that assigns to Agile or Lean the different framework/methodologies. All of them are Lean because ***Agile***

Table 6.6 Adaptive frameworks/methodologies/toolkits

Framework/ methodology	Type	Agile	Lean	Team	Scalable
Scrum	Prescriptive framework for small teams	X		X	
XP (eXtreme Programming)	Flexible framework for small teams	X		X	
DSDM (Dynamic System Development Method)	Prescriptive framework for medium to large teams	X		X	
FDD (Feature-Driven Development)	Flexible framework for medium team	X		X	
Crystal	Flexible frameworks for several types of teams' size	X			X
AUP (Agile Unified Process)	Prescriptive framework for medium teams	X		X	
Scrumban	Integrated approach between Scrum and Kanban methods	X			X
DevOps, Continuous Delivery	Flexible set of methods and practices for Continuous Delivery and collaboration between Development teams and Operational Teams		X		X
Disciplined Agile	Flexible toolkit of hundreds of practices described for several team size	X	X		X
SAFe (Scaled Agile Framework)	Prescriptive scaled Agile framework for organizing Agile approaches at Enterprise scale, applicable homogeneous to all teams of the enterprise	X	X		X
Kanban	Flexible set of methods and practices applicable for continues flow of working to several teams' sizes	X	X	X	

is a sub-set of Lean, but the table wants to highlight which of those are strictly Agile, which of them are strictly Lean, and which of them can be considered both Agile and Lean, because they describe practices compliant to both (ref. Agile Practice Guide – Figure 2-4 – "Agile is a blanket term for many approaches"). Also, the table relate the frameworks/methodologies with their scalability, that is, if the framework is to Team level and/or Scalable to Program or enterprise level.

In the next sections, we will describe the introduction to several of the above Adaptive approaches.

6.2 Terms

Table 6.7   Glossary of some important terms used in this chapter

Terms	Source	Page
Adaptive approach	*PMBOK® Guide* 7th Edition	35,37
Agile life cycle	*Agile Practice Guide*	
Agile Manifesto	*Agile Practice Guide*	8,9
Agile Mindset	*Agile Practice Guide*	10
Hybrid approach	*PMBOK® Guide* 7th Edition	36
Incremental life cycle	*PMBOK® Guide* 7th Edition	37
Iterative life cycle	*PMBOK® Guide* 7th Edition	37
Lean frameworks/methodologies	*Agile Practice Guide*	11

6.3 Mapping the exam content outline to the readings

Here is Table 6.8 with the list of Tasks defined in the CAPM® ECO – Exam Content Outline for the domain Agile framework/methodologies related to some of the referenced books where you can read details about the contents, we are going to describe in the next chapters of this book. The number of questions in the CAPM® exam related to the Agile framework/methodologies are 20% of the total number of questions of the whole CAPM® exam.

The next sections will describe one by one the tasks and sub-tasks defined in the above table

Table 6.8   Mapping the ECO Domain #3 to the PMI reference books' chapters

Domain 3: Agile frameworks/methodologies (20%)	The Standard for Project Management 7th edition	PMBOK® Guide 7th Edition	Agile Practice Guide	Process Groups: A Practice Guide	Choose Your Wow! 2nd ed
Task/items			*Chapters*		
Introduction		2.3.3; 2.3; 2.3.2	2.2; Fig. 2.4; 3.1.2; 3.1.3; 3.1.4; Fig 2.3; 3.1		2; 6
Task 1 - Explain when it is appropriate to use an adaptive approach.	3.7	3		2.1; 2.2	
• Compare the pros and cons of adaptive and predictive, plan-based projects.	3.9	2.8; 4.2.5.1; 4.2.5.2	2.4		Fig. 3.6
• Identify the suitability of adaptive approaches for the organizational structure (e.g., virtual, co-location, matrix structure, hierarchical, etc.)			4.3; 4.2; 6.7	2.5.1;	
• Identify organizational process assets and enterprise environmental factors that facilitate the use of adaptive approaches.				2.1;2.2	
Task 2 - Determine how to plan project iterations		Fig. 2–17; 2.4; 4.6.2; 2.6.2.2	5.1	5.5	
• Distinguish the logical units of iterations		2.6.2.2	5.2		
• Interpret the pros and cons of the iteration			5.3		

(Continued)

Table 6.8 (Continued) Mapping the ECO Domain #3 to the PMI reference books' chapters

Domain 3: Agile frameworks/methodologies (20%)	The Standard for Project Management 7th edition	PMBOK® Guide 7th Edition	Agile Practice Guide	Process Groups: A Practice Guide	Choose Your Wow! 2nd ed
• Translate this WBS to an adaptive iteration.		2.6.2.2			
• Determine inputs for scope		4.6.1	5.1		
• Explain the importance of adaptive project tracking versus predictive, plan-based tracking.		2.3.3; 2.7			
Task 3 - Determine how to document project controls for an adaptive project		2.7; 4.4.2; 2.7.2.2	5.4	7	
• Identify artifacts that are used in adaptive projects.		2.7.3; Fig. 2–28; Fig. 2.29; 4.6.6	5.4.1; Fig. 5–7		
Task 4 - Explain the components of an adaptive plan			A3.14		
• Distinguish between the components of different adaptive methodologies (e.g., Scrum, eXtreme Programming (XP), Scaled Adaptive Framework (SAFe®), Kanban, etc.).			A3.2; A3.3; A3.4; A3.14		2; 5
Task 5 - Determine how to prepare and execute task management steps	3				
• Interpret success criteria of an adaptive project management task	3.4; 3.8	2.7.2.5; 2.6.3; 2.6			
• Prioritize tasks in adaptive project management		4.4; 2.2.2.4			

6.4 Task 1 – Explain when it is appropriate to use an adaptive approach

Adaptive approaches suit projects with uncertain, volatile requirements and unknown technologies. They're ideal for high uncertainty or complexity contexts, while Predictive approaches are better for low uncertainty or complexity. (ref. *PMBOK® Guide* 7th Edition – section 2.8 – "Uncertainty Performance Domain", ref. The Standard For Project Management – section 3.9 – Principle "Navigate Complexity")

Selecting the appropriate approach for a project involves analyzing its complexity and contextual factors via EEFs and OPAs. The upcoming chapter details how to assess project complexity for tailoring the right Adaptive Approach.

6.4.1 Compare the pros and cons of adaptive and predictive, plan-based projects

Several complexity models can be used to assess and analyze the context of the project, their EEFs and OPAs, to understand better what the best approach to use within the project could be. We are going to explain here: The Cynefin framework or Cynefin Model by Dave Snowden (ref. *PMBOK® Guide* 7th Edition - section 4.2.5.1), the Stacey Matrix or Stacey Complexity model by Ralph Stacey (ref. *PMBOK® Guide* 7th Edition – section 4.2.5.2 – "Stacey Matrix", ref. Agile Practice Guide – section 2.4 – "Uncertainty, risk, and life cycle selection"), the Disciplined Agile Delivery Tactical Scaling Factors by Scott Ambler and Mark Lines (ref. *Choose Your WOW! A Disciplined Approach to Optimizing Your Way of Working*, 2nd Edition – Fig 3.6)

6.4.1.1 Cynefin

The **Cynefin model** by Dave Snowden assesses problem complexity subjectively. Complexity levels change with acquired knowledge, making classifications temporary and dynamic. Problems may shift through complexity classes over time.

The Cynefin model defines the following five classes or domains of complexity:

- ***Clear***: The "Clear" domain involves problems with known solutions, suitable for ordered, predictable systems. It's one of the "Ordered" domains, along with "Complicated." Projects with known solutions and advanced planning belong to this domain.
- ***Complicated***: The "Complicated" domain involves problems with known unknowns, requiring analysis and experimentation for solutions. It lacks predefined solution categories due to novel problem characteristics. Planning for a project in this domain focuses on the clear scope, deferring planning for unclear aspects until they become clearer.
- ***Complex***: The "Complex" domain entails uncertainty, emergent outcomes, and intricate interactions. It lacks clear cause-and-effect relationships and requires adaptive experimentation due to nonlinear dynamics. Complex situations demand ongoing sense-making, involving diverse perspectives, quick experiments, and rapid feedback for understanding and adaptation.
- ***Chaotic***: The "Chaotic" domain signifies extreme disorder and unpredictability, demanding urgent, bold actions to restore stability. No patterns or predictions are feasible, requiring strong leadership to make quick decisions. Transitioning to a less chaotic domain like "Complex" or "Complicated" is necessary before applying a project approach, but if not possible, a "start to work" approach can help.
- ***Confusion***: "Confusion" is distinct from "Chaos," involving creating Aporia to escape confusion. Unintentionally being in the Confusion domain is risky. Decisions made here can address problems spanning multiple domains, and illogical thinking might help transition to other Cynefin domains.

6.4.1.2 Stacey complexity model

The **Stacey Matrix or Stacey complexity model** is quite related to the Cynefin complexity model; indeed, it describes four complexity domain at the same scale of the five Cynefin domains. In the Stacey Matrix, the Approaches to projects can be identified starting from two parameters of the environment: The degree of the project' requirements uncertainty (from Low to High uncertainty), the degree of technical unknowns.

In Table 6.9, Stacy Matrix is applied to selection of project approaches.

Table 6.9   Stacey matrix

Stacy matrix complexity area	*Degree of requirements uncertainty*	*Degree of technical unknowns*	*Suggested approaches in projects*
Simple	Low	Low	Predictive or Hybrid
Complicated	Low	High	Adaptive Agile or Hybrid
Complicated	High	Low	Adaptive Agile or Hybrid
Complex	High	High	Adaptive Lean, continuous flow, continuous delivery
Chaos	Very high	Very High	Fundamentally risky, not applicable

6.4.1.3 *Disciplined Agile delivery tactical scaling factors*

The Disciplined Agile Delivery Tactical Scaling Factors are several parameters applicable to delivery teams; through their combined evaluation we can understand the more appropriate approach to project. Table 6.10 illustrates the list of those factors with related brief description and scales of evaluation:

Table 6.10   Discipline Agile delivery tactical scaling factors

Disciplined Agile Delivery - tactical scaling factor	*Factor description*	*Scale of evaluation of the factor from lower to higher*
Team Size	The number of people composing the project teams	10; 25; 100; 250+
Geographic distribution	The geographical distribution of the people composing the project teams	Co-located; Same building; Same time zone; Global (worldwide, different time-zones)
Organizational distribution	The type of organization hosting the projects teams	Startup; Single Organization; Paid Partners; Coalition Partners
Skill Availability	The scale of availability in time of the people skilled in the required scope of work to realize with the project	Available now; Available soon; easy to acquire; Difficult to acquire
		(Continued)

Table 6.10 (Continued)   Discipline Agile delivery tactical scaling factors

Disciplined Agile Delivery - tactical scaling factor	Factor description	Scale of evaluation of the factor from lower to higher
Compliance	The measure of compliance to standards required by the product, or service, or result of the project	Informal; Internal oversight; External standards; Regulatory oversight; Existential
Solution complexity	The scale of architectural complexity of the product to realize with the project	New stand-alone; New integrated; Legacy; Multi-environment legacy
Domain complexity	The scale of uncertainty and dynamics of the solution domain	Straightforward; Complex; Very complex; Rapidly evolving

The combined evaluation of such factors gives the understanding of the approaches that can be selected for the project. There is no general rule to apply to select the best approach to project, and we need to evaluate the combination of the values of the scaled tactical factors with reference to the principles described in this chapter to understand which approach best fit to the project.

6.4.2 Identify the suitability of adaptive approaches for the organizational structure (e.g., virtual, co-location, matrix structure, hierarchical, etc.)

Adaptive approaches require **project teams with the following base characteristics,** for both Agile and Lean approaches (ref. Agile Practice Guide, section 4.3 – "Team composition")

- **Small teams**: usually an Agile team is less the ten people, this is to minimize the complexity of the communications within the team. A project team larger than ten should be decomposed in several team with less than ten people. This is because small teams are more effective in communication and collaboration.
- **Stable teams (or product teams)**: the longer the time the teammates are in the same team, the more they are effective in collaboration and communication.

- **Co-location** (physical or virtual): they need to exchange frequent feedback and information with others, and they need to share information in a transparent way using easy technologies to radiate information.
- **Full-time engagement**: Agile project team members work focused 100% on the tasks of the project, minimizing any possible task-switch or project-switch, to reduce any time waste.
- **Self-management**: Agile encourage each project team member to be accountable to others on the work they do, to decide their way of working, and take decisions collectively.
- **Cross-functionality**: each team member is highly skilled in the work he or she does and has knowledge about the work the other teammates are doing ("T-Shaped" people, ref. Agile Practice Guide – section 4.3.3 – "Generalizing specialist") so that they could take charge of several types of work, or they could support the other team members in case of need, maximizing the efficiency of the workflow.
- **Safe work environment**: people in teams need not be afraid to fail. A psychological safe environment is required because Agile teams execute empirical processes with several experiments and explorations where the outcomes are in any case newly acquired knowledge useful to progress in the project, and never a failed experiment should be considered a mistake of someone.

Also, Adaptive approaches like Agile or Lean requires the team leaders to learn and apply a Servant Leadership style (ref. Agile Practice Guide – section 4.2 – "Servant Leadership empowers the team"). Servant Leadership is the practice of leading the team through service, by focusing on understanding and addressing the needs and development of team members to enable the highest possible team performance. Following are some of the characteristics of the **Servant Leadership**.

- **Shield the team from interruption**: Servant leaders need to isolate and protect the team members from diversions, interruptions, and request for work that aren't part of the project.
- **Remove impediment to progress:** Servant leaders need to clear obstacles from the team's path that would cause delay or waste. In Lean terms, removing impediments is about minimizing the efforts that do not directly contribute toward delivering business value.

- **Communicate (and recommunicate) the project vision**: Only if stakeholders have a clear vision of the goals for the completed product and projects can they align their decisions with, and work toward, the common project objective.
- **Carry food and water:** Not literally, it's about providing the essential resources a team needs to keep them nourished and productive.
- **Practice transparency** through visualization of information.
- **Create a safe environment** for experimentation, and experiment with new techniques and processes.
- **Share knowledge** through collaboration and encourage emergent leadership via a safe environment.

Not all the types of organizational structures (see Section 5.4.1 of this book) we find in companies enable the shifting of people to an Agile mindset or the shifting to a Servant Leadership style by the leaders, within projects and at the larger scale of the organization (ref. Agile Practice Guide – section 6.7 – "Organizational Structure").

Table 6.11 relates the possible organizational structure with the **level of enablement to Adaptive approaches**.

Table 6.11 Adaptive approaches enablement by organizational structure types

Organizational structure type	Project team stability	Project team cross functionality	Project team engagement	Project manager role	Adaptive approaches enablement level
Functional	**Low.** Project teams are frequently created and dismissed	**Low.** People are specialized by organizational functions	**Part-time.** No full commitment in project work	**Part-time.** Facilitator, not Responsible	**Low.** It can be challenging to implement fully due to functional silos and potential delays in decision-making.
Matrix	**Moderate.** Good probability to work in teams with same people	**Low.** People are specialized by competence centers	**Part-time.** No full commitment in project work	**Full-time.** Facilitator, not Responsible	**Moderate.** It requires careful attention to communication, decision-making processes, and team stability to create an enabling environment
Project-Oriented	**Moderate.** Good probability to work in teams with same people	**Moderate.** People in projects are skilled in several scopes of work	**Full-time.** Full commitment in project work	**Full-time.** Responsible in any project performance domain	**Moderate/High.** Teams are formed mainly around projects, programs, or initiatives
Product-oriented	**High.** Teams are long term due to long product life cycle	**High.** People in projects are skilled in several technical domains	**Full-time.** Full commitment in project work	**Full time.** Responsible mainly of projects for product implementations	**High.** Enablement of dedicated, stable, and long-term teams to deliver value iteratively and respond to customer needs quickly.
Procurement-heavy	**Not applicable.** Supplier' project teams	**Not applicable.** Supplier' project teams	**None.** Supplier' project teams	**Part-time.** Supplier' proxy, mainly contract management	**None/Low.** Supplier' project teams

6.4.3 Identify organizational process assets and enterprise environmental factors that facilitate the use of adaptive approaches

Earlier chapters introduced EEFs and OPAs as project context components, influencing uncertainty and complexity. Some factors cause uncertainty while others impose constraints. Higher uncertainty calls for the adoption of Adaptive approaches based on complexity models discussed earlier. Let's take a deeper look at some of the examples of the EEFs and OPAs we introduced earlier to see how these factors impact on the approaches we can adopt in projects.

- **Marketplace conditions** drive project initiation for new products or services, but can fluctuate during execution. Unexpected competitors emerging can impact projects. If an Adaptive approach was chosen, adapting the product features to changing market conditions is more feasible.
- **Social and cultural factors** affect workplace conditions and product acceptance. Projects impacting society require robust Change Management Plans, engaging stakeholders to negotiate societal needs with project goals. Such plans enhance project adaptability to diverse societal demands.
- **Financial factors**, influenced by local/global economics, significantly affect project ROI, NPV, IRR, and feasibility. Adapting the project approach (Adaptive, hybrid, predictive) depends on the flexibility to reassess and reset these business variables during execution.
- **Organizational culture, structure, and governance** impact Adaptive project approaches. Hierarchical structures delay decisions, hindering team ownership. Flat structures and outcome-focused culture enable self-management and self-organization within project teams, while micro-management restricts autonomy.
- **Resource availability** impacts project approaches. Budget flexibility with contingency reserves allows adaptable scope. Full-time, skilled teams with reduced task-switching lead to collaborative, efficient project execution and increased agility.

6.5 Task 2 – Determine how to plan project iterations

Adaptive Agile life cycles involve a sequence of iterations like Scrum's "Sprints" with pre-defined time-box. Teams plan and execute work within each iteration to achieve a valuable product increment, benefiting users and stakeholders. Incremental progress aims for usable results with added business and user value.

Planning in an Agile life cycle is a frequent effort done by the project team that start with a Product Vision at high level, then continue in deeper details with Product Roadmap, Release Plan, Iteration Plan, Daily plan (ref. *PMBOK® Guide* 7th Edition – section 2.4 – "Planning performance domain" – Figure 2-17 – "Release and Iteration Plan").

Planning starts with defining a **Product Vision** (ref. Agile Practice Guide – section 5.1 – "Charter the Project and the Team" of the product to realize, usually done by a Product Manager or a Product Owner. The Vision could be a formal or informal document and it describes information usually described in a Project Charter like goals and intended business value of the product, initial budget, scope statement, principal milestones, project team composition, high- level risks, constraints, assumptions, dependencies with other project teams, etc.

The Product Vision is usually decomposed in Releases of product scheduled at higher level using **Product Roadmaps** to create a **Release Plan**. Releases are medium term batches of work that are composed by several Iterations. At the end of one Release, a certain increment of product is released to the users. From the value proposition perspective, a Release *must* give value to the users via an increment of product, while an Iteration *can* give value to the users via an increment of product. Time-box of iterations in a project are constant, it is pre-defined by the project team at the start of the project, and usually it goes from few days, or one week for the shortest iterations to few weeks like one month for the longest one, depending on the agreement with the project' stakeholders.

The whole scope of the work to do in a project that use Adaptive Agile approaches is defined in an artifact called Product Backlog. The **Product Backlog** in Adaptive Agile approaches describes the whole scope of the work to realize as the Work Breakdown Structure (WBS – ref. Process

Groups: A Practice Guide – section 5.5 – "Create WBS") is in a project that use Predictive approaches. The Product Backlog is defined as an ordered list of user-centric requirements (ref. Agile Practice – chapter "Definitions"), or an ordered list of work to be done (ref. *PMBOK® Guide* 7th Edition – section 4.6.2 – "Logs and Registers"),

The Product Backlog derives from Product Vision and Roadmap, divided into small Product Backlog Items (PBIs). PBIs are prioritized by a Product Owner based on stakeholder value, often placing the most valuable at the top. Product Owner frequently refines the Backlog. Each PBI includes feature descriptions, release details, priority, complexity, and value estimation. The Product Backlog can serve as a Release Plan, grouping PBIs by release for a prioritized project scope.

Product Backlog Item is the generic term to define a requirement that, based on their complexity, could be of several types. Following are the most common name used in Agile projects for requirements:

■ **Theme or Initiatives**: a set of Epics of the product to realize.
■ **Epic**: a set of integrated Features within a Theme or Initiative
■ **Feature**: a set of User Stories that provide value to the users
■ **User Story**: the description of a single, small functionality of the product

User Stories can be broken down into "**Tasks**" by the project team, typically during Iteration Planning. Tasks detail activities for implementing User Stories in the upcoming Iteration and can be part of the Iteration Backlog or Kanban/Task Board.

The above types of requirements are also defined by their complexity, that is, the large grained estimated effort to realize the requirement. Table 6.12 relates the type of requirements with their complexity (ref. *PMBOK® Guide* 7th Edition – section 2.6.2.2 – "Scope definition"):

Table 6.12   Agile requirement types

Agile requirement type	Rough estimated effort to realize the requirement	Example
Theme or Initiative	Effort do not fit in one Release; it is usually spanned to several Releases	The high-level description of a whole software system like a collaboration tool composed by several sub-systems like email, calendar, chat
Epic	Effort fit in one single Release	The high-level description of the email sub-system within the collaboration system
Feature	Effort fit in one Iteration	The description of the "write an email" feature of the email sub-system within the collaboration system
User Story	Small effort, less than a couple of days of work to realize	The description of the "send message" pushbutton of the "write an email" feature within the email sub-system of the collaboration system

Defining a Product Roadmap or a Release Plan require to decompose requirements using **Decomposition Analysis'** techniques so that the closest scheduled requirements are decomposed at the deeper details of User Stories, while the farthest scheduled requirements are not yet decomposed, but they remain at Theme' level until we get to the time to start the planning and development of those releases.

User Stories can be written with some characteristics:

■ **3C**: Card, Conversation, Confirmation
■ **INVEST**: Independent, Negotiable, Valuable, Estimable, Small, Testable

A User Story requires a *Small* description because is easy to implement, and its description usually stay in a little *Card* like a sticky note. The description is not in deep detail, but it is just enough detailed to start a *Conversation* or *Negotiation* between the project team and the stakeholders to get clarifications or to agree on the *Estimation* to realize it; a User Story is a promise for conversation to clarify details. The implementation of the User Story will provide value to the users, that is *Valuable* for the users. Finally, the implementation of a User Story must be *Testable,* that is, it must include the description of a *Confirmation* criteria or Acceptable Criteria.

User Stories can be written using several templates and one of the most common is the following:

- As a <role of the user>
- I want <description of the functionality>,
- so that <description of the value or benefit received by the user>
- Acceptance criteria (optional): *Given* <description of the context of the test>, *When* <description of the action to take to stimulate the system>, *Then* <description of the expected result given the stimulus in the context>

The above format of the Acceptance Criteria is a meta-language called Gerkin, mostly used in Automated Testing of software within a practice called *Behavior-Driven Development* (BDD).

The provided ordered **Product Backlog example** you read in Table 6.13 showcases items with explicit priority through their order. It includes rough effort estimates, planned release, and a "Notes" field. Larger requirements are decomposed when timely, while Features and User Stories stem from earlier decomposed Themes and Epics due to higher priority for closer Releases.

Table 6.13   Ordered product backlog example

ID	Rough effort estimation	Planned release	Notes
Feature 1	6	1	
User Story 1.1	3	1	
User Story 1.2	3	1	
Feature 2	8	1	
User Story 2.1	2	1	
User Story 2.2	3	1	
User Story 2.3	3	1	
Epic 1	To estimate	To assign	Breakdown and plan at the start of next release
Epic 2	To estimate	To assign	Breakdown and plan at the start of next release
Theme 1	To estimate	To assign	Breakdown and plan at the start of next release

6.5.1 *Distinguish the logical units of iterations*

In Adaptive Lean approaches, the Product Backlog outlines the scope without fixed iterations. Lean, like Kanban, teams commence early by *pulling* the high-priority PBIs to work on, creating a continuous flow. Upon completing some high-priority PBIs, the team and stakeholders assess their value for integration and release. This *Continuous Flow* is also known as *Continuous Delivery* approach in software project, and it emphasizes delivering frequent valuable increments.

In Adaptive Agile approaches, the Product Backlog isn't the final scope planning artifact due to time-boxed Iterations. Each Iteration resembles a small project with practices (ref. Agile Practice Guide – section 5.2 – "Common Agile Practices") like Iteration Planning, Execution, Daily stand-ups, Backlog refinement, Review, and Retrospective. These practices focus on planning, re-planning, and iterative work processes.

Iteration Planning is a time-boxed workshop where the team and stakeholders analyze the Product Backlog, determining which PBIs to work on next based on priority. This results in the creation of Iteration Backlog. This workshop typically lasting a couple of hours for each week duration of the time-boxed Iteration.

The **Iteration Backlog** is a sub-set of the Product Backlog, containing PBIs for the next Iteration. It includes prioritized PBIs whose estimated effort fits the team's capacity. Stable teams have known capacity. For high-accuracy estimations, the team decompose PBIs tasks during Iteration Planning, with stakeholder help, often from the Product Owner, providing detailed requirements.

Referring to the example Product Backlog in Table 6.13, in Table 6.14 is an **example of Iteration Backlog**. As you can see in the "notes" field of the Iteration Backlog, the project Team decided not to commit themself in the current iteration (but in the next iteration) on the User Stories 2.2 and 2.3, because the effort required exceeds the current team iteration capacity.

Table 6.14   Iteration backlog example

ID	Effort estimation	Planned release	Planned iteration	Notes
Feature 1	6	1	Current	
User Story 1.1	3	1	Current	
Task 1.1.1	1	1	Current	
Task 1.1.2	2	1	Current	
User Story 1.2	3	1	Current	
Task 1.2.1	2	1	Current	
Task 1.2.2.	1	1	Current	
Feature 2	8	1	Current	
User Story 2.1	2	1	Current	
Task 2.1.1	2	1	Current	
User Story 2.2	3	1	Next iteration	Out of capacity
Task 2.2.1	1	1	Next iteration	Out of capacity
Task 2.2.2	2	1	Next iteration	Out of capacity
User Story 2.3	3	1	Next iteration	Out of capacity
Task 2.3.1	3	1	Next iteration	Out of capacity

Iteration execution follows Iteration Planning, where the team works on pulled items from the Iteration Backlog, completing Tasks defined earlier. Self-organized throughout, they aim to create a valuable product increment for release. Integration, verification, and testing of realized features occur during execution, leading to the next step, Iteration Review.

The **daily standup** is a brief daily meeting, often in the morning, involving the entire project team and possibly a Process Coach like a Scrum Master. Team members discuss the previous day's work, encountered impediments, and their plans for the current day. For unresolved impediments, the team seeks the Process Coach's help for solutions.

Throughout Iteration Execution, the **product backlog is frequently refined**, updating details based on current work progress. This could include revised estimations, priority changes, improved requirements, or new PBIs arising from ongoing work. Product Backlog refinement is supervised by a key stakeholder like a Product Owner, often assisted by a Process Coach.

The **iteration review** involves the team and stakeholders, particularly the Product Owner. The team demonstrate the product increment's value and collect feedback. Feedback prompts changes planned into the Product Backlog for prioritization in future iterations. This review confirms realization of planned product increment and is typically time-boxed, such as one hour per week of Iteration duration.

The **retrospective**, involving the project team and potentially a Process Coach like a Scrum Master, focuses on process reflection. It assesses past iteration processes, identifies strengths and areas for improvement, and plans for enhancements in subsequent iterations. This practice doesn't concern product planning but addresses work methods, communication, skills, and more. Retrospectives are typically time-boxed, like 45 minutes per week of Iteration duration.

6.5.2 Interpret the pros and cons of the iteration

The most important benefit in having iterations is the frequent feedback exchanged between stakeholders and project team. Indeed, the Adaptive Agile approach involves an Iterative and Incremental lifecycle, fostering frequent feedback, communication, and trust between stakeholders and the project team. Iteration Review gathers stakeholder feedback, Retrospective improves processes, and Daily meetings provide daily updates. Product Backlog refinement is ongoing, updating requirements and priorities based on stakeholder information. Iteration Planning involves stakeholders, enabling detailed requirement planning using the Iteration Backlog.

But applying the iterative life cycle is challenging (ref. Agile Practice Guide – section 5.3 – "Troubleshooting Agile project challenges"). As said, the Adaptive approaches are appliable to complicated or complex projects, the project team and the leadership needs to respond to some characteristics, and the organization hosting the project (the environment) must enable the Adaptive approach, so these challenges must be addressed before deciding to apply the Adaptive approach.

Common challenges in the adoption of an Adaptive approach are: Maintaining continuous Vision communication, defining work processes, ensuring context clarity for stakeholders, engaging users, fostering team accountability, delivering high-quality increments with regular refactoring, addressing incomplete work, minimizing waste, resolving workflow bottle-necks, and promoting cross-functional teams with diverse skill sets.

6.5.3 Translate WBS to an adaptive iteration

In contrast to the Predictive approach with hierarchical WBS, Adaptive approach outlines product requirements in the Product Backlog. This involves decomposing into Themes, Epics, Features, and User Stories. Usually, Themes, and, depending on their size also Epics, are described in advance to the start of the project in the Product Vision, Product Roadmap, or Project Charter (ref. *PMBOK® Guide* 7th Edition – section 2.6.2.2 – "Scope definition").

WBS is decomposition of the work to do, while a Product Backlog is a decomposition of the product to realize, that is, a Product Backlog is more like a sort of Product Breakdown Structure (PBS).

The key distinction between a WBS and a Product Backlog is that the former is pre-defined for Predictive projects, while the latter is frequently refined in Adaptive projects. WBS outlines hierarchical work packages for project end, while a Product Backlog details items (PBIs like Epics, Features, or User Stories) for product realization, ordered by time of release and priority.

The scope of the work of the next in time Iteration is described in the Iteration Backlog that is a sub-list of the Product Backlog. The Iteration Backlog of one Iteration is whole defined at the start of the Iteration. From this standpoint, the Iteration Backlog is more like a WBS where the work packages are components of the product (that is, more like a Product Breakdown Structure).

6.5.4 Determine inputs for scope

The scope of work in a project with Adaptive approach is described within the Product Backlog. Usually, the project team get the product requirements talking to the stakeholders and refining requirements on-going. The scope of work in the Product Backlog can be the output of several processes and artifacts: Project Vision. Project overview statement, Project Charter, Project Kick-off meeting, Iteration planning, Product Backlog refinement, Iteration Review, Retrospective.

At the start of a project, for any of the approaches we can adopt within the project, we need a clear vision of the desired objectives. We also need to understand and appreciate how the vision aligns with the organization's strategic goals. That is, with the Vision, the project team have a document where they can clearly understand why they are doing the project.

A Product or **Project Vision** statement (ref. *PMBOK*® 7th edition – section 4.6.1 – "Strategy artifacts") might include, product or solution description, initial project budget for the release of the first usable version or the *Minimum Viable Product* (MVP), time to market for the first version of the product, intended users or consumers of the solution, key desired objectives, differentiators from competitive approaches, key features, benefits for the users, business value for the organization.

The information described in the Project Vision is usually summarized in the Project overview statement**.** The **Project overview statement (**or Project Brief – ref. *PMBOK*® 7th edition – section 4.6.1 – "Strategy artifacts") is a very short recap written to communicate enterprise-wide (mainly to the executives of the organization) the intent and vision of the project. Written with brevity and clarity, it captures the project's objective, problem or opportunity, and criteria for success.

To formally start the project, the Project Manager and the project team need a formal document called Project Charter authorized by the Project Sponsor. The **Project Charter** (ref. *PMBOK*® 7th edition – section 4.6.1 – "Strategy artifacts") describe in more deeper details, compared against the project Vision, the requirements, the product' features, and the scope of the work.

The Project Charter for a project with an Adaptive Approach (ref. Agile Practice Guide – section 5.1 – "Charter the project and the team") is usually less formal compared against the one for Predictive approaches; it is more focused on the description of the processes, life cycle, the project team's way of working during the project, with less details about the requirements of the work because they will be discovered during the project, and it could contain information, such as, measurable project objectives in long-term and related success criteria, high-level requirements, high-level project description, boundaries, and key deliverables, overall project risks, pre-approved financial resources, key stakeholders register, project exit criteria.

Also, the project team can decide to have a separate **Team Charter**. A Team Charter is a document written by the project team, for the project team, that acts as a compass, guiding the team members toward effective communication, decision-making, and overall project management. It is especially useful for setting ground rules to follow within the project. For instance, project teams might adopt the **Wideband Delphi** method for consensus on effort estimates, with Team Charter ground rules customized to their needs. These rules can include time-boxed meetings, voting system type, privacy or transparency level, iteration limits, accuracy boundaries for ending votes, and discussion trigger conditions. The Team Charter is a living document that should evolve as the project progresses. It should be regularly revisited and refined based on feedback and changing circumstances to ensure its relevance and effectiveness.

Project kickoff activities are often initiated through authorization via a project charter or approved project overview statement. The **Kickoff meeting**, attended by stakeholders and team members, establishes context, team alignment, and can include discussing the vision statement, communication rules, refining the team charter or project charter, aiding in User Story writing, prioritization, and setting up the initial product backlog.

The other input of the scope of work to the Product Backlog are Iteration planning, Product Backlog refinement, Iteration Review, and Retrospective. They are all activities where the scope of the work for the next iterations is reviewed, refined, updated, added, as we have already written in the previous chapters. Also, the Retrospectives meeting, where the project team reflect on possible improvements in their way of working, ends having as outcome the improvement to apply described as updates to the Team Chart, or Project Chart, or directly as User Stories into the Product Backlog.

6.5.5 Explain the importance of adaptive project tracking versus predictive, plan-based tracking

Most of the cases when an Adaptive approach is better to use against a Predictive approach have been described in the section "Task 1 - Explain when it is appropriate to use an adaptive approach", especially in the section "6.4.1 Compare the pros and cons of adaptive and predictive, plan-based projects". In summary, adaptive project tracking offers flexibility, customer satisfaction, continuous improvement, and early risk identification. On the other hand, predictive, plan-based tracking provides clarity, predictability, efficient resource allocation, and compliance adherence. The choice between these approaches depends on the specific project context, objectives, and constraints.

6.6 Task 3 – Determine how to document project controls for an adaptive project

Monitoring and Control of the work progress (ref. Process Groups: A Practice Guide – chapter 7 – "Monitoring and Controlling process group", ref. *PMBOK® Guide* 7th Edition – section 2.7 – "Measurement Performance Domain") in projects with Adaptive approaches are activities the project team execute mainly to verify the efficiency of the work' processes. The project team can use some metrics, and measurements as noted in Table 6.15 (ref. Agile Practice Guide – section 5.4 – "Measurements in Agile projects").

Table 6.15   Some adaptive metrics

Metric	Unit of measure	Mainly adopted in	Brief description
Velocity	Story Points in Time	Agile	It could be the Velocity of Story Points done during one Iteration or the Velocity of Story Points done in one Release.
Throughput	Number of items in Time	Lean/Kanban, Continuous Delivery	It could be the Input Throughput of incoming items to the workflow or the Output Throughput of done items outcoming from the workflow
Work In Process/Work In Progress (WIP)	Number of Items	Lean/Kanban, Continuous Delivery	The number of Items the project team is working in one step of the workflow
Cycle Time	Time	Lean/Kanban, Continuous Delivery	The mean time to complete the workflow starting from the time the items were pulled from the Product Backlog by the project team
Lead Time	Time	Lean/Kanban, Continuous Delivery	The mean time to complete the workflow starting from the time the items were queued into the Product Backlog
Deployment frequency	Number of Deployments in time	Lean/Kanban, Continuous Delivery	The number of Deployments (Releases) of increments of product per time
Mean Time To Recover (MTTR)	Time	Lean/Kanban, DevOps	The mean time to recover a failure starting from the failure notification

Story Points and Relative estimations (ref. *PMBOK® Guide* 7th Edition – section 4.4.2 – "Estimating").

In Adaptive Agile approaches, Relative Estimation is a common practice for estimating and measuring work complexity. Work items are estimated by comparing their complexity against a reference item with a value of 1. For example, if a User Story US1 is set as reference with a complexity of 1, and another User Story US2 is estimated to be four times more complex, its relative estimation is 4. This approach helps gauge complexity ratios rather than absolute values.

Story Point is the standard name given to the complexity to realize the User Story taken as reference. The name Story Point is given because it is explicitly used to size User Stories, while Relative estimation is a more general appliable method to estimate (not only User Story but any kind of object). So, in the above example, the User Story US2 is 4 Story Points because the reference User Story US1 is 1 Story Point.

Each project team establishes its own criteria for estimating User Story sizes and selecting a reference Story for 1 Story Point. *Story Point estimations are team-specific and shouldn't be compared between different teams.* For instance, if Team A's velocity is 100 Story Points per Iteration and Team B's velocity is 150 Story Points per Iteration, it doesn't imply that Team A is slower than Team B, as their criteria and context may differ.

Story point estimations are useful inside a single team to allow them to measure their current Velocity with their past Velocity so that they can analyze the causes of possible delays during time (during a series of Iterations) and find workarounds.

Little's Law (ref. *PMBOK® Guide* 7th Edition – section 2.7.2.2 – "Delivery – Queue size").

In projects with Adaptive Lean approaches, *Little's Law* relate the Throughput with mean Cycle time and Work in Process (or Work in Progress), so that

■ mean Cycle Time = mean Work in Process / Throughput

That is, the mean Cycle Time of the items, from the start of their work to their completion, is proportional to the mean Work in Process. Assuming a constant Throughput, an increased number of items in work-in-progress gives an increased mean Cycle Time to complete the items themself.

That's why it is important in Projects adopting Lean/Kanban, or Continuous Delivery approaches, to have a limited Work in Process (**WIP**

Limit) to avoid that too much work-in-process increase the mean cycle time delaying the whole workflow. The steps of the workflow that cause decrease in the mean Cycle Time of the workflow are called **Bottlenecks**. Bottlenecks in a workflow always must be avoided, that's why it is important to limit the work in progress using the WIP Limit..

6.6.1 Identify artifacts that are used in adaptive projects

Project monitoring and control in Adaptive project is usually done using the following artifacts (ref. *PMBOK® Guide* 7th Edition – section 2.7.3 – "Presenting Information", ref. Agile Practice Guide – section 5.4.1 – "Agile teams measure results"): Kanban Board used in all adaptive approaches, Burnup/Burndown chart mainly used in Adaptive Agile projects, Cumulative Flow Diagram (CFD) mainly used in Lean/Kanban projects.

6.6.1.1 Kanban board

A Kanban board is a visual tool (ref. *PMBOK® Guide* 7th Edition – Figure 2.29 – "Task Board or Kanban Board") used in the Adaptive Lean and Adaptive Agile approaches to manage and track work in progress. It provides a clear and organized representation of the workflow, allowing teams to visualize and manage their tasks or work items effectively. Here's a description of a typical Kanban board when used with Adaptive Lean/Kanban approaches:

- **Columns**: The Kanban board is divided into columns that represent different stages of the workflow. These columns typically include labels such as "To Do", "In Progress", and "Done". The number of columns can vary depending on the specific workflow and team preferences.
- **Cards**: Work items or tasks are represented by cards, which are placed in the appropriate columns based on their status. Each card represents a specific task or work item that needs to be completed. Cards usually contain essential information such as a brief description, assigned team member, due date, and any other relevant details.
- **Limiting WIP**: Each column on the Kanban board has a Work in Progress (WIP) limit, which defines the maximum number of tasks or work items allowed in that column at any given time. WIP limits help prevent overloading team members and encourage a smooth flow of work throughout the workflow.

▪ **Visual signals**: Kanban boards often use visual signals to provide additional information or indicate specific conditions. For example, color-coded labels or stickers can be used to indicate task priorities, different types of work, or specific project categories. Flags or icons may also be used to represent urgent tasks or blocked items that require attention.

As work progresses, cards are moved across the columns from left to right, representing the transition from one stage to the next. Team members can easily see the status of each task, identify bottlenecks, and collaborate effectively by visually tracking the movement of cards. Kanban boards promote continuous improvement by encouraging teams to regularly review and optimize their workflow. Through regular retrospective meetings or discussions, teams can identify areas for improvement, such as adjusting WIP limits, streamlining processes, or optimizing the flow of work across the board.

Figure 6.1 shows an example of Kanban Board. There are no bottlenecks because both the column/steps of the workflow "Development" and "Test" have Work in Process Limit (WIP Limit) set to a higher number than the number of the tasks that for each column are in work in progress. The total Work in Progress is 5, that is, the number of the tasks 2, 4, 5, 6, 7, in progress in steps Development and Test.

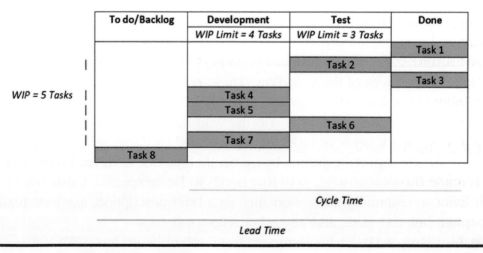

Figure 6.1 Kanban board example

Overall, a Kanban board serves as a visual representation of the team's workflow, providing transparency, clarity, and an effective way to manage and track work items. It promotes collaboration, efficiency, and continuous improvement, enabling teams to visualize their work, identify bottlenecks, and deliver value more effectively.

When used with Adaptive Agile approaches, like Scrum, the Kanban Board can take the name of Scrum board or Task Board. Here are some conceptual differences between a Scrum board and a Kanban board:

- *Timeboxing*: Scrum operates on time-boxed iterations called sprints, typically lasting 1–4 weeks. A Scrum board represents the work planned for a single sprint. In contrast, Kanban is more continuous and does not have time-boxed iterations, allowing for a continuous flow of work.
- *Work Planning*: Scrum boards are typically used for planning the work within a sprint. The columns on a Scrum board reflect the different stages of work for that particular sprint, and the focus is on completing the planned sprint backlog items. Kanban boards, on the other hand, often have columns that represent the different stages of the overall workflow, irrespective of specific time-bound iterations.
- *Work in Progress Limits (WIP Limits)*: Kanban boards typically incorporate explicit WIP limits for each column, which are designed to prevent overloading and maintain a smooth flow of work. Scrum boards usually do not enforce WIP limits explicitly.

It's important to note that these differences are not absolute, and teams can adapt and customize their boards based on their specific needs and preferences. The choice between Scrum and Kanban boards depends on the Adaptive approach used, the team's workflow requirements, and the level of flexibility desired in managing and tracking work.

6.6.1.2 Burndown/Burnup chart

A **release burndown chart** is visual representation (ref. *PMBOK® Guide* 7th Edition – figure 2-28 – "Information Radiator") commonly used in Adaptive projects to track and communicate the progress of a project's release. It provides a clear depiction of the amount of ***work remaining*** over time and helps the team understand if they are on track to complete the release within the desired time frame. Here's a description of a typical release burndown chart:

- **Horizontal axis**: The horizontal axis represents time and is divided into iterations number or sprints number. Each iteration corresponds to a specific time period within the project's release.
- **Vertical axis**: The vertical axis represents the amount of work remaining. It is usually measured in units that reflect the project's scope, such as story points, user stories, or tasks.
- **Ideal burndown line**: The chart begins with an ideal burndown line that represents the total amount of work planned for the release. This line shows how the remaining work to do should decrease linearly over time if everything goes according to the plan. The slope of the line indicates the rate at which the work should be completed.
- **Actual burndown line**: As the project progresses, the actual burndown line is plotted on the chart. This line represents the cumulative amount of work remaining at each end of the iteration. It shows how the team is progressing in completing the remaining work.
- **Total work**: Another line or bar on the chart represents the total work for the release. It starts at the total planned work time and could change over time because of the changes in the scope of the work during the release. It is the whole amount of work present within the Product Backlog for the release.
- **Sprint/iteration boundaries**: If the project is divided into sprints or iterations, the chart may include vertical lines to indicate the boundaries of each sprint. This provides a visual reference for tracking progress within each sprint.

By regularly updating and analyzing the release burndown chart, the team can assess their progress, identify any deviations from the plan, and make necessary adjustments to meet their release goals. It serves as a visual indicator of whether the team is on track to complete the work within the allocated time, helping them make informed decisions and take corrective actions when needed.

Figure 6.2 illustrates an example of release burndown chart. The release is composed of six Iterations and the total amount of work at the start is 200 Story Points. You can see a delay during the Iteration 1 that the project team is recovering during the iteration 2; it is visualized by the Actual Burndown line above the Ideal Burndown line. The execution of the work is currently during the Iteration 4, that's why the last Actual Burndown value is at Iteration 3 (the Actual burndown line ends currently in Iteration 3).

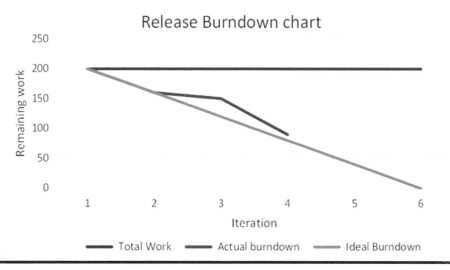

Figure 6.2   Release burndown chart example

When the actual burndown line is above the ideal burndown line in a release burndown chart, it indicates that the project's progress is behind schedule or slower than expected. Several issues could contribute to this situation. Here are some possible causes:

- **Scope creep**: Additional work or changes in requirements that were not accounted for in the initial plan can lead to increased effort and slower progress, causing the actual work line to rise above the ideal burndown line.
- **Underestimated effort**: Insufficiently estimating the effort required for the planned work can result in slower progress than anticipated. It could be due to incomplete understanding of the requirements, complexity, or dependencies that were not considered during estimation.
- **Resource constraints**: Limited availability of resources, such as team members or necessary tools, can impact productivity and delay progress. If the resources allocated are insufficient or are facing bottlenecks, it can contribute to the actual work line exceeding the ideal burndown line.
- **Unforeseen dependencies**: Dependencies on external teams, stakeholders, or systems that were not accounted for in the initial plan can cause delays and disrupt the expected progress. Any delays in receiving dependencies can result in the actual work line being above the ideal burndown line.

- **Technical challenges**: Technical difficulties, such as unexpected technical issues, architectural complexities, or integration problems, can lead to slower progress. These challenges may require additional time and effort to overcome, causing the actual work line to deviate from the ideal burndown line.
- **Lack of collaboration or communication**: Inadequate collaboration within the team or poor communication can lead to misalignments, misunderstandings, and delays. When team members are not working efficiently together or are not effectively communicating, it can impact progress and result in the actual work line being above the ideal burndown line.
- **External factors**: External factors beyond the team's control, such as changes in market conditions, regulations, or unforeseen events, can impact the project's progress. These factors can introduce delays or additional work, causing the actual work line to exceed the ideal burndown line.

Identifying the specific causes of the deviation between the actual burndown line and the ideal burndown line is crucial for the project team to address the issues, reassess the plan, and make necessary adjustments to get back on track and achieve the desired project goals.

In the above example Release Burndown Chart, the total work remain constant over time, so the delay we see during Iteration 2 is not due to a Scope Creep but the other possibly causes the project team has to analyze.

A **Release Burnup Chart** (ref. *PMBOK® Guide* 7th Edition – figure 2-28 – "Information Radiator") is quite like the Release burndown chart. The main difference is that *a Release Burndown Chart focuses on tracking the decrease in remaining work over time, while a Release Burnup chart focuses on **tracking completion of the work***. The former provides insights into the progress of work remaining, while the latter highlights the overall scope and completion of work.

Figure 6.3 illustrates an example of Release Burnup Chart. Here, the total Work Line increase in Iteration 2 and the Ideal Burnup has been adjusted from there to the end in iteration 6. The Actual Burnup is the actual work completed and in Iteration 2, due to the scope creep or increase in the work, the line goes below the Ideal Burnup. So, the project team is having issues in absorbing the augmented work. They must find some workaround to try to compete the whole work at the end of iteration 6, that is, they have

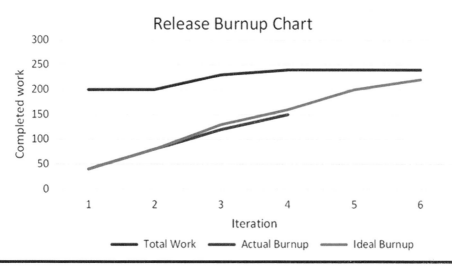

Figure 6.3   Release burnup chart example

to find some workaround to try to move the trend of the Actual Burnup to the Ideal Burnup line in the next Iteration 4 and 5.

Release Burndown and Burnup Chart can both be applied to Iterations, becoming **Iteration Burndown Chart and Iteration Burnup Chart**. The difference between Release Burn* Charts and Iteration Burn* Charts is that the first type in the horizontal axis has Iteration indicators, while the second type in the horizontal axis has days or weeks within the time-box of one Iteration. The meaning and logic of both types are the same.

Both Burndown and Burnup charts are useful in Adaptive approaches and serve different purposes in monitoring and visualizing the progress of project's releases or iterations.

6.6.1.3 Cumulative Flow Diagram (CFD)

A cumulative flow diagram (CFD – ref. *PMBOK® Guide* 7th Edition – section 4.6.6 – "Visual data and information", ref. Agile Practice Guide – Fig. 5–7 – "Cumulative Flow Diagram of completed features") is a visual representation that provides insights into the flow and status of work items over time in a process. It is commonly used in Adaptive Lean/Kanban approaches to track the progress and identify bottlenecks in the workflow. Here's a description of a typical CFD:

- **Vertical axis**: The vertical axis of the diagram represents the quantity or count of work items. It can be measured in units such as number of tasks, Story Points, or any other relevant work item type.

■ **Horizontal axis**: The horizontal axis represents time and is divided into time unit days or weeks.
■ **Flow lines**: Flow lines connect the data points on the diagram. Each flow line represents the cumulative count of work items in a specific stage at a given point in time. The flow lines are Burnup line types of lines, and each flow line is the Actual Burnup line of the related step of the workflow (that is, the related column in the Kanban Board)
■ **Lanes or areas**: The CFD consists of multiple lanes or areas between two different flow lines. Usually, the lanes are distinct, where each one has a different color. Each lane represent a different stage or state in the workflow. These stages are usually mapped with the columns of the Kanban Board.

The width or height of each lane represents the quantity or count of work items in a particular stage at a specific time. By analyzing the width or height of the lanes, it is possible to identify the distribution of work items across different stages at any given point in time. The CFD helps identify bottlenecks and imbalances in the workflow by examining the gaps or irregularities in the flow lines. If certain stages consistently have a higher count of work items compared to others, it indicates potential bottlenecks that may require attention.

The thinnest area below a widening area of the CFD is the bottleneck of the workflow. There could be several bottlenecks in a workflow but only the harder (that is, only the thinnest area in the workflow) is the most urgent to solve. After solving the harder bottleneck, we can focus on the next bottleneck (ref. *The Goal* – Eliyahu Goldratt – the book is a novel that introduce to the Theory of Constraints – TOC). By observing the trend and slope of the flow lines, it is possible to forecast and predict the future progress of work items. This allows the team to estimate when certain stages or the entire project/process might be completed based on historical data. In a well-functioning and efficient workflow, the ideal trend of the flow lines in a CFD would generally exhibit the following characteristics:

■ *Smooth and Balanced Flow*: The work items should flow steadily through the different stages of the workflow without significant fluctuations or spikes in any stage. A smooth and balanced flow indicates a stable and predictable workflow.
■ *Consistent Slope*: The slope of the flow lines should be consistent or gradually decrease over time. It indicates that the team is consistently making progress and maintaining a sustainable workflow.

■ *Even Distribution*: The distribution of work items across different stages should be relatively even. Ideally, the flow lines should have a similar width or height, indicating that work items are being evenly distributed and progressing through the workflow stages in a balanced manner. This suggests that there are no significant bottlenecks or delays in any stage.

■ *Continuous Improvement*: Over time, the flow lines should exhibit an upward trend, indicating progress and the completion of work items. This demonstrates that the team is continuously improving and delivering value by steadily moving work items from backlog to done.

Figure 6.4 shows an example of CFD.

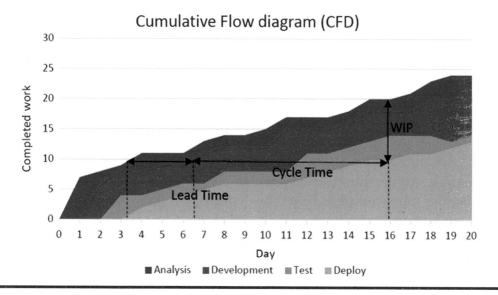

Figure 6.4   Cumulative flow diagram example

In the above example CFD, we can see a bottleneck in the Test stage between the 18th and 20th day because "Test" is the thinnest area below the widening area that is "Development".

6.7 Task 4 – Explain the components of an adaptive plan

We've written about the components of Adaptive Plan in section 4.5 Task 2 – Determine how to plan project iterations. In the current chapter, we'll see which Adaptive planning components are in specific Adaptive frameworks/methodologies.

6.7.1 Distinguish between the components of different adaptive methodologies (e.g., Scrum, eXtreme Programming (XP), Scaled Adaptive Framework (SAFe®), Kanban, etc.)

We are going to give a brief introduction in terms of values, principles, practices, artifacts, roles, components of the following: Scrum, eXtreme Programming (XP), Kanban, Disciplined Agile (DA). Scrum, XP, and Kanban as examples of Team framework, and DA as an example of scaled framework.

6.7.1.1 Scrum

Scrum (ref. Agile Practice guide – A3.2 – "Scrum") is one of the most popular Agile frameworks. It was created in 1995 by Jeff Sutherland and Ken Schwaber. The whole framework is described in a very small document, few pages more than 10 pages called Scrum Guide (scrumguides.org). The Scrum Guide is so small because Scrum is explicitly not completed, and it needs to be tailored on the specific needs within the project. The theory of Scrum is founded on ***empiricism*** and ***lean thinking***.

The Scrum life cycle is Adaptive Agile, that is, Iterative with time-box and incremental. An Iteration is called "Sprint". A Sprint can have a time-box of one month or less. Scrum is based on 3 pillars, 5 values, 3 roles, 5 events or ceremonies, 3 artifacts.

Scrum Pillars

They are three core components that serve as the foundation of the framework:

- **Transparency**: It involves making all information and work visible to the relevant stakeholders.
- **Inspection**: The Scrum Team frequently inspects the product, progress toward the sprint goal, and the processes being used.
- **Adaptation**: Scrum encourages adaptation based on the inspection results.

Scrum Values

The Scrum values guide the behavior and mindset of individuals and teams practicing Scrum. These values, as defined in the Scrum Guide, are as follows:

- **Commitment**: Scrum team members are dedicated in achieving the goals of the sprint and the project. They commit to complete the work they have agreed upon within the defined time frame.
- **Courage**: The courage to address challenges, provide feedback, and make decisions. It involves taking risks and being open to experimentation and learning from failures.
- **Focus**: The team concentrates on the work agreed upon for the sprint and strives to minimize distractions. They focus on delivering value and achieving the sprint goal.
- **Openness**: Scrum promotes transparency and openness among team members. It encourages sharing of information, ideas, and progress to foster collaboration and trust within the team and with stakeholders.
- **Respect**: Scrum emphasizes mutual respect and appreciation for the skills, knowledge, and perspectives of all team members. It recognizes that each person's contribution is valuable and promotes a positive working environment.

Scrum Roles

Scrum defines three primary roles within the framework:

- **Product owner**: The Product Owner represents the stakeholders, customers, and users. Their main responsibility is to define and prioritize the product backlog. The Product Owner collaborates with the development team to ensure that the product backlog items are well-understood and delivered effectively. They make decisions about the features of the product.
- **Scrum master**: The Scrum Master is a servant-leader for the Scrum team. Their role is to ensure that Scrum is understood and followed, and to facilitate its practices and processes. The Scrum Master removes any obstacles or impediments that hinder the team's progress, helps the team stay focused and motivated, and fosters a culture of continuous improvement. They also facilitate Scrum events, such as the daily stand-up, sprint planning, sprint review, and sprint retrospective.
- **Developers** (former Development Team): The Developers are professionals who do the work of delivering a potentially releasable product increment at the end of each Sprint. They are self-organizing and cross-functional. They collaborate closely with the Product Owner to understand and refine the product backlog items, and they decide the works

to plan for the Sprint during the Sprint Planning. They are account-able for delivering high-quality work and continuously improving their processes.

Scrum Events (Ceremonies)

Scrum defines several events, or ceremonies, in addition to the **Sprint** itself, that provide opportunities for collaboration, synchronization, and adaptation within the Scrum framework. These events help to structure the work and provide transparency and regularity to the project. The key Scrum events are as follows:

- **Sprint planning**: It's an Iteration Planning meeting as we described in previous chapters.
- **Daily scrum** (or Daily Stand-up): It's a Daily meeting as we described in previous chapters.
- **Sprint review**: It's an Iteration review meeting as we described in pre-vious chapters.
- **Sprint retrospective**: It's Retrospective meeting as we described in previous chapters.

Additionally, there are other optional events that can be used as needed, such as Product Backlog Refinement to review, clarify, and estimate back-log items, and the Sprint Cancelation if a sprint is deemed unachievable or unnecessary.

Scrum Artifacts

- **Product backlog**: As we described in the previous chapters.
- **Sprint backlog**: It's an Iteration Backlog as we described in previous chapters.
- **Increment**: The Increment is the sum of all the completed and poten-tially releasable Product Backlog Items (PBIs) at the end of each Sprint.

6.7.1.2 eXtreme Programming (XP)

Extreme Programming (XP, ref. Agile Practice Guide – A3.3 – "Extreme Programming") is a software development methodology that emphasizes close collaboration between customers, developers, and other stakeholders throughout the development process. It was first introduced by Kent Beck in the late 1990s as a response to traditional software development methods that often-faced challenges in delivering quality software on time. In 1999, Kent Beck published his book titled *Extreme Programming Explained: Embrace Change*. This book introduced the principles and practices of XP to a wider audience, outlining the key ideas and techniques.

XP is an Adaptive Agile approach.

It is founded to five core values: **Courage, Feedback, Simplicity, Communication, Respect** for that the meaning is very similar to the five Scrum' values.

XP Practices

XP encompasses a set of 13 practices that support its core values.

- **Whole team**: The Whole Team Collaboration practice emphasizes the importance of collaboration and shared responsibility among all members of the development team.
- **Planning game**: The Planning Game involves the active participation of customers and developers in the planning process. Customers define user stories, which represent desired features or functionality, and prioritize them. Developers estimate the effort required for each user story, and together with the customers, they determine the scope of work for each iteration.
- **Small releases**: XP promotes frequent, small releases of working software. Instead of waiting for a large, monolithic release, small increments of functionality are delivered regularly. This allows for quicker feedback from customers and enables incremental value delivery.
- **On-Site customer/customer tests**: Having an on-site customer, or at least frequent and direct customer involvement, is a crucial practice in XP. It enables real-time communication, quick feedback, and helps ensure that the development team understands and meets customer requirements effectively.
- **Collective code ownership**: In XP, all team members have the responsibility and authority to modify any part of the codebase. Collective Code Ownership require to have a central source code repository where each team member can pull the latest version of the central source code, and push back to it the updated source. This is the foundation of the XP Continuous Integration practice.
- **Coding standards**: XP encourages the establishment of coding standards and conventions to maintain consistency and readability in the

codebase. Consistent coding practices facilitate code comprehension and make the codebase more maintainable.

- **Sustainable pace**: XP emphasizes maintaining a sustainable pace of work, avoiding overwork and burnout. This practice recognizes that sustainable productivity is more valuable in the long run than short bursts of intense effort. It promotes a healthy work-life balance and supports the well-being of team members.

- **Metaphor**: The Metaphor practice involves using a shared conceptual framework or analogy to describe the software system. This metaphor helps align the understanding of the system's purpose, structure, and behavior among team members, facilitating effective communication and decision-making.

- **Continuous Integration (CI)**: It is the practice of regularly merging (integrating) code changes from multiple developers into the Collective Code repository. CI includes automated building, testing, and frequent integration of very small software modifications done by the team. It helps to identify and address integration issues early, ensuring a stable and functioning codebase. The usual pipeline/workflow offered by a Continuous Integration system to each team member is:
  a. pull the latest version of the source code from the central code repository,
  b. synch the local source code to the central repository code,
  c. add or modify the source code in an isolated environment (local environment),
  d. test locally the modifications using the XP Test-Driven Development practice,
  e. push back to the central repository the updated source code to merge (integrate) with possible concurrent modifications to the central source code done by the other teammates,
  f. automatically build the binaries of the source code,
  g. deploy the binaries to testing, integration, or staging environments.

- **Simple design**: XP emphasizes keeping the design of the software system as simple as possible. The focus is on fulfilling current requirements rather than attempting to predict future needs. Simple design reduces complexity, improves maintainability, and enables easier adaptation to changing requirements.

- **Pair programming**: Pair Programming involves two developers working together at a single workstation. One developer writes the code, while the other reviews it in real-time, providing immediate feedback. They are the "Pilot" and the "Navigator" and they frequently exchange the roles.

■ **Test-Driven Development (TDD)**: XP promotes extensive and automated testing throughout the development process. Test-driven development (TDD) is a common practice in XP, where tests are written before the corresponding code. These help to ensure the correctness and quality of the software. The TDD workflow is composed of three steps, also known as Red, Green, Blue:
  – Red: Write a test for a small feature and see that it fails
  – Green: Develop the feature that pass the test
  – Blue: Refactor the feature' code and see that it passes the test

■ **Refactoring**: Refactoring involves improving the internal structure of the code without changing its external behavior. This practice allows for continuous code improvement, making it more maintainable, extensible, and efficient over time.

Most of the XP practices, especially Collective Code Ownership, TDD, and CI, were the foundation for what today we know in software realization projects as Continuous Delivery (CD), and later DevOps.

XP Roles

Here are the primary roles in XP:

■ **Customer**: The Customer represents the stakeholders, end-users, and business representatives who have a vested interest in the software being developed. The Customer works closely with the development team to define and prioritize user stories, provide feedback, and make decisions regarding the product's features and requirements.

■ **Developer**: Developers are responsible for designing, coding, and implementing the software. They work closely with the Customer to understand requirements, participate in planning sessions, and deliver working software increments. Developers also collaborate with other team members, engage in pair programming, and contribute to the collective code ownership and continuous improvement of the codebase.

■ **Tester:** They collaborate with the Customer and the Developer to define acceptance criteria, create test cases. Testers also contribute to the automation of tests and work closely with the development team to address issues and defects.

■ **Coach**: The Coach, also known as the XP Coach or Agile Coach provides guidance and mentorship to the team. The Coach helps the team understand and adopt XP practices effectively, resolves conflicts, and assists in continuous improvement efforts. They bring expertise in XP principles and practices, helping the team refine their skills and achieve higher levels of productivity and quality.

It's important to note that in XP, there is an emphasis on a collaborative and self-organizing team structure. While these roles exist, the team members are encouraged to work closely, communicate openly, and share responsibilities. The goal is to foster a whole-team approach where individuals with different skills and perspectives collaborate effectively to deliver high-quality software in an iterative and incremental manner.

One of the important concepts introduced by XP, that is, at the base of most of the Adaptive approaches, is the **Planning/Feedback Loop**. It is a continuous improvement cycle that highlight the time to receive feedbacks from peers and stakeholders, to have efficiency in collaboration within an Adaptive project. In the Planning/Feedback loop we have:

■ Less than months to receive feedback from stakeholders because the Release Plan is closed with a small release of product increment
■ Less than weeks to receive feedback from Product Owners or Product Managers because the Iteration Plan is closed with a potentially releasable product increment
■ Less than Days to get feedback on the quality of teamwork because Customer on site/Customer Tests XP practices
■ Less than 1 day because the Daily Stand-up meetings
■ Less than hours because the Pair changing roles (*Pair Negotiation*) during the Pair Programming practice
■ Less than minutes because the Test-Driven Development and Unit Tests practices
■ Scale of seconds the feedback exchanged by the Pilot and Navigator during a Pair Programming session
■ Scale of seconds the feedback received by each developer from the Continuous Integration System because of the Continuous Integration and Collective Code Ownership practices

A very important concept introduced with XP is the **Spike**. A Spike is a particular Iteration (time-boxed), that the project team exceptionally execute to discover something they do not know. A Spike could be of several types, the most used are Architectural Spikes and Risk Spikes. The Architectural Spike is used by the team to learn something they need to learn from a new technology they are going to use or to verify some performance. For example, the team can decide to experiment the performance of a new database they have to use within the project. A Risk Spike is one where the team experiment something to mitigate some risk they have identified. For instance, they could run a Risk Spike to verify what happens to the system under some trigger event and how those trigger events could be avoided or mitigated. Spikes are experiments where some hypothesis is set by the team and actions are taken to prove or disprove the hypothesis during a time-box.

6.7.1.3 *Kanban*

Kanban (ref. Agile Practice Guide – A3.4 – "Kanban Method") is a popular workflow system that originated in the manufacturing industry but has since been applied to various domains, including software development, marketing, and personal productivity. The history of Kanban can be traced back to the Toyota Production System (TPS), developed by Toyota in the 1940s and 1950s, introduced by Taiichi Ohno, an engineer and executive at Toyota, to improve efficiency and eliminate wastes in the manufacturing process; it was originally used as a scheduling system to manage inventory and production flow on the shop floor. The word "Kanban" itself translates to "visual card" or "signboard" from Japanese.

Kanban places a strong emphasis on managing the flow of work. The goal is to achieve a steady and predictable flow from the start of a task to its completion. Teams actively monitor the flow, identify any issues or delays, and take steps to resolve them. Managing flow reduces lead times, improves efficiency, and enables faster delivery of value. Kanban follows a pull-based system, where work is pulled into the workflow based on capacity and demand. **Team members pull work from a prioritized backlog as they have the capacity to take on new tasks**. This approach helps balance workloads, prevents overcommitment, and promotes a smoother workflow.

Kanban principles (or Kanban properties)

Kanban is based on the following principles, also known as Kanban properties, that aim to improve efficiency, productivity, and collaboration within a team.

- **Visualize the workflow**: This typically involves using a Kanban board, which is divided into columns representing different stages of work. Each column contains cards or sticky notes representing tasks or work items, allowing team members to see the status of each item briefly.
- **Limit work in progress (WIP)**: By setting WIP limits for each stage of the workflow, teams can prevent overloading themselves and ensure that work is flowing smoothly. This helps to avoid bottlenecks and improves focus on completing tasks rather than starting new ones.
- **Manage flow**: The goal is to achieve a steady and predictable flow of work from start to finish, minimizing delays and interruptions. Teams should continuously monitor and measure the flow of work, identifying and addressing any obstacles or inefficiencies that arise.
- **Make policies explicit**: This includes defining the criteria for moving tasks from one column to another, prioritization rules, and any specific rules or agreements the team follows. By making these policies clear and transparent, everyone on the team can understand and adhere to them, fostering consistency and reducing ambiguity.
- **Implement feedback loops**: Kanban encourages the establishment of feedback loops to gather data, insights, and feedback, which inform decision-making and drive continuous improvement.
- **Improve collaboratively**: Kanban promotes a culture of continuous improvement. Team members are encouraged to collaborate and actively participate in identifying bottlenecks, suggesting improvements, and experimenting with changes to the workflow.

Kanban encourage leadership at all levels. It recognizes that leadership and decision-making should not be limited to a few individuals. Instead, it encourages leadership at all levels within the team. Team members are empowered to make decisions and take ownership of their work. This distributed leadership fosters a sense of responsibility, engagement, and accountability among team members. That's why **in Kanban there are no explicit roles defined** except the Team role.

6.7.1.4 Disciplined Agile

Disciplined Agile (ref. Agile Practice Guide – A3.14 – "Disciplined Agile (DA)", ref. *Choose Your WoW!* 2nd edition – chapter 2 "Being Disciplined", and chapter 5 "The Process Goals") is an agnostic, hybrid tool kit that harnesses hundreds of Adaptive Agile, Lean, and Predictive strategies to guide you to the best way of working (WoW) for your team, program, or organization. DA is context-sensitive; rather than prescribing a collection of "best practices", it teaches you how to choose and later evolve a fit-for-purpose WoW that is best for you given the situation you face. The DA tool kit provides straightforward guidance to help organizations streamline their processes in a context-sensitive manner, providing a solid foundation for business agility. It does this by showing how the various business functions such as Finance, Portfolio Management, Solution Delivery (software development), IT Operations, Enterprise Architecture, Vendor Management, and many others work together. The reference book for the DA toolkit is *Choose Your WoW! A Disciplined Agile Approach to Optimize Your Way of Working* – second edition – by Scott Ambler and Mark Lines (creators of the toolkit).

The mindset of DA is composed by several Principles, Promises, and Guidelines. The **DA principles** are Delight Customers, Be Awesome, Be Pragmatic, Context Counts, Optimize Flow, Enterprise Awareness, Choice is Good, Organize around product/services.

The toolkit describes practices classified in four organization **layers**:

- **Foundation**: in this layer the DA mindset with principles, promises, general guidelines for the Way of Working in Agile, Lean, "Serial" approaches, and high-level product' life cycle: Concept->Inception->Construction->Transition->Production->Retire, are described.
- **Disciplined DevOps**: here are described processes and practices of the **Discipled Agile Delivery (DAD)** toolkit describing in detail the six DA lifecycle we introduced in the previous chapter, and the practices applicable to Security, Data Management, Release Management, Support, and IT operation processes within an organization.
- **Value stream**: Value Streams (as we defined previously in this book) layer include practices for the common processes usually existing within an enterprise organization: Research & Development, Business Operation, Strategy, Governance, Marketing, Continuous Improvement Sales, Portfolio Management, Program Management, Product Management.
- **DA Enterprise (DAE)**: Descriptions of the enterprise executive processes: People management, Enterprise Architecture, Information Technology, Asset Management, Transformation, Finance, Vendor Management, Legal.

Within the DAD toolkit there is the description of 24 "Process Goal", each one describing dozens of practices that can be decided to apply in projects on the basis of the context (principle "Context count"). A "Process Goal" is a decision tree with Decision name at the root, Decision Points in the middle, Options (practices) that can be selected for each Decision Point. The "DAD Browser" is publicly available as an open-source document in the PMI website. The 24 Process Goal of DAD are classified on the basis of the high-level product development phases you can read in Table 6.16

Table 6.16   Disciplined Agile Delivery process goals

Product development high-level phases	DAD process goals
Inception	Form Team, Align with Enterprise Direction, Explore Scope, Identify Architecture Strategy, Plan the release, Develop test strategy, Develop common vision, Secure funding
Construction	Prove architecture early, Address changing stakeholder needs, Produce a potentially consumable solution, Improve quality, accelerate value delivery
Transition	Ensure production readiness, Deploy the solution
On-Going	Grow team members, Coordinate activities, Address risks, Evolve Way of Working, Leverage and enhance existing infrastructure, Govern Team, intake work, Organize metric, Measure outcome

Two very important concepts introduced in Disciplined Agile as customizations of previously existing concept are the Minimum Viable Product (MVP) and Guided Continuous Improvement process (GCI)

Minimum Viable Product (MVP)

Several definitions of MVP are available in literature, most of them conflicting with the others, and this is the one from Disciplined Agile: An MVP is an investment in creating a new product or service, to create or to explore a hypothesis, often starts as a functional prototype where some functionality is simulated or permed manually; the aim is to do just enough work to get something in front of potential customers to learn what they really want.

Guided Continuous Improvement (GCI)

Several Continuous Improvement cycles have been defined in history, for instance,

■ the **PDSA loop** – Plan, Do, Study, Act – of Edward Deming (ref. *Choose Your WoW!* 2nd edition – chapter 1 – "Choosing your Wow", "Guided Continuous Improvement [GCI]")

■ the **POOGI** – Process Of On-Going Improvements – of Eliyahu Goldratt, also known as the "Five Focusing Steps of Theory of Constraints" (TOC - ref. *The Goal* - Eliyahu Goldratt)

■ the **Kaizen** from the Lean Thinking mindset.

■ the **Discipline Agile Guided Continuous Improvement** (DA GCI) cycle – of Scott Ambler and Mark Lines (ref. *Choose Your WoW!* 2nd edition – chapter 1 – "Choosing your Wow", "Guided Continuous Improvement (GCI)"

Table 6.17 illustrates the definition of the DA Guided Continuous Improvement cycle represented by a conceptual map with the Deming' PDSA cycle.

Table 6.17   Mapping PDSA loop with DA guided continuous improvement cycle

Deming' PDSA continuous improvement cycle	*DA guided continuous improvement (GCI) cycle*
Plan	Identify an issue -> Identify a potential improvement
Do	Try out the new Way of Working (WoW) experimenting
Study	Assess effectiveness
Act	If effective for us, then adopt the new WoW, else abandon the new WoW; In any case, share learning with Others and **Repeat the cycle**

6.8 Task 5 – Determine how to prepare and execute task management steps

In previous chapters, we wrote that User Stories are usually decomposed in "Tasks" by the project team; they are usually not part of the Product Backlog, they could be the items of the Iteration Backlog, and Kanban Board or Task Board. Project Teams decompose User Stories in Tasks during the Iteration Planning. "Tasks" describes the activities the projects team do to implement the User Stories. As the User Stories usually take less than a couple of days of effort to implement, the breakdown of them into smaller "Tasks" takes the Tasks to have an estimated effort, each one, not more than

1 to 4 hours of work. Usually, the management of tasks by the project team is via a Task Board, where the tasks are pulled from the initial Iteration Backlog represented by the first column on the left in the Task Board, also called "Backlog" or "To Do". Each Task can have some information or meta-data describing it, for example: Brief description of the task to do, assigned team member to do the work, estimations of the effort, due dates, etc.

The team is self-organized, so they decide in autonomy which tasks self-assign to themselves. This requires a certain level of skills to be prepared to manage the Tasks. Those skills are mainly related to the team capability to define Success criteria for the completion of the Tasks (Done criteria) and Prioritization techniques.

6.8.1 Interpret success criteria of an adaptive project management task

Success criteria in adaptive projects are at two different layers: Quality and processes efficiency, Business Value and project efficacy.

Definition of Done (DoD)

Quality in adaptive project is successful when the increment of products released, or the features/user stories realized, match some "done criteria" defined in the DoD – "Definition of Done" checklist (ref. *PMBOK® Guide* 7th Edition – section 2.6 – "Delivery Performance Domain").

The term DoD refers to a set of conditions or requirements that must be met for an increment of product, or a user story, or a task to be considered complete or done. It helps provide a clear definition of what it means for work to be finished and ensures a shared understanding among the project team members. DoD serves as a guideline or checklist against which the team can assess their progress and determine when a particular item is truly complete. Example of Done Criteria: The product increment meets all the planned user stories/tasks; the defined acceptance criteria have been met; the work has been tested and meets the established quality standards; user documentation has been created or updated; the product increment has been integrated successfully with the other components of the system; the user story/tasks has been demonstrated to, and accepted by the stakeholders or the product owner.

It's important for the project team to define the DoD early on and revisit and refine them throughout the project as needed.

Business Value metrics

How can we recognize a project is Successful? Well, we could say the project is successful if the users of the product realized with the project are receiving value by the product released, and if the stakeholders who are investing in the project are receiving Business Value.

It's not easy to measure the success of a project, probably it's also not really feasible due to the different stakeholders' perspectives who looks to the project's outcomes, also considering a product can be really appreciated (or not) by the users after long time since the project is closed. But we, as project management practitioners, must continuously assess and verify the Business Value measures during the ongoing of the project. Business Value measures are planned before the project starts for assessing the feasibility of the project, during the ongoing of the project to verify that the Business Value measures are aligned with the external Enterprise Environmental Factors (EEF) such as marketing condition, social impacts, laws or legal restrictions, etc., and if they are not aligned with that, then we have to take all the needed actions to align them or decide to terminate the project.

Also, in Adaptive projects, the Business Value is the most important metric used to prioritize the work in the project. The prioritization of the Product Backlog Items (PBIs) in the Product Backlog is usually driven by the value or business value the PBIs realize (ref. The Standard for Project Management in *PMBOK® Guide* 7th Edition section 2.3.6 – "Provide business direction and insights", ref. The Standard for Project Management in *PMBOK® Guide* 7th Edition – section 3.4 – Principle "Focus on Value", ref. *PMBOK® Guide* 7th Edition – section 2.7.2.5 – "Business Value")

Example of Business Value metrics are **Return on Investmen**t (**ROI**), it indicates the gain or loss generated relative to the amount invested; **Net Present Value** (**NPV**), it calculates the present value of future cash inflows and outflows associated with an investment, discounted to the present time using a predetermined discount rate; **Internal Rate Return** (**IRR**), it represents the discount rate at which the present value of expected cash inflows equals the present value of cash outflows, resulting in a net present value of zero. The higher the values are, the most profitable is the project.

Also, it is very important to estimate the **Cash Flow** to assess the continuous feasibility of the project. Cash-flow refers to the movement of money coming into or going out of a project or business. It includes revenue generated, expenses incurred, investments made, and payments received or paid during different project stages.

6.8.2 Prioritize tasks in adaptive project management

Planning the scope of the work in Adaptive projects is done mainly using some prioritization techniques. The PBIs in a Product Backlog can be prioritized in several ways. The "Explore Scope" Process Goal of the Disciplined Agile Delivery toolkit identify the following different types of Product Backlogs on the base of the way the PBIs are ordered within it:

- **Unsequenced backlog**: With an unsequenced backlog all the work is effectively at the same priority. There may be the concept of two priorities – what is in the current release and what needs to be in future releases.
- **Requirements (product) backlog**: A unique, ranked stack of requirements that need to be addressed. Requirements at the top of the list should be captured in greater detail than lower-priority requirements at the bottom of the list. Some teams would include defects and some form of quality requirements (often captured as technical stories) on the backlog, as they were considered valid requirement types as well.
- **Agile backlog**: Work items are managed as an ordered list/stack. Work items at the top of the list should be captured in greater detail than lower-priority work at the bottom of the list. Work items potentially include all types of requirements (usage, technical/quality, defects, …), technical debt removal, team health events (e.g., training workshops), work to help other teams (e.g., reviewing their work, mentoring others, …)
- **Lean backlog**: It contains work items and is typically organized into four groupings: Potential work items the team knows about, work items that the team has committed to work on, work items that the team is currently working on, work that has been completed.

PBIs at higher priorities are the *most important and urgent to realize.* Importance and urgency of PBIs in Adaptive project is usually related to some combination of the following parameters:

- **Business values** given to stakeholders accountable for the realization of the product and/or Benefits/Value given to the stakeholders impacted by the release of the product. The higher the business value or benefit, the higher is the priority.

- **Uncertainty** (unknown unknowns), and **risks** (known unknowns) impacting the realization of the PBIs. The higher the uncertainty or risks, the higher is the priority assigned to the PBIs. This is because Adaptive teams want to augment their knowledges on the PBIs they know less as soon as they can, because demonstrating ambiguous, volatile, uncertain features to users or stakeholders allow them to receive feedbacks to refine the requirements and improve the product.

Several Prioritization Schema can be used to prioritize the work, like for instance, MoSCoW (Must have, Should have, Could have, Would have) techniques, Kano analysis, Paired compared analysis, Relative ranking (ref. *PMBOK® Guide* 7th Edition – section 4.4.4 – "Other methods"). The decision on which type of schema to select depends also on which type of detailed approach and Product Backlog the project has.

Also, to decide collectively which priorities are to be assigned to the PBIs, several collective decisional strategies or collaborative "games" can be used (ref. *PMBOK® Guide* 7th Edition – section 2.2.2.4 – "Interpersonal Skills", "Decision Making") like: Monopoly money, 100 points schema, Dot voting/ Multi voting, Roman voting, Fist of five.

6.9 Sample test questions on Agile frameworks/methodologies

Question 1

Which attributes of a project team are the best to have to enable an Adaptive approach?

- A. Large team, part-time engaged, working in different time-zone, in a functional organizational structure
- B. Small team, stable, co-located, cross-functional
- C. Small team, part-time engaged, co-located, cross-functional
- D. Small team, full-time engaged, provided by the supplier' organization, in a fixed price contract

Question 2

Which practices usually do the project team within an Iteration?

A. Iteration Execution, Daily stand-ups, Iteration Review or demo, Retrospective
B. Create Project Vision, Create Project Charter
C. Plan the budget of the Iteration
D. Create the Statement of Work

Question 3

What is the order of complexity (effort estimation), from the most complex one on the left to less complex one to the right, of the following type of requirements?

A. Epic, Feature, Theme, User Story
B. User Story, Feature, Theme, Epic
C. Theme, Epic, Feature, User Story
D. Feature, Epic, User Story, Theme

Question 4

Which of the following are all Events of Scrum?

A. Visualize the Workflow, Limit WIP, Make policies explicit
B. Continuous Integration, Sustainable pace, Collective ownership
C. Courage, Commitment, Focus, Openness, Respect
D. Sprint Planning, Sprint Review, Daily scrum

Question 5

Which of the following is a Prioritization Schema?

A. IRR
B. NPV
C. MoSCoW
D. DoD

Answer to Question 1: The correct answer is B.
A project team can be successful adopting Adaptive approaches if it's stable, co-located, cross-functional, and small (ref. Agile Practice guide, section 4.3 – "Team composition")

Answer to Question 2: The correct answer is A.
Inside one Iteration the project team usually follows the following practices (ref. Agile Practice Guide – section 5.2 – "Common Agile Practices"), where most of those practices are about planning and re-planning the work to do: Iteration Planning, Iteration Backlog creation, Iteration Execution, Daily stand-ups, Product Backlog refinement, Iteration Review or demo, Retrospective

Answer to Question 3: The correct answer is C.
Theme, or Initiative effort do not fit in one Release. Epic effort fits in one single Release. Feature effort fits in one Iteration. User Story is a small effort, less than a couple of days of work to realize (ref. *PMBOK® Guide* 7th Edition – section 2.6.2.2 – "Scope definition").

Answer to Question 4: The correct answer is D.
Scrum defines several events, or ceremonies, in addition to the **Sprint** itself, that provide opportunities for collaboration, synchronization, and adaptation within the Scrum framework. The key Scrum events are as follows: Sprint Planning, Daily Scrum (or Daily Stand-up), Sprint Review, Sprint Retrospective (ref. Agile Practice Guide – A3.2 – "Scrum").

Answer to Question 5: The correct answer is C.
Several Prioritization Schema can be used to prioritize the work, like for instance, MoSCoW (Must have, Should have, Could have, Would have) techniques, Kano model, Paired compared analysis, Relative ranking (ref. *PMBOK® Guide* 7th Edition – section 4.4 – "Other methods").

6.10 Summary of Agile frameworks/methodologies

In Chapter 6 of this book, we described the knowledges required to attend the Domain #3 questions of the CAPM® exam defined in the CAPM® – ECO – Exam Content Outline.

The Introduction section contains the Agile values, principles and mindset description, the Lean Principles, the Lean Software development principles, and Wastes, what's the meaning of Adaptive approaches, the correlations between Adaptive, Agile, Lean, what's the meaning of Life cycles in projects, and a list of the most significant Adaptive frameworks/methodologies.

In the Terms section, we have definitions of the words coming from the Adaptive domain most used within this chapter of the book.

The Mapping the Exam Content Outline section maps the tasks of the CAPM® ECO with the references books useful to read to better prepare for the CAPM® exam.

The Task 1 section describes when it's appropriate to use Adaptive approaches in projects, how to understand which Adaptive approach fits better with the context using some complexity models, the External Environmental Factors, and Organizational Process Assets to consider when deciding the approaches to select.

The Task 2 section is the description of the Planning performance domain within and Adaptive projects, including, Vision, Roadmap planning, Release planning, Iteration planning, the description of the main components of Iterations within and Adaptive Agile approach, and the description of the main components of Incremental approaches.

The Task 3 section describes some of the principal artifacts used in Adaptive projects like Kanban Boards, Burnup/burndown charts, CFDs.

The Task 4 section gives introduction to Scrum, eXtreme Programming (XP), Kanban, and Disciplined Agile (DA).

The Task 5 section explains some of the competencies that are needed to prepare and execute for managing an Adaptive project with focus on DoD, Business Value, and Prioritization.

Chapter 7

Business analysis frameworks

7.1 Introduction

The Business Analysis Frameworks is the fourth and final domain of the new CAPM® certification. The domains are high-level knowledge where the fundamental, predictive, and agile approaches have been covered in chapters 4–6. The Business Analysis Frameworks build upon this knowledge including the six underlying responsibilities of the project team member within each domain area, also labeled tasks in the PMI Certified Associate of Project Management Examination Content Outline. Each of the 6 tasks includes a total of 13 enablers which are examples to illustrate the topics.

The readings for this domain is covered in Section 7.3; however, if you have previous experience within this field or are considering specializing in Business Analysis, you will be able to find extensive knowledge supporting the PMI Professional in Business Analysis (PMI-PBA)® exam and content from competing organizations such as International Institute of Business Analysis (IIBA) or International Requirements Engineering Board (IREB). These sources could be used as supplementary reading, not mandatory for taking the exam:

- *Business Analysis: Best Practices for Success* by Steven Blais (Wiley)
- *Business Analysis Techniques: 72 Essential Tools For Success* by James Cadle, Paul Turner, Debra Paul (British Informatics Society Ltd)

DOI: 10.4324/9781003462378-7

- *Seven Steps to Mastering Business Analysis* by Barbara Carkenord (J. Ross Publishing)
- *The Software Requirements Memory Jogger: A Pocket Guide to Help Software and Business Teams Develop and Manage Requirements* by Ellen Gottesdiener (Goal Q P C Inc)
- *Unearthing Business Requirements: Elicitation Tools and Techniques* by Kathleen Hass, Rosemary Hossenlopp (Management Concepts, Inc.)
- *Customer-Centered Products: Creating Successful Products through Smart Requirements Management* by Ivy F. Hooks and Kristin A. Farry (AMACOM)
- *The Business Analyst's Handbook* by Howard Podeswa (Cengage Learning PTR)
- *Mastering the Requirements Process: Getting Requirements Right* by Suzanne Robertson and James Robertson (Addison-Wesley Professional)
- *Data Modeling Essentials* by Graeme Simsion and Graham Witt (Morgan Kaufmann)
- *Software Requirements 2* by Karl Wiegers (Microsoft Press)

7.2 Terms

In the beginning of each chapter, the key terms are highlighted (see Table 7.1), as required by the Project Management Institute (PMI) for the CAPM® exam. Hence, you should start with these terms. If you already have solid knowledge of them, you may consider skipping this or part of this chapter. However, once you have finished reading the chapter, you can refer to this list and test your knowledge. Table 7.1 includes the term, source, and page number for the reference in that source. Some terms might be found in several sources, but definitions are the same in all PMI publications. If you want to read about the terms, you need to access the books mentioned which is where the PMI membership comes in handy for easy access. The list of terms is extensive; however, you may still find terms now and then during your reading that are relevant and not described in Table 7.1.

Table 7.1 Business analysis frameworks terminology

Terms	Source	Page
Acceptance criteria	PMI *Business Analysis for Practitioners*	183
Affinity Diagram	PMI *PMBOK® Guide* 7th Edition	235
Benchmarking	PMI *PMBOK® Guide* 7th Edition	236
Benefits	*The PMI Guide to Business Analysis*	389
Business Case	PMI *PMBOK® Guide* 7th Edition	236
Brainstorming	PMI *Business Analysis for Practitioners*	184
Business value	PMI *Business Analysis for Practitioners*	185
Business need	*The PMI Guide to Business Analysis*	390
Capability	*The PMI Guide to Business Analysis*	390
Cause and effect diagram	PMI *Business Analysis for Practitioners*	185
Context Diagram	PMI *Business Analysis for Practitioners*	186
Compliance standard	*The PMI Guide to Business Analysis*	409
Cost-Benefit Analysis	PMI *PMBOK® Guide* 7th Edition	237
Creative thinking	*The PMI Guide to Business Analysis*	393
Definition of Done	PMI *Agile Practice Guide*	151
Document Analysis	*The PMI Guide to Business Analysis*	395
Elicitation	PMI *Business Analysis for Practitioners*	187
Epic	PMI *PMBOK® Guide* 7th Edition	239
Export Judgment	PMI *Business Analysis for Practitioners*	187
Five Whys technique	PMI *Business Analysis for Practitioners*	188
Force Field Analysis	*The PMI Guide to Business Analysis*	398
Interviews	PMI *Business Analysis for Practitioners*	188
Kano classification	*The PMI Guide to Business Analysis*	400
Minimum Viable Product	*The PMI Guide to Business Analysis*	401
Multivoting process	PMI *Business Analysis for Practitioners*	190
		(Continued)

Table 7.1 (Continued)   Business analysis frameworks terminology

Terms	Source	Page
Persona	PMI *Business Analysis for Practitioners*	191
Problem solving	*The PMI Guide to Business Analysis*	405
Product roadmap	*The PMI Guide to Business Analysis*	407
Proof of Concept	*The PMI Guide to Business Analysis*	407
Prototype	PMI *Business Analysis for Practitioners*	192
RACI model	PMI *Business Analysis for Practitioners*	192
Requirement	PMI *PMBOK® Guide* 7th Edition	247
Requirements documentation	*The PMI Guide to Business Analysis*	410
Requirement Management Plan	PMI *PMBOK® Guide* 7th Edition	247
Requirement Traceability Matrix	PMI *PMBOK® Guide* 7th Edition	247
Scope	PMI *Business Analysis for Practitioners*	194
Stakeholder	*The PMI Guide to Business Analysis*	412
Stakeholder Analysis	*The PMI Guide to Business Analysis*	412
SWOT analysis	PMI *Business Analysis for Practitioners*	196
Traceability	The *PMI Guide to Business Analysis*	415
Use case	PMI *Business Analysis for Practitioners*	197
User Story	*The PMI Guide to Business Analysis*	416
Validation	PMI *Business Analysis for Practitioners*	197
Value Stream Mapping	PMI *Agile Practice Guide*	155
Verification	PMI *Business Analysis for Practitioners*	197
Wireframes	*The PMI Guide to Business Analysis*	417

7.3 Mapping the exam content outline to the reading

The reading for this domain is based on the four PMI publications: the *PMBOK®*, the guide, and the two practice guides; see Table 7.2 for details.

Table 7.2 Business analysis frameworks readings

	Domain 4: Business Analysis Frameworks (27%)	*PMI PMBOK® Guide 7th Edition (July 2021)*	*PMI Agile Practice Guide (2017)*	*PMI Business Analysis for Practitioners: A Practice Guide (2015)*	The PMI Guide to Business Analysis *(December 2017)*
Task 1	Demonstrate an understanding of business analysis (BA) roles and responsibilities	10–15, 17–19		11–36, 72	229–236
Task 2	Determine how to conduct stakeholder communication			132, 144	109–152, 223, 232–235, 368
Task 3	Determine how to gather requirements	192	52, 84–87	7, 11–36, 69–136, 137, 145, 157–176	112, 159–163, 212–215, 251–276, 277–300
Task 4	Demonstrate an understanding of product roadmaps	93–114, 137–144 184	52	37–38, 72–75, 77–86, 151–154	92–95, 182–207, 281–282
Task 5	Determine how project methodologies influence business analysis processes	98–105, 33, 153–196			
Task 6	Validate requirements through product delivery	72, 80–92, 188–190		111–117, 146–147, 157–158, 169	66–72, 175–250

The PMI reference materials list also refer to *Effective Project Management: Traditional, Agile, Extreme, Hybrid* by Robert K. Wysocki; however, the Business Analysis Framework content is limited in the book and covered elsewhere, while the last book on the PMI reference materials list *Project Management Answer Book, 2nd Edition* by Jeff Furman contains no relevant content for this domain.

The four books needed are all available from PMI part of the membership. Table 7.2 include the full list of recommended reading for the Business Analysis Frameworks domain. Table 7.2 include a mapping of the six tasks and which pages in the four recommended sources that you should read.

This can save you a lot of time, so you just read what is needed. Some topics are covered in multiple books, but we still recommend that you read the listed pages. The total amount of readings is 400–500 pages for this domain.

7.4 Brief introduction – business analysis frameworks

Every project starts with a need; projects without a need don't fail at the end, they fail at the beginning.

This is why we need the business analyst to connect the dots and ensure project success, as unclear or incomplete requirements are one of the main causes of project failure. In the list of reasons for top five indicators in challenged IT projects by The Standish Group Chaos report for 2021 is incomplete requirements and specifications and top five factors in successful IT projects include clear statement of requirements. Back in 2014 the PMI annual global Pulse of the Profession® study revealed that 47% of unsuccessful projects fail to meet goals due to poor requirements management. Furthermore, the same study revealed that "inaccurate requirements gathering" remained a primary cause of project failure (37%) in 2014 (up from 32% in 2013). The PMI research highlights that when executive sponsors give value to requirements management as a critical competency, it leads to better project performance, as poor requirements equal to poor performance. However, only 49% of organizations report that they have the necessary resources in place, to properly perform requirements management. The research indicates that high-performer organizations are significantly more likely to value requirements management as a critical competency versus low-performer organizations. This highlights the importance of effective requirements management as one of the key factors in determining project success. Some of these data may seem dated however in recent years not much have changed. We need business analysts and Business Analysis Frameworks more than ever. This chapter will get you started.

7.5 Task 1 – Demonstrate an understanding of business analysis (BA) roles and responsibilities

The business analyst is the person who manages requirements. However, requirements change rapidly. A survey of 4,000 European companies back in 2000, indicates the lack of proper management of changing requirements as one of the main drivers and links to project success. With an increase in complexity due to a wide range of factors such as globalization, technology, systems, processes, and resources – the role of the business analyst is more vital and complex than ever before. A survey by McKinsey and Company, "Big Data Report" indicates that by 2018, the United States alone needs between 140,000–190,000 professionals with deep analytical skills, such as the business analyst.

The business analyst can be of many types, known as an independent assessor or a catalyst for change that can create a positive attitude of collaboration, to overcome internal inertia against change. The business analyst is a self-confident analyst of change, which requires analytical thinking and conflict resolution skills. Often, creative problem-solving is also needed, combined with empathy and communication skills. To be successful the business analyst requires the following important skills and expertise:

- Analytical skills
- Business and industry knowledge
- Communication skills
- Conflict management
- Creative and critical thinking
- Cultural awareness
- Decision-making
- Facilitation
- Project and development approaches
- Influence
- Issue management skills
- Leadership skills
- Negotiation skills
- Organizational skills
- Political awareness

One of the basic objectives of this domain is to correlate business analysis and project management activities together. These roles share many responsibilities, and this is why some people get confused about what differentiates the two roles. The relationship between the business analyst and the project manager is often not clear – at best slightly confusing. The project manager manages the project, while the business analyst conducts business analysis –however, it's not that simple, nor should it be, as it is an opportunity to bridge the gap and shine.

A project manager is accountable for the successful completion of a project, which is measured by the fact that objectives of the project have been achieved. A business analyst, on the other hand, is accountable for the product scope of the project, which needs to be defined correctly and delivered. Therefore, requirement processes will be seen in elaborated form in the domain, and the business analyst will ensure that product vision is in line with the benefits mentioned in the business case.

The activities of the business analyst are a subset of activities in the project which need to be aligned and managed collaboratively. If the business analyst activities fail, the project will most likely fail, with scope challenges resulting in the wrath of the stakeholders. If the business analyst activities are successful, the likelihood of success for the project increases, with product scope well-defined and managed.

The business analyst needs to identify and manage stakeholders, risks, communication, and a range of business analysis planning activities which also are activities involving the project manager. In PMI *Business Analysis for Practitioners* (2015), these points are defined as collaboration points. Collaboration points are activities where the business analyst and the project manager should work together; combined resources may increase the value of the work more than can be conducted individually. The project manager and business analyst are both leaders within their area of expertise, which requires some degree of alignment and cooperation to work. To make the partnership work, to avoid rework and stakeholder confusion, the roles and responsibilities of the business analyst and the project managers need to be coordinated and communicated. Some may see the relationship between the business analyst and the project manager as a competition; however, that should not be the case, as each one is needed for the other to be successful. As a result, more and more successful business analysts and project managers have experience with both roles.

Business analysis as a discipline is the evaluation of an organization's needs, followed by the identification and management of requirements, to arrive at a solution. In other words, it is the discipline of working with stakeholders to define an organization's requirements, to shape the output of projects, and ensure that the output delivers the expected business benefits.

The business analyst works closely with both the business and the development community. The business analyst defines the product or solution, which solves a business problem. The defined solution is then produced by the development community and project.

The purpose of this first tasks is to understand the roles and responsibilities of being the business analyst, and all the various internal and external stakeholders we interact with during the work and who does which tasks.

The main points being that Business analysis is the application of knowledge, skills, tools and techniques to

- determine problems and identify business needs;
- identify and recommend viable solutions for meeting those needs;
- elicit, document, and manage stakeholder requirements to meet business and project objectives; and
- facilitate the successful implementation of the product, service, or result of the program or project.

These are the main responsibilities of the business analysis.

7.5.1 Distinguish between stakeholder roles

The first enabler has emphasis on the Business Analysis being able to distinguish between stakeholder roles. During the needs assessment or early stages of the project, the stakeholder analysis focus has been on stakeholder identification, assessment, and management.

Stakeholder analyses no doubt have always been important. Pulitzer prize-winning historian Barbara Tuchman illustrates this in her sobering history *The March of Folly: From Troy to Vietnam,* which recounts a series of disastrous misadventures that followed in the footsteps of ignoring the interests of, and information held by, key stakeholders. Stakeholders are vital for project success. However, the project and business analyst need to ensure that the right stakeholders are involved, that they are used at the right time, and that stakeholder resources are used in the right way. This means that the Business analysts should work with the project manager or similar role in developing the stakeholder register.

We need to identify stakeholders to ensure that the appropriate parties are represented, informed, and involved. Stakeholders are one of the key sources for requirements and for this, you need to know the number of stakeholders that you are eliciting information from. By knowing the number, you can determine which elicitation techniques work best.

Stakeholders are vital for project success. Some may recall the butterfly effect, where a butterfly may spread its wings in China and cause a flood in Europe. Stakeholders – identified and analyzed or not – have a similar capability to influence the project. Typical stakeholders would have the following roles:

- Business analyst,
- Product manager,
- Product owner,
- Process owner,
- Process manager,
- Customer,
- End user,
- Subject-matter experts,
- Project managers,
- Sponsors,
- Suppliers,
- Testers.

Table 7.3 illustrates the common PMI tools and techniques for stakeholder identification and assessment.

Table 7.3 Stakeholder identification and analysis

Stakeholder identification	*Explanation*
Brainstorming	Brainstorming is a creative technique by which group or individual efforts are made to find stakeholders by gathering a list of possible stakeholders spontaneously contributed by its member(s). A variant is brainwriting or Edward de bono's six thinking hats.
Interviews	One-on-one interviews (i.e., ask your sponsor).
Delphi	The original version of the Delphi method was first applied in the 1960s and the concept was to ask a range of experts for an estimate. The expert was not located in the same location and was unable to communicate and influence the other expert estimate
SWOT analysis	Strengths, weaknesses, opportunities, and threats.
PEST/PESTLE	Political, economic, social, and technological analysis. Legal and environment.
Analogy	Comparison with similar projects. Documentation analysis and prior business analyst experience
	(Continued)

Table 7.3 (Continued)   Stakeholder identification and analysis

Stakeholder analysis	Explanation
Stakeholder cube	The stakeholder cube is a three-dimensional analysis. The cube accounts for the power, interest, and attitude of the stakeholder. They may hold either influential or insignificant power and have active or passive interest
Stakeholder salience	A classification model that groups stakeholders on the basis of their level of authority, their immediate needs, and how appropriate their involvement is in terms of the project. The stakeholder salience model was introduced by Ronald K. Mitchell, Bradley R. Agle and Donna J. Wood in 1997
Power/interest grid	Groups stakeholders on the basis of their levels of authority and interest in the project. Stakeholders are mapped toward low or high power and low or high interest fx. high power and high interest.
Direction of influence	This tool is used to classify the Stakeholders according to their influence on the project. Upward. Senior management, the Sponsor, the Steering Committee. Downward. The Team or specialists contributing knowledge or skills in temporary capacity. Sideward toward fellow project managers or Outward toward the market, competitors and such.
CATWOE	Customer, actor, transformation, worldview, owner, environment
VOCATE	Viewpoint, owner, customer, actor, transformation, environment
PARADE	Perspective, activity, recipient, actor, decision-maker environment

7.5.2 Outline the need for roles and responsibilities

The second enabler for this task has emphasis on outlining the need for roles and responsibilities, while the third enabler focuses on differentiating between internal and external role. PMI typically illustrate the various roles using an Onion Diagram, see Figure 7.1.

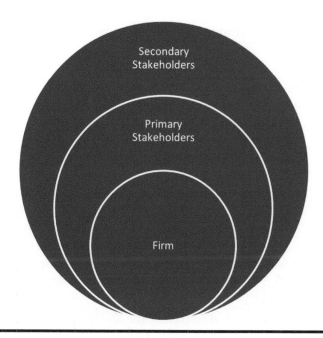

Figure 7.1   Onion diagram

The Onion Diagram is based upon the two-tier Freemanns model, which is a common way to show the findings in terms of primary and secondary stakeholders of the project. As a business analyst, primary stakeholders might include end user, subject-matter expert, product owner and such which are sources of requirements and finding the right solution. Secondary stakeholders might be process owner, business representatives, and others with less knowledge of the requirement and say when it comes to defining the solution. This can vary significantly depending on the context you are in. Internal and external roles may also be a matter of the level of engagement to expect knowledge to be shared and similar considerations which emphasize the importance of this work.

Here you need to keep in mind that various roles do exist depending on the approach the project is using, e.g., agile might include Scrum roles like Scrum master and product owner, team lead from Disciplined agile, while a predictive approach may include more traditional roles like a project manager, business analysis and such. Also know which role in which approach should manage the business analysis tasks, e.g., consider if it is appropriate for the product owner in Scrum to collect requirement as part of the voice of the customer or if another arrangement is better for your organization fx more involvement of the team. For clear roles and responsibilities, a good PMI tool and technique is the use of a RACI chart (A common type of responsibility assignment matrix that uses responsible, accountable, consult, and informs statuses to define the involvement of stakeholders in project activities) or similar type of Responsibility Assignment Matrix (RAM) diagrams, e.g., RASI to clearly illustrate roles and responsibilities. This is commonly applied when working predictive.

7.5.3 Differentiate between internal and external roles

You can also define internal and external roles as project stakeholders, those internal and those external to the client/your organization. The internal stakeholders are your coworkers and people within your own organization, which may sometimes be more problematic to manage. External stakeholders are the individuals or organizations who are not part of the client/your organization, but nevertheless have an interest in the project. They are perhaps the stakeholder groups most readily recognized.

7.6 Task 2 – Determine how to conduct stakeholder communication

The second task – Determine how to conduct stakeholder communication includes two enablers, recommend the most appropriate communication channel/tool ref. Section 7.5.1, and demonstrate why communication is important for a business analyst between various teams ref. Section 7.5.2.

7.6.1 Recommend the most appropriate communication channel/tool

Communication is the exchange of information, intended or involuntary. The information exchanged can be in the form of ideas, instructions, or emotions. This content is mainly derived from the Project Communication Management knowledge area described back in the *PMBOK® Guide* 6th Edition and in bits and pieces in the *PMBOK® Guide* 7th Edition. When it comes to recommending the most appropriate communication channel/tool for reporting, presentation, and such, you need to ensure to cover the topics included in Table 7.4.

Table 7.4   Project communication management

Key terms	Explanation
Communication Management Plan	A component of the project, program, or portfolio management plan that describes how, when, and by whom information about the project will be administered and disseminated.
Communication Requirement Analysis	The analytical technique to determine the information needs of the project stakeholders through interviews, workshops, study of lessons learned from previous projects, etc. Sources of information typically used to identify and define Communications Requirements Analysis include but are not limited to: • Stakeholder information and communication requirements from within the stakeholder register and stakeholder engagement plan; • Organizational charts; • Project organization and stakeholder responsibility, relationships and interdependencies; • Disciplines, departments, and specialties involved in the project; • Logistics of how many persons will be involved with the project and at which locations; • Internal information needs (e.g., when communicating within organizations); • External information needs (e.g., when communicating with the media, public, or contractors).
Communication Types	Face-to-face meetings, video and voice conferencing (virtual meetings), email, fax, instant messaging (IM), text messaging, print media and documents, social media, company website and such.
Communication Channels	Number of Communications Channels is an indicator of the complexity of project Communications. The formular is $N*(n-1)/2$ where N = The number of people.
Communication Models	A description, analogy, or schematic used to represent how the communication process will be performed for the project. Read Communication model for cross-cultural communication ref. *PMBOK®* 6 Edition, figure 10-4.
Communication Methods	A systematic procedure, technique, or process used to transfer information among project stakeholders. These being interactive, pull and push.

The following guidelines has been applied throughout the PMP exam covering this field and is also relevant here:

- Gather and distribute contact information for all involved parties.
- Determine the communication needs of project stakeholders.
- As a rule of thumb, project team members require more detail on a more frequent basis. Senior management typically requires summary information on a less frequent basis.
- Analyze the value to the project of providing the information.

- Evaluate any constraints and assumptions to determine their possible impact on communication planning.
- Determine the appropriate communications technologies to use for communicating project information.
- Make sure your communications management plan includes all key elements.
- Integrate the communications management plan into the overall project plan.
- Distribute the plan to project stakeholders.

7.6.2 Demonstrate why communication is important for a business analyst

The second enabler within this task focuses on demonstrating why communication is important for a business analyst between various teams and stakeholders. The business analyst needs to capture team and stakeholder feedback and perceptions. This is all about communication scope from the stakeholders to the team. Without proper communication the business analyst might not be able to identify and define the right solution for the stakeholders. Even so, if the business analyst gets this right but is unable to communicate the stakeholder's need to the team in terms of requirements and communication, the team may end up producing a solution that does not meet the stakeholder's expectations. This may sound basic and standard; however, 90% of all we do is based around communication which often tends to fail for one or the other reason, meaning delivering of the project scope may fail.

Ways and means of communication can vary depending on the approach, e.g., predictive, or agile. In an agile approach the communication might be supported by user stories and wireframe, while the predictive approach would focus on requirements. Consider where the team is located, co-located versus distributed and the distribution of the team, are they self-organized and cross-function? The reading will emphasize the importance of this communication to ensure that scope is managed according to the requirements of the various stakeholders.

7.7 Task 3 – Determine how to gather requirements

In this task, requirements are elicited, analyzed, developed, modeled, and managed in all possible forms. The basis for requirements elicitation is the knowledge gained during requirements engineering, about the system context of the system to be developed, which comprises the requirements sources that are to be analyzed and queried. These sources include:

- Stakeholders – people or organizations that directly or indirectly influence the requirements of the system.
- Documents – often containing important information that can be a source for attaining requirements.
- Systems in operation – can be legacy, predecessor, or competing systems. Providing the stakeholders with a chance to try the system out, will help them gain an impression of the current system and they can then request extensions or changes based on their impressions.

However, the task has closer ties to the project management activities and most of the activities are conducted in close collaboration with the stakeholders and various parts of the project.

Business Analysis for Practitioners (2015) illustrates the requirement elicitation and analysis as the following steps:

- Plan for elicitation;
- Prepare for elicitation;
- Conduct elicitation activities;
- Document outputs from elicitation activities;
- Complete elicitation;
- Elicitation issues and challenges;
- Analyze requirements;
- Model and refine requirements;
- Document the solution requirements;
- Validate requirements;
- Verify requirements;
- Approval sessions; and
- Resolve requirement-related conflicts.

Here, the business analyst needs to elicit or identify requirements, using individual and group elicitation techniques to discover and capture requirements with supporting details. Requirement elicitation, requirement gathering, requirement discovery, and requirement definition are core activities in requirements engineering. However, while requirement elicitation is critical for the success of our project, it is also one of the most difficult activities. It is error prone, which emphasizes the need for a structured approach and proper documentation. It is also communicatively intensive and should be aligned with stakeholder needs and constraints. Although we need stakeholder input for elicitation, we need to ensure the loudest voice in the room is not the only one that is heard and elicited.

Determine how to gather requirements is central in what the business analyst does. First, it is relevant to understand the process. The common business analysis work process starts with the need assessment which may end up with a business case or similar kind of document. When work commences the business analyst needs to gather requirements from stakeholders, documentation or living artifacts like an IT system. We call this elicitation. When the business analyst has gathered the requirements, he or she needs to document them, this is the analysis part. This task focus on elicitation and analysis. To complete the process ongoing monitoring and controlling will occur until the solution is ready for evaluation. During the whole process the business analyst should engage the various internal and external stakeholders previously discussed.

This task focus on elicitation and analysis of requirements implying gathering and documenting them. The elicitation of requirements represents an early but continuous and critical stage in the development of software systems. Requirements engineering can be defined as a group of activities, which help us to find and communicate the need, purpose, and context of a system. The requirements for a software system may be spread across many sources. Techniques for requirements elicitation are derived mostly from the social sciences, organizational theory, group dynamics, knowledge engineering, and very often, from practical experience.

The main goal of all elicitation techniques is to support the business analyst in ascertaining the knowledge and requirements of the stakeholders. Every project is mostly unique, with individual constraints and individual characteristics, but there are always common elicitation techniques that are compatible with most projects. There is no universal method for requirements elicitation. Several factors influence the choice of elicitation technique. They are listed as follows:

- Distinction between conscious, unconscious, and subconscious requirements.
- Time and budget constraints, and stakeholder availability.
- The business analyst's experience with a particular elicitation technique.
- Chances and risks of the project.

These activities are covered by the PMI *Business Analysis for Practitioners: A Practice Guide*, just highlighted to illustrate the process.

- Plan for elicitation (4.3)
- Prepare for elicitation (4.4)
- Conduct elicitation activities (4.5)
- Document outputs from elicitation activities (4.6)
- Complete elicitation (4.7)
- Elicitation issues and challenges (4.8)
- Analyze requirements (4.9)
- Model and refine requirements (4.10)
- Document the solution requirements (4.11)

7.7.1 Identify the requirements gathering approach for a situation

The first enabler of this task focuses on identifying the requirements gathering approach for a situation, but requirements are not just requirements.

Requirements may range from a high-level abstract statement of a service or of a system constraint, to a detailed mathematical functional specification. First, the business analyst might have identified a wide range of requirements and is in the process of elaborating on them. To do so, the business analyst needs to consider what kind of requirements he or she is working with. Most models for requirements consider two types of requirements; Functional requirements, i.e., what are its behaviors; and Non-functional requirements, i.e. how does it perform them. PMI defines the following types of requirements:

- Business requirements fx. high-level needs of the organization.
- Stakeholder's requirements fx. needs of the stakeholders.
- Solution requirements (functional and non-functional requirements).
- Project requirements (The agreed-upon conditions or capabilities of a product, service, or outcome that the project is designed to satisfy).
- Transition requirements (temporary capabilities such as training or data conversion).
- Requirements assumptions, dependencies, and constraints.

To complete the requirements classification, the business analyst also needs to consider the following factors:

- Source;
- Product or process requirements;
- Priority;

- Scope in terms of affected components;
- Volatility vs stability.

Other classification schemes also describe requirement attributes, such as, the level of detail of a requirement, the priority, or the degree of legal obligation of requirements. CARA'S SOUPS stands for vital requirement attributes, which makes them easier to memorize:

- Complexity;
- Absolute reference;
- Risks;
- Author;
- Source;
- Stability;
- Ownership;
- Urgency;
- Priority;
- Status.

Early identification of the requirements is important, as this has direct bearing on the design and architecture of the system. Unfortunately, requirements' attributes are often overlooked and underspecified in early requirement documents and may cause serious impact in later stages of the Software Development Life cycle. Requirements that are not documented, inadequately documented, or improperly negotiated can lead to circumstances that can threaten the project's success or the subsequent acceptance of the system under development. A business analyst should place special emphasis on the elicitation, documentation, and negotiation of requirements during the development process. Low requirements quality can have expensive consequences during the software development life cycle. Especially, if iterations are long and feedback comes late, the faster a problem is found, the cheaper it is to fix.

Let us turn our attention back to elicitation of various approaches to elicitate requirements. The elicitation of requirements represents an early but continuous and critical stage in the development of software systems. Requirements engineering can be defined as a group of activities, which help us to find and communicate the need, purpose, and context of a system. The requirements for a software system may be spread across many sources. Techniques for requirements elicitation are derived mostly from the social sciences, organizational theory, group dynamics, knowledge engineering, and very often, from practical experience.

The main goal of all elicitation techniques is to support the business analyst in ascertaining the knowledge and requirements of the stakeholders. Every project has individual constraints and individual characteristics, and is mostly unique, but there are always elicitation techniques that are compatible with the project. There is no universal method for requirements elicitation. Several factors influence the choice of elicitation technique. They are:

■ Distinction between conscious, unconscious, and subconscious requirements.
■ Time and budget constraints, and stakeholder availability.
■ Business analyst's experience with a particular elicitation technique.
■ Chances and risks of the project.

Selection of a suitable elicitation technique is dependent on the risk factors involved in a project. These factors can result from the following influences:

■ Human influences;
■ Organizational influences;
■ Additionally, also from operational influences of the content.

Combination of different techniques helps minimize many risks inherent to the project. Risk factors are constraints that are critical to a project. They result from human, organizational, and professional influences, and from operational influence of the content, and desired level of requirement details.

Table 7.5 contains the common requirement elicitation techniques applied in the industry and documented in the *PMBOK®* 6 Edition.

Table 7.5   Requirement elicitation techniques

Techniques	Explanations
Benchmarking	The comparison of actual or planned products, processes, and practices to those of comparable organizations to identify best practices, generate ideas for improvement, and provide a basis for measuring performance
Document analysis	A technique used to gain project requirements from current documentation evaluation
Facilitated workshops	Organized working sessions held by project managers to determine what a project's requirements are and to get all stakeholders together to agree on the project's outcomes

(Continued)

Table 7.5 (Continued)   Requirement elicitation techniques

Techniques	Explanations
Focus groups	An elicitation technique that brings together prequalified stakeholders and subject-matter experts to learn about their expectations and attitudes about a proposed product, service, or result
Interview	A formal or informal approach to elicit information from stakeholders by talking with them directly
Observation	A technique used to gain knowledge of a specific job role, task, or function in order to understand and determine project requirements
Prototype	A method of obtaining early feedback on requirements by providing a working model of the expected product before actually building it
Storyboarding	A prototyping method that can use visuals or images to illustrate a process or represent a project outcome
Questionnaires	Written sets of questions designed to quickly accumulate information from a large number of respondents

The following introduces two (Table 7.6 and Figure 7.2) approaches to categorize the requirement elicitation techniques. The categorizations

Table 7.6   Requirement elicitation methods

Requirement elicitation methods	Techniques
Conversional methods	Interviews Workshops Focus groups
Observational methods	Protocol analysis Ethnography analysis
Analytical methods	Requirement reuse Laddering Card sorting Repertory grid
Synthetic methods	Scenarios Storyboards Prototyping JAD/RAD Contextual inquiry

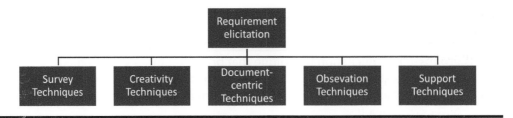

Figure 7.2   Requirement elicitation techniques

do contain additional requirement elicitation techniques not included in Table 7.6 and not expected to be included in the CAPM® exam.

Another influencing factor on the choice of elicitation techniques is the desired level of detail of the requirements. For abstract requirements, creativity technique is suitable. Inquisitive or observational techniques can be used to get medium-level detail of requirements, and document-centric techniques can be used for detailed requirements. Combination of different techniques helps minimize many risks that are inherent to the project. Weaknesses and pitfalls of a particular technique can be balanced out using another technique whose strong points lie where the first technique may have deficits. Figure 7.2 illustrates the requirement elicitation techniques that form the toolbox of a business analyst.

Survey technique

The survey techniques help to elicit precise and unbiased statements from stakeholders, which are then derived by the business analyst. The survey techniques are interviews, such as personal interviews or group interviews with several stakeholders at once; customer site visits or task analysis; and written survey in terms of questionnaires. Table 7.7 and Table 7.8 contain

Table 7.7   Advantages and disadvantages of using interviews for requirement elicitation

Advantages of interviews	Disadvantages of interviews
Scripted discussion Promote dialogue Encourage participants Observation of nonverbal behavior Allow immediate feedback	Require access to committed stakeholders Require training and skills to work well Documentation is subject to interpretation Conflicts are unresolved as they only heard their own points of views Stakeholders may not be able to describe the future, so limited to describe the current situation

Table 7.8 Advantages and disadvantages of using surveys for requirement elicitation

Advantages of surveys	*Disadvantages of surveys*
Require limited stakeholders' time Effective at reaching stakeholders globally shattered Relative fast and inexpensive Scale	Relatively low response rate Poorly worded questions may provide misinformation Require training and business domain knowledge

some of the advantages and disadvantages of using interviews and surveys for requirement elicitation.

Creativity technique

The creativity techniques for requirement elicitation help in developing innovative requirements and elicit excitement factors. The creativity techniques are not suitable for eliciting fine-grained requirements of system behavior. The creativity technique of brainstorming can be used in several variances, such as individual brainstorming sessions, open brainstorming during a workshop, structured brainstorming using WBS for a structured approach, or silent brainstorming using yellow stickers. In addition to this, the brainstorming paradox, as well as the change in perspective and analogy techniques, can also be used as creativity techniques for requirements elicitation. Table 7.9 demonstrates advantages and disadvantages of using interviews for requirement elicitation.

Table 7.9 Advantages and disadvantages of using brainstorming for requirement elicitation

Advantages of brainstorming	*Disadvantages of brainstorming*
Generates multiple ideas quickly Involves multiple perspectives Promotes equal participants	Ideas are not discussed or explored. The true meaning may be misunderstood or ambiguous

Document-centric technique

Document-centric techniques begin with existing documents and systems, which means that solutions and experiences made with existing systems may be reused. The techniques can also be combined with other elicitation

Table 7.10   Advantages and disadvantages of using document review for requirement elicitation

Advantages of document review	Disadvantages of document review
Current process documentation for a starting point	Documentation may be old and outdated Domain knowledge in order to judge the documentation Can be time-consuming

techniques to determine the validity of elicited requirements and to identify new requirements for the new system. The most common document-centric techniques are as follows:

- System archaeology;
- Document review;
- Perspective-based reading; and
- Reuse.

The documents used as part of the techniques can vary from old specifications and designs to problem reports and current list of changes.

Observation technique

The observation techniques are useful when domain specialists are unable to share their knowledge and when it is possible to observe stakeholders as they perform their work. The observation techniques help to formulate the potential requirements, identify inefficient processes, and elicit detailed requirements and dissatisfiers. However, they may not be suitable for development of new processes.

The most common observation techniques are:

- Field observation;
- Apprenticing.

Table 7.11 illustrates the advantages and disadvantages of using observations and apprenticing for requirement elicitation.

Table 7.11 Advantages and disadvantages of using observations and apprenticing for requirement elicitation

Advantages of field observation and apprenticing	*Disadvantages of field observation and apprenticing*
Getting a good feeling about the environment Discover practical issues and unintended uses Simulate dialogue Seeing that a given approach may not work	Not many new requirements Events may not be typical

Support technique

Support techniques serve as an addition to the elicitation techniques and help to balance out the weaknesses and pitfalls of the selected technique.

The support techniques include:

- Mind mapping,
- Workshops,
- CRC Cards,
- Audio/Video recordings,
- Personas,
- Use-Case modeling,
- Wikis, blogs,
- Discussion forums,
- Requirements prototypes,
- Reverse engineering,
- Requirement reuse.

Table 7.12 illustrates the advantages and disadvantages of using workshops for requirement elicitation.

Table 7.12 Advantages and disadvantages of using workshops for requirement elicitation

Advantages of workshops	*Disadvantages of workshops*

Effective at getting real requirements
Can neutralize a predominant voice
A greater chance of getting consensus
Feedback is immediate
Documentation is completed quickly
	Difficult getting the appropriate
	  stakeholders
	Can be costly
	Success very much depends on the
	  facilitator
	Logistic difficulties

With the agile methodologies, the use of prototypes has increased over the years. Table 7.13 illustrates some of the advantages and disadvantages of using prototypes for requirement elicitation.

Table 7.13 Advantages and disadvantages of using prototypes for requirement elicitation

Advantages of prototypes	Disadvantages of prototypes
Reduced time and cost Improved and increased user involvement	Poor documentation Changes to user expectation Unmanageability Exclusion of some users Poor system performance Over-optimistic estimates based upon a prototype

According to *The PMI Guide to Business Analyst* (2017) the following are the key issues and challenges when eliciting requirements:

■ Conflicting viewpoints;
■ Conflicting information;
■ Unstated or assumed information;
■ Stakeholders fails to cooperate;
■ Inability to schedule time for interviews;
■ Inability by the stakeholders to express what they do or what they would like to do; and
■ Inability by the stakeholders to focus on the current solution.

7.7.2 Match tools to scenarios

The first enabler which is placed second match tools to scenarios (e.g., user stories, use cases, etc.) which is the analysis and documentation of the elicited requirements. The business analyst needs to document the outputs from the requirement elicitation activities.

The business analyst selects the models and organizes requirements to understand which models are appropriate to include, based on the business need, and to understand and clearly communicate the interdependencies and relationships between the various requirements. In addition to this, the business analyst verifies that we are following standards, document dependencies, and interrelationships among requirements; and develops concepts for a consistent set of models and templates to document the requirements.

The PMI Business Analysis for Practitioners: A Practice Guide includes various tools and techniques grouped as scope, process, rule, data, and interface models; ref Table 7.14. This is how the business analysis document the requirements.

Table 7.14   Models organized by category

Category	Definition	Examples
Scope models	Models that structure and organize the features, functions, and boundaries of the business domain being analyzed	Use case SWOT diagram
Process models	Models that describe business processes and ways in which stakeholders interact with those processes	Use case User story
Rule models	Models of concepts and behaviors that defines or constrain aspect of a business in order to enforce establish business policies.	Decision tree
Data models	Model that documents the data used in a process or system and its life cycle	State diagram
Interface models	Models that assist in understanding specific systems and their relationship with the solution	User-interface flow Wireframe

After a successful elicitation of the requirements (and documentation), the business analyst needs to analyze, decompose, and elaborate requirements using techniques, such as, dependency analysis, interface analysis, and data and process modeling, in order to collaboratively uncover and clarify product options and capabilities.

Elaborating requirements is a matter of examining, going into details, and adding knowledge into the elicited requirements. Elaborating requirements can be done with the help of a requirements analysis. Requirements analysis, also called requirements engineering, is the process of determining user expectations for a new or modified product. It is a process of discovery, refinement, modeling, and specification, to maximize future exploitation possibilities. Requirements analysis also involves frequent communication with stakeholders and system users to determine specific feature expectations. As we expand upon the requirements, the business analyst examines the high-level ones and determines if they are clear, complete, and free of contradictions, before defining the strategy to address these issues. In addition, the business analyst needs to specify software's operational characteristics that indicate software's interface with other system elements and establish constraints that the software must meet.

Requirements analysis allows the business analyst to:

- Elaborate on basic requirements established during earlier requirement engineering tasks.
- Build models that depict user scenarios, functional activities, problem classes and their relationships, system and class behavior, and the flow of data as it is transformed.
- Identify essential "real world" information.
- Remove redundant, unimportant details.
- Clarify unclear natural language statements.
- Fill remaining gaps in discussions.
- Detect and resolve conflicts between requirements.
- Discover bounds of software.
- Define interaction with the environment.
- Elaborate high-level requirements to derive detailed requirements.
- Distinguish data and operations.

7.7.3 Explain a requirements traceability matrix/product backlog

The third enabler has emphasis on explaining requirements traceability matrix/product backlog. These are two various and important tools but somewhat related. The requirement traceability matrix illustrates how, e.g., requirements are linked to elements such as business needs, project objectives, and WBS deliverables.

Traceability is important when documenting the life of the requirements. The documentation or traceability may help control the force of change and avoid runaway requirements turning into a scope creep. Traceability helps the business analyst get the updated status on the current requirements and all its cross-references. With traceability, the business analyst can explain why a requirement has been changed, then use the documentation as a basis for testing and as ongoing system documentation. Furthermore, traceability can enhance our ability to understand where requirements are built in. Traceability can improve quality, reduce risks, and reduce development costs – which may increase our ability to embrace change. This means we have a clear view of the requirements, what being delivered and what to test. This is all about scope.

Business Analysis for Practitioners (2015) has identified collaboration points indicating that the requirements traceability matrix is an area where the business analyst and the project manager should work together, in coordination with key stakeholders to determine content and application.

In an agile Scrum environment, the scope is managed by the Product Owner in the Product backlog where requirements in terms of user stories, features, epics, and such are linked with the business needs or even WBS deliverables in a Hybrid set-up.

7.8 Task 4 – Demonstrate an understanding of product roadmaps

This task has emphasis on demonstrating an understanding of product roadmaps and which components go to which release.

7.8.1 *Explain the application of a product roadmap*

The product roadmap serves as a high-level visual summary of the product or products of the project. The product roadmap is an overview that shows an overall plan with each planned release and the relevant features associated with those releases. The product roadmap is essential during the analysis and design as the user stories are derived from the product roadmap.

- Roadmaps can vary in appearance and presentation.
- Objective is to display the strategy and direction of the product being built and value to be delivered.
- Roadmaps start with the overarching vision of the product.
- Over time, the roadmap is progressively elaborated as more information is known, work is being completed or not completed, and vision is refined.
- Themes, which equate to goals, emerge to provide structure and associations.
- Product roadmaps provide short-term and long-term visualization of the product.

If we take one step back and look at the multiple levels of agile planning, then we can see the larger context. In an agile environment, the highest level of planning is the product vision which is envisioned in the product roadmap. The product roadmap is then the basis for planning releases. Each release consists of X number of iterations/sprints which consists of X number of days.

- Product Vision,
- Product roadmap,
- Release planning,
- Iteration/sprint planning,
- Daily planning.

7.8.2 Determine which components go to which releases

The second enabler has emphasis on determining which components go to which releases. This ties back to the product roadmap. The product roadmap among other information contains epics which are broken down into user stories in the product backlog. This means based upon the Product roadmap and product backlog the product owner can plan which components go to which releases.

7.9 Task 5 – Determine how project methodologies influence business analysis processes

The project methodologies have major impact on the work and processes of the business analysis which is what is in focus with this fifth task.

7.9.1 Determine the role of a business analyst in adaptive and/or predictive, plan-based approaches

This is described to some degree in the literature with materials on the Continuum of Project Life Cycles and such. Table 7.15 highlights the central aspect and differences between working predictive or agile as a business analysis. When using a predictive approach requirements are elicited early on, in great details and detailed documented by the business analyst. The validation of the requirements happens at the end of the project when the full solution is delivered. The adaptive approach is the opposite of the predictive approach. Various roles may identify and document requirements throughout the project. Documentation is lightweight with user stories and wireframes. The requirements are constantly validated after each iteration.

Table 7.15 Predictive and Agile

Question	Predictive	Agile
When are requirements elicitated?	Early on	Ongoing
How often are requirements elicitated?	Early on, possible one time	Ongoing
How are requirements documented?	More heavyweight/detailed approaches e.g., use cases	Epics, user stories, features, and tasks
Are requirements easy to change?	No, change them early on or work with changes	Yes, just update the Product backlog
Who elicitate and document requirements?	The business analysts	The product owner is responsible, but multiple roles can do the work
How do you validate requirements?	End of project	End of iteration

In the predictive environment the business analysis work and processes are somewhat clearly defined, while in the agile and dynamic environment multiple roles can perform these tasks continuously.

7.10 Task 6 – Validate requirements through product delivery

This sixth and final task of the Business Analysis Frameworks include two enablers, define acceptance criteria, ref. Section 7.10.1, and determine if a project/product is ready for delivery based on a requirements traceability matrix/product backlog, ref. Section 7.10.2.

7.10.1 Define acceptance criteria

Firstly, it's important to understand how we manage quality. In an adaptive/agile Scrum environment, the product owner would define the acceptance criteria uniquely for each user story (in the product backlog with high prioritization) which functions as the acceptance criteria for each user story at the end of the sprint, the sprint review. If the product is ready for delivery is delivered or it might have been accepted earlier if DevOps or such technologies are applied. This is supported by the Definition of Done while regulating the quality covering all user stories for the whole sprint.

In the predictive approach, acceptance criteria are defined for the key deliverables and validated before delivery. Validation is defined as the assurance that a product, service, or system meets the need of the customer and other identified stakeholders. It often involves acceptance and suitability with external customers.

7.10.2 Determine if a project/product is ready for delivery based on a requirements traceability matrix/product backlog

The requirement traceability matrix is important as it helps to ensure that each requirement adds business value, meets customers' expectation, and helps to manage scope. The requirement traceability matrix aligns requirements with objectives, work break structure work packages, testcases and such. This means that acceptance criteriacan be aligned with requirements, deliverables, and testcases.

7.11 – Sample test questions on business analysis frameworks

This section contains five short exam questions in the CAPM® format for you to check your knowledge of the content presented in this chapter and to check your readiness for the CAPM® exam. The answers will be provided in the next section. If you make mistakes, you should go back and learn why mistakes were made. Do not learn the questions and answers, learn the content.

Question 1
Pete is the Business analysis on a big IT project. Currently he is preparing to communicate with various stakeholders, but as it is a globally shattered organization, he is not sure about all the details of them yet. Mary is working with Pete as a project manager. Mary, Pete, and the team has identified the stakeholders. What should they do next?

A. Examine the Project Charter for new insights
B. Identify more stakeholder
C. Analyze the stakeholder to fill in the details
D. Ask the sponsor for details on the key stakeholders

Question 2

Pete, the business analysis on a big IT project is getting ready to start elaboration requirements. His few key stakeholders are shattered around the world in a global organization. People in the organization are busy. The product is all new, so nobody is using it or something like be observed. Pete has access to an old contract somewhat related, market data, and a bunch of research. Which technique should he use next to start gathering requirements?

A. Document analysis
B. Focus group
C. Interview
D. Workshops

Question 3

Petra is working Agile with a couple of teams on a big pharma project. She is struggling to get an overview of what is going on and the direction the teams are heading. She had a brief talk with the product owner who quickly provided her with the product vision. She is still a bit confused. What should she do next?

A. Follow up on the activities in the Gannt diagram
B. Get hold of the roadmap
C. Arrange a session with the teams to develop a WBS
D. Start taking part in the daily stand-ups to understand the status and concerns the teams are facing

Question 4

Petra is working Agile, Scrum to be precise. The maturity of her teams is low, and they are not using DevOps or a similar methodology. When would it be a good time for her and her product owner to validate requirements?

A. Any time during the sprint when a user story has been completed
B. To go through the requirements with the full team during the Sprint retrospective
C. Validate the requirements during the Sprint Review meeting
D. Validate the requirements daily with the team during the daily stand-ups

Question 5

Sweet Farm is a new innovative pharma company working with cutting-edge technology. The IT department is trying to keep up with the business where key stakeholders have a lot to say; however, they rarely know what they want or may quickly change their minds. The business analysis processes are not defined. Which project methodology would be a good starting point for this organization?

A. This is Chaos. Changes are needed before methodology might work
B. Order and structure are needed, so recommend working predictive
C. Considering working hybrid to bring in the best of both worlds
D. Speed and adaptability are required, go Agile

Answer to Question 1: The correct answer is C.
Answer A is wrong. Mary should have read the project charter now and the project charter only contains the initially identified stakeholders which should have been identified. Answer B is wrong. Stakeholders have been identified and more seems not like the issue. Answer C is correct. The team should analyze the stakeholders to fill in the details when the stakeholder identification has been completed. Answer D is wrong. The sponsor might have some details on the key stakeholders but not all and the teams needs to do this work. (ref. *Business Analysis for Practitioners: A Practice Guide*, Section 2.3.1 – "Identify stakeholders")

Answer to Question 2: The correct answer is A.
Answer A is correct. Documents are available and a good starting point. Answer B, C, and D are all wrong. These are conversional methods which are difficult to apply with the stakeholders with limited availability, globally shattered, and possible limited knowledge. These might work well after the document analysis has been completed. (ref. *Business Analysis for Practitioners: A Practice Guide*, Section 4.5.5.2 – "Document Analysis")

Answer to Question 3: The correct answer is B.
Answer A is wrong. The teams are working Agile and might not have Gantt diagrams. Also, it is too detailed to the content she might be looking for. Answer B is correct. The product vision is supported by the roadmap which should answer her question about direction. Answer C is wrong. A WBS might have been a finer choice in a Hybrid set-up, but she is working Agile

where it might not be used. Also, option B is a better choice. Answer D is wrong. This is too detailed and would not provide her with the bigger picture. (ref. *PMBOK® Guide* 7th Edition, section 2.4.2.1 – "Delivery")

Answer to Question 4: The correct answer is C.
Answer A is wrong. This might have worked out if the team was more mature and using DevOps where validation could happen ongoing; however, this is not possible with these teams. Answer B is wrong. Requirements are not validated during the Spring retrospective, which is a team meeting that focuses on continuous improvements. Answer C is correct. Scrum requirements are validated at the Sprint Review. Answer D is wrong. Requirements are not validated during the daily stand-ups where only the three questions are answered. (ref. *Business Analysis for Practitioners: A Practice Guide*, Chapter 6 – "Solution Evaluation")

Answer to Question 5: The correct answer is D.
Answer A is wrong. This is not Chaos according to the Stacy matrix. Answer B is wrong. Order and structure may be needed; however, other factors are more important. Answer C is wrong. This might work well, but Answer D is the better choice as a fully Agile environment is required. Answer D is correct. Speed and adaptability are required. (ref. *PMBOK® Guide* 7th Edition, section 2.3 – "Development approach and Life cycle")

7.12 – Summary of the business analysis framework domain

The purpose of the domain is to demonstrate an understanding of business analysis (BA) roles and responsibilities. Every project starts with a need; projects without a need don't fail at the end, they fail at the beginning. This is why we need the business analyst to connect the dots and ensure project success. According to the PMI global standard, *Business Analysis for Practitioners* (2015),

> a business analyst is the application of knowledge, skills, tools, and techniques to:

■ Determine problems and opportunities;
■ Identify and recommend viable solutions for meeting those needs;

- Elicit, document, and manage stakeholders requirements in order to meet business and project objectives; and
- Facilitate the successful implementation of the product, service, or end result of the program or project.

The British Computer Society proposes the following definition of a business analyst: An internal consultancy role that has the responsibility for investigating business systems, identifying options for improving business systems, and bridging the needs of the business with the use of IT.

Overall, the project or business needs the business analysis to define the problem or opportunity, recommend a good solution, define and document the requirements to deliver the solution and finally validate the delivery of the final solution to meet the stakeholders' needs, this is what this section is all about.

Furthermore, we know from PMI research that effective business analysis helps addressing business needs, managing risks, and reducing rework, have a positive effect on the amount of product defects and increased stakeholder satisfaction.

The business analysis (BA) roles and responsibilities might seem like those of a project manager as both roles identify and assess stakeholders, conduct planning, manage risks, and so forth; however, the BA focus on the product which needs to solve a problem or opportunity. However, it does require constant collaboration between the project manager and the business analysis. The PMI *Business Analysis for Practitioners: A Practice Guide* (2015) uses the term "collaboration points" for all these interactions as works need to be planned, coordinated, and communicated together.

The relationship between the business analyst and the project manager is often not clear. The project manager manages the project, while the business analyst conducts business analysis – however, it's not that simple. Some may see the relationship between the business analyst and the project manager as a competition; however, that should not be the case, as each one is needed for the other to be successful.

Keep in mind project management is the application of knowledge, skills, tools, and techniques to project activities to meet project requirements. Requirements are an inherent aspect of project management (and program management) and business analysis is an important function that identifies, analyzes, and manages those requirements in order to ensure the goal of the project is achieved. Business analysis is a discipline of the broader practice of requirements management. Risk, complexity, change, and stakeholder and communications management are components of requirements management but are only useful if you successfully identify and plan for them within the project and/or program plan.

One of the main tasks for the business analyst is to elicit, document, and manage stakeholder's requirements to meet business and project objectives. To do so the business analysis need to determine how to conduct stakeholder communication. This is also a good example of a collaboration point with the project manager who also has ongoing stakeholder communication, has a communication management plan, stakeholder engagement plan, and so forth. Requirements are mainly elicited from stakeholders, documentation, and real-life uses, where stakeholders for many are the main source of requirements. The need for collaboration with the stakeholders is to determine how to gather requirements and consequently which tools and techniques are we going to apply. Factors like availability, knowledge, location, power, interest, use of technology and such may have an impact on the choice of tools and techniques. The business analyst needs to be able to identify and recommend viable solutions for meeting the needs of the stakeholders based on the gathering and documentation of the requirements.

When the requirements have been elicited from the stakeholders and documented, the business analysts need to support the planning of the delivery. This is why the business analysis needs to demonstrate an understanding of product roadmaps which often are part of the planning process. The planning might start off with a product vision (think multiple level of planning) which is broken down into a product roadmap to illustrate and plan which components of the products are to be delivered at which time and as a vehicle for stakeholder's communication. The product roadmap is also a powerful tool because it works regardless of project methodologies; see next section on this topic. Later the team or project manager may use the product roadmap to plan releases, iterations, and such.

The fifth task focuses on the need to determine how project methodologies influence business analysis processes. This is important because the project methodologies influence business analysis processes significantly. The plan-based approach involves early involvement of the business analysis in a detailed process, often workshop heavy to ensure all requirements are elicited and documented before moving on. The tools and techniques are often comprehensive like use-cases and such to ensure all details are included. In contrast, the agile approach is a lightweight ongoing approach where the business analyst would support the product owner or like to grasp the voice of the customer and document the requirements in a lightweight manner like user stories with wireframes. This underlies the importance early on and in collaboration with the project manager (collaboration point) determine the project methodology to be applied in the project.

The final task we need to emphasize on for the exam is the need to facilitate the successful implementation of the product, service, or end result of the program or project. The examination content outline states this as "validate requirements through product delivery". The business analyst knows the requirements better than anyone and what we are trying to achieve. At this point in time, the business analyst helps to ensure requirements are solved as expected and deliver the envisioned solution; that's why the final validation is important and a task with the involvement of the business analysts.

Chapter 8

Full practice exam one

The CAPM® full practice exam one consists of 135 questions which should be completed in not more than 3 hours in total. The PMI exam do contain 150 questions; however, 15 questions are not scored. Table 8.1 gives the overview of the CAPM® exam breakdown which you should use if you need to go back and revisit the chapter and as a confirmation if all content has been covered, understood, and mastered.

Table 8.1 CAPM® practice exam one breakdown

Domain	Split	Questions	Test questions
Project Management Fundamentals and Core Concepts	36%	49	1–49
Predictive, Plan-Based Methodologies	17%	23	50–72
Agile Frameworks/Methodologies	20%	27	73–99
Business Analysis Frameworks	27%	36	100–135
Summary	**100%**	**135**	**1–135**

Section 8.1 contains the questions and space for answering the questions. Each question includes four possible answers, however, only one is correct. Section 8.2 includes all the answers and explanations. At this stage you should have at least 95 correct questions before moving on to the actual certification exam.

Do not attempt to take the full practice exams before you are ready. You will not get the full benefits and retaking the exam may result in flawed

DOI: 10.4324/9781003462378-8

results. These are the last practice exams you should take before getting above average on the actual PMI exam.

Some of the questions you find below could not be relatable to topics discussed explicitly in this book, but in the answers, you'll always find the references to the external books in the CAPM® reference list, to motivate the correct answers. So, the practice exams of this book are to verify your learning by this book, and to learn something else useful for taking the CAPM® exam.

8.1 Full practice exam one – questions

Question 1
What best describes the term "issues" in the context of project management?

A. Known uncertainties that can impact project objectives
B. Ethical dilemmas faced by project managers during a project
C. Current problems or challenges that are impacting the project and need to be addressed
D. Potential future events that might have a negative impact on the project if they occur

Question 2
Which of the following best describes the "adaptive approach" in project management?

A. An approach primarily based on a set sequence of phases with well-defined requirements from the start
B. A management structure where related projects are coordinated to obtain synergistic benefits
C. An iterative method where requirements and solutions evolve through the collaborative effort of cross-functional teams
D. The process of regularly checking the accuracy and completeness of the project scope

Question 3
What does the term "program" primarily refer to in the context of project management?

A. A set of ethical guidelines and standards for project management professionals
B. A methodology primarily based on a set sequence of phases
C. A group of related projects, subprograms, and program activities managed in a coordinated way to obtain benefits not available from managing them individually
D. The temporary endeavor undertaken to create a unique product, service, or result

Question 4

What is the primary focus of "operations" within an organization in relation to projects?

A. Managing a set of ethical guidelines for professionals
B. Overseeing the group of related projects and programs
C. Handling the day-to-day activities to maintain the ongoing functionality of an organization
D. Coordinating changes and transitions from project outputs to ongoing operations

Question 5

In project management, what is the main intent behind "assumptions"?

A. To provide ethical standards for all project professionals
B. To represent things that are believed to be true but are not confirmed, forming the basis for planning and decision-making
C. To identify uncertain events that might positively or negatively impact project objectives
D. To confirm that the project has delivered all requirements as outlined in the scope

Question 6

What is the primary distinction between "issues" and "risks" in project management?

A. "Issues" are ethical challenges faced by project managers, while "risks" are uncertain events that might impact project objectives.
B. "Issues" are known challenges or problems currently impacting the project, while "risks" are uncertain events that, if they occur, might impact project objectives

C. "Issues" refer to day-to-day operations, whereas "risks" pertain to projects and programs

D. "Issues" are used in the predictive approach, while "risks" are used in the adaptive approach

Question 7

Which statement best differentiates between a "program" and a "project"?

A. A program is a temporary endeavor with a start and finish, while a project is an ongoing operation

B. A program is a collection of related projects managed in a coordinated manner to obtain benefits not available from managing them individually

C. A program deals exclusively with software development, while a project can be in any domain

D. A program and a project are the same, with no distinct differences

Question 8

Which of the following statements best captures the purpose of the "PMI Code of Ethics and Professional Conduct"?

A. The PMI Code of Ethics and Professional Conduct defines the life cycle and stages of a project

B. It is a document used to review and critique the project's scope

C. The PMI Code of Ethics and Professional Conduct sets guidelines and standards for project management professionals in their professional conduct and interactions

D. It is a methodology used for project risk assessment

Question 9

You are a project manager leading a team to implement a new software system for a client. During the project, you discover that a team member has been sharing confidential information about the client's business with a competitor. What should you do as per the PMI Code of Ethics and Professional Conduct?

A. Ignore the situation since it does not directly impact the project's progress

B. Confront the team member privately and ask him/her to stop sharing confidential information

C. Report the situation to the client and let them handle the matter internally
D. Report the unethical behavior to the appropriate authority within your organization or the client's organization

Question 10
What is the key characteristic of a "portfolio" in project management?

A. A portfolio consists of a collection of related projects and programs managed together to achieve strategic objectives
B. A portfolio is a temporary endeavor with a defined beginning and end, similar to a project
C. A portfolio focuses on ongoing operations and repetitive tasks
D. A portfolio is managed by internal teams only

Question 11
Which of the following activities is typically NOT performed during the project closure phase?

A. Handing over project deliverables to the customer
B. Conducting a final project performance review
C. Identifying lessons learned for future projects
D. Creating the project charter

Question 12
What is the primary purpose of a project management plan?

A. To define the project scope
B. To allocate project resources
C. To guide project execution and control
D. To identify project risks

Question 13
Which of the following is NOT a common technique used in the qualitative risk analysis process?

A. Probability and impact matrix
B. Risk probability assessment
C. Monte Carlo simulation
D. Risk categorization

Question 14
Which of the following is an essential component of a project management plan?

A. Organizational chart
B. Project schedule
C. Product backlog
D. Marketing strategy

Question 15
Which of the following documents provides a high-level overview of the project's objectives, scope, and deliverables?

A. Project charter
B. Project management plan
C. Work breakdown structure (WBS)
D. Stakeholder register

Question 16
What is the primary purpose of stakeholder engagement in a project?

A. To minimize the influence of stakeholders on the project
B. To involve stakeholders in project decision-making processes
C. To avoid communication with stakeholders to reduce project complexity
D. To decrease the project's visibility among stakeholders

Question 17
Which of the following documents defines how project resources will be estimated, acquired, and managed?

A. Project charter
B. Resource management plan
C. Project scope statement
D. Stakeholder register

Question 18
What is the primary purpose of a work breakdown structure (WBS) in project management?

A. To identify potential project risks

B. To define project objectives and scope

C. To outline how project resources will be acquired and utilized

D. To decompose project work into smaller, manageable components

Question 19

What is the main purpose of a milestone in a project schedule?

A. To represent the critical path of the project

B. To divide the project into phases or stages

C. To monitor the project's progress and performance

D. To indicate the completion of a significant project event or deliverable

Question 20

Which of the following is a technique used to identify and document project risks by gathering inputs from team members and subject-matter experts?

A. Brainstorming

B. Control Chart

C. Delphi Technique

D. Pareto Chart

Question 21

How does emotional intelligence (EQ) primarily influence project management?

A. EQ helps in estimating the project budget accurately

B. EQ assists in the technical problem-solving aspects of the project

C. EQ plays a significant role in managing stakeholder expectations and team dynamics

D. EQ ensures that the project adheres to its timeline without any delays

Question 22

In the context of project management, which of the following best describes the role of the project manager as a "listener"?

A. The project manager listens to music to help them concentrate on project tasks

B. The project manager takes feedback only from the senior stakeholders to make decisions

C. The project manager attentively listens to all stakeholders, understanding their needs and concerns, and uses this information to guide project direction

D. The project manager listens only to the project team and bases decisions solely on their feedback

Question 23

Which of the following statements best distinguishes the roles of a project manager and a project sponsor?

A. A project sponsor manages day-to-day operations of the project, while the project manager provides financial support

B. The project manager is responsible for the execution of the project, while the project sponsor acts as a key supporter and decision-maker, especially when strategic direction or resources are concerned

C. Both the project manager and the project sponsor are responsible for creating the project schedule

D. A project sponsor resolves all team conflicts, while the project manager focuses only on project documentation

Question 24

Why is emotional intelligence (EQ) considered vital for a project manager's success?

A. Because EQ allows project managers to predict project risks more accurately

B. Because EQ directly helps in the technical aspects of project management tools and software

C. Because EQ enhances a project manager's ability to understand, communicate with, and manage the emotions of themselves and others, leading to better team dynamics and stakeholder relationships

D. Because EQ ensures that projects are always completed on time and within budget

Question 25

Which of the following best describes the primary responsibility of a project team in relation to a project?

A. The project team is mainly responsible for securing project funding and aligning the project with strategic objectives

B. The project team is responsible for executing tasks, producing deliverables, and providing expertise to ensure the project meets its objectives
C. The project team is responsible for approving or rejecting changes to the project scope
D. The project team's primary duty is to market the project outcomes to external stakeholders

Question 26

Which of the following statements best distinguishes the concepts of leadership and management in the context of project management?

A. Leadership is about executing tasks on time, while management is about inspiring and motivating the team
B. Leadership focuses on maintaining processes and systems, while management is about setting a vision and direction
C. Leadership involves setting a vision, inspiring the team, and driving change, whereas management deals with planning, organizing, and controlling processes to achieve specific goals
D. Leadership and management are essentially the same, and the terms can be used interchangeably in a project context

Question 27

Which of the following best contrasts the roles of the project team and the project sponsor?

A. The project team focuses on high-level strategic decisions, while the project sponsor focuses on day-to-day operational tasks
B. The project team is responsible for providing the budget and resources, while the project sponsor is responsible for executing tasks and deliverables
C. The project team specializes in executing tasks, producing deliverables, and handling technical aspects, while the project sponsor champions the project at higher levels, ensuring alignment with organizational goals, and makes critical business decisions
D. The project team and project sponsor share the same responsibilities and roles, and there is no distinct difference between them

Question 28

Which of the following roles is NOT typically associated with a project manager in the context of project management?

A. Initiator
B. Negotiator
C. Facilitator
D. Financial Auditor

Question 29
Which statement best summarizes the role of a project manager as both a leader and a manager?

A. As a leader, the project manager sets the project schedule, and as a manager, they inspire the team
B. As a leader, the project manager is responsible for resource allocation, while as a manager, they handle conflict resolution
C. As a leader, the project manager motivates, influences, and drives change, whereas as a manager, they plan, organize, and ensure project tasks are executed efficiently
D. As a leader and manager, the project manager only focuses on ensuring project deliverables are met on time

Question 30
In the context of a project, who is typically responsible for securing necessary resources, championing the project's cause within the organization, and making high-level decisions?

A. Project Sponsor
B. Project Coordinator
C. Project Team Member
D. Stakeholder

Question 31
Explain communication management in project management.

A. Communication management involves developing a risk register to track project risks
B. Communication management focuses on creating a detailed project schedule and allocating resources
C. Communication management is the process of planning, executing, and monitoring project communication
D. Communication management involves identifying and analyzing project stakeholders

Question 32

In an Agile project, the team encounters unexpected technical challenges that could delay the project. What is an appropriate response to this situation?

A. Conduct a retrospective to identify the root causes and collaboratively find solutions
B. Revert to traditional project management methods to address the challenges
C. Add more features to the project scope to compensate for the delays
D. Ignore the challenges and continue with the original plan

Question 33

What is the main objective of benefit realization in a project?

A. To create a detailed project schedule and allocate resources
B. To identify potential project risks and develop mitigation strategies
C. To define the project objectives and deliverables
D. To ensure that the project delivers the intended benefits and value to the organization

Question 34

What is the main purpose of a project charter?

A. To create a detailed project schedule and allocate resources
B. To identify potential project risks and develop mitigation strategies
C. To define the project objectives, scope, and authorization
D. To establish communication channels with stakeholders

Question 35

Which document formally authorizes the existence of a project and provides the project manager with the authority to apply organizational resources to project activities?

A. Project Charter
B. Work Breakdown Structure
C. Project Management Plan
D. Risk Register

Question 36
When following a planned risk management strategy, if a team decides to purchase insurance for a potential risk or enter into a partnership to share the risk, which risk response strategy are they employing?

A. Acceptance
B. Avoidance
C. Transfer
D. Mitigation

Question 37
During project execution, you realize that a planned communication strategy isn't effectively reaching all stakeholders. What is the most appropriate action to take?

A. Continue with the strategy and document it as a lesson learned
B. Re-evaluate and adjust the communication management plan
C. Increase the frequency of communications without changing the strategy
D. Inform only the most important stakeholders about the communication issues

Question 38
Which of the following is a key responsibility of the project manager during project execution?

A. Developing the project charter
B. Creating the work breakdown structure
C. Managing changes to the project scope
D. Planning the project schedule

Question 39
Explain project initiation and benefit planning in project management.

A. Project initiation involves creating a detailed project schedule, while benefit planning focuses on identifying project stakeholders
B. Project initiation is about securing project funding, and benefit planning is about determining project objectives
C. Project initiation includes defining the project scope and objectives, while benefit planning involves identifying the expected value and benefits from the project
D. Project initiation is all about creating the project communication plan, and benefit planning is about managing project risks

Question 40

Give an example of how it is appropriate to respond to a planned communication strategy in a project

A. The project manager shares all project-related information with stakeholders without considering their communication preferences
B. The project team conducts regular status meetings and provides stakeholders with relevant and timely project updates
C. The project manager decides not to communicate any project-related information to stakeholders
D. The project team delays communication until the end of the project to avoid any potential conflicts

Question 41

Which of the following is primarily used in agile frameworks to discuss what was done the previous day, what is planned for the current day, and any impediments?

A. Focus group
B. Brainstorming session
C. Stand-up meeting
D. Retrospective meeting

Question 42

Which problem-solving technique involves the spontaneous contribution of ideas from all members of a group?

A. Focus group
B. Pareto analysis
C. Stand-up meeting
D. Brainstorming

Question 43

Which of the following is a qualitative method of gathering information on opinions, perceptions, and beliefs from a diverse group of people?

A. Brainstorming
B. Stand-up meeting
C. Pareto analysis
D. Focus group

Question 44

At the end of an iteration, which meeting is primarily used to discuss what went well, what could be improved, and how to incorporate the improvements in future iterations?

A. Stand-up meeting
B. Brainstorming session
C. Focus group
D. Retrospective meeting

Question 45

Which of the following techniques assists in visualizing the cause-and-effect relationships that might lead to a particular problem or outcome?

A. Pareto chart
B. Flow chart
C. Fishbone diagram
D. Affinity diagram

Question 46

In the context of agile methodologies, which event provides an opportunity for the team to inspect their work and adapt the product backlog, based on feedback and learning from the last sprint?

A. Daily Standup
B. Sprint Review
C. Sprint Planning
D. Retrospective

Question 47

Which of the following tools visually depicts relationships among variables to determine if a correlation exists?

A. Flow chart
B. Pareto chart
C. Fishbone diagram
D. Scatter plot

Question 48
Which of the following agile practices involves the team working on a specific set of user stories or product backlog items within a fixed time frame, typically ranging from one to four weeks?

A. Kanban
B. Sprint or Iteration
C. Continuous Integration
D. User Story Mapping

Question 49
In a project, when stakeholders with different backgrounds and perspectives come together to provide feedback about project requirements, products, or issues, which tool or technique is being used?

A. Brainstorming
B. Stand-up meetings
C. Focus group
D. Pareto analysis

Question 50
Which of the following is an enabling factor for using a predictive plan-based approach in projects?

A. Emphasis on adaptability and flexibility
B. Rapidly changing market conditions
C. Well-documented historical project data
D. Continuous customer collaboration

Question 51
Which of the following is NOT a Process Group in project management?

A. Initiating
B. Planning
C. Monitoring and Controlling
D. Reviewing and Evaluating

Question 52
What are Phase Gates in project management?

A. Checkpoints that determine whether a project can proceed to the next phase
B. Documents from previous similar projects
C. Factors that affect the organization's structure and culture
D. External conditions that can influence the project

Question 53
Which organizational structure is characterized by functional departments that operate independently, with little integration or coordination across departments?

A. Projectized organization
B. Matrix organization
C. Functional organization
D. Composite organization

Question 54
What are the enabling factors for using a predictive plan-based approach in projects?

A. High degree of uncertainty and rapidly changing requirements
B. Flexible and adaptable project team
C. Well-defined scope and stable project environment
D. Emphasis on collaboration and customer feedback

Question 55
What is the purpose of a project schedule network diagram?

A. To identify the critical path and determine project duration
B. To track the progress of project activities
C. To allocate resources to project tasks
D. To define the sequence and dependencies of project activities

Question 56
What is the purpose of a project budget determination technique?

A. To allocate resources to project activities
B. To track and control project costs

C. To estimate the duration of project activities

D. To define the sequence and dependencies of project activities

Question 57

What are the types of estimation techniques commonly used for determining project duration and costs?

A. Analogous Estimating, Parametric Estimating, Three-Point Estimating

B. Critical Path Method, Earned Value Management, Monte Carlo Simulation

C. Resource Leveling, Resource Smoothing, Critical Chain Method

D. Control Charts, Trend Analysis, Variance Analysis

Question 58

Which schedule compression technique involves allocating additional resources to activities to shorten the project schedule?

A. Crashing

B. Fast tracking

C. Resource leveling

D. Monte Carlo simulation

Question 59

What is the primary purpose of a Gantt chart in project management?

A. To track project costs and expenses

B. To visualize the project schedule and task dependencies

C. To assess project risks and develop risk mitigation strategies

D. To monitor and control project quality and performance

Question 60

In earned value analysis, what does a negative Schedule Variance (SV) indicate?

A. The project is ahead of schedule

B. The project is behind schedule

C. The project is on schedule

D. The project is at risk of cancellation

Question 61

What is the purpose of creating a Work Breakdown Structure (WBS) in project management?

A. To define project deliverables and organize project work
B. To allocate resources and manage project costs
C. To identify project risks and develop risk mitigation strategies
D. To monitor and control project quality and performance

Question 62

A project has a planned duration of 10 weeks and a planned cost of 50,000 Euro. At the end of Week 6, the actual cost incurred is 30,000 Euro, and the work completed is 60% of the planned work. Calculate the Schedule Variance (SV) for the project.

A. −15,000 Euro
B. −20,000 Euro
C. 20,000 Euro
D. 30,000 Euro

Question 63

Consider a project with the following Activity durations:

■ Activity F: 3 days
■ Activity G: 5 days
■ Activity H: 2 days
■ Activity I: 4 days
■ Activity L: 6 days

and consider the following Finish-To-Start dependencies:

■ F -> G
■ F -> H
■ G -> I
■ H -> I
■ I -> L

Calculate the total duration of the Critical Path.

A. 12 days
B. 15 days

C. 16 days

D. 18 days

Question 64

What is the purpose of a Quality Management Plan in project management?

A. To define the processes, procedures, and resources required to ensure project quality

B. To identify and assess project risks and develop risk mitigation strategies

C. To monitor and control project schedule and progress

D. To track and manage project costs and expenses

Question 65

What does the term "percentage of completion" refer to in project management?

A. The proportion of the project budget spent

B. The estimated time remaining to complete the project

C. The progress made on a project in terms of completed activities

D. The ratio of planned duration to actual duration

Question 66

Which of the following formulas correctly represents the calculation of Estimate At Completion (EAC) in Earned Value Method (EVM)?

A. EAC = Budget at Completion (BAC) – Cost Performance Index (CPI)

B. EAC = Actual Cost (AC) + Estimate to Complete (ETC)

C. EAC = Earned Value (EV) / Cost Performance Index (CPI)

D. EAC = Budget at Completion (BAC) – Actual Cost (AC)

Question 67

Which of the following statements regarding control charts is correct?

A. Control charts are used to monitor cost performance only

B. Control charts are used to monitor schedule performance only

C. Control charts are used to monitor both cost and schedule performance

D. Control charts are used to monitor quality performance only

Question 68
Which of the following statements best describes Root Cause Analysis?

A. Root Cause Analysis is a reactive approach used after the project is completed to analyze project performance
B. Root Cause Analysis is a proactive approach used at the beginning of a project to identify potential risks
C. Root Cause Analysis is a technique used to identify the primary causes of project issues or problems
D. Root Cause Analysis is a qualitative analysis technique used to assess project stakeholders' satisfaction

Question 69
Which of the following statements regarding variance analysis is correct?

A. Variance analysis is only concerned with cost deviations in the project
B. Variance analysis compares actual values with earned values
C. Variance analysis is used to identify trends and patterns in project performance
D. Variance analysis focuses on the differences between planned and actual values

Question 70
Which of the following statements regarding status reports is correct?

A. Status reports are only shared with the project team and not with external stakeholders
B. Status reports are typically prepared at the beginning of a project to outline the project plan
C. Status reports provide a summary of completed tasks without any analysis of project performance
D. Status reports communicate project progress, risks, issues, and other relevant information to stakeholders

Question 71
What is the primary purpose of trend analysis in project management?

A. To compare actual project performance against the project plan
B. To identify the root causes of project issues or problems

C. To assess stakeholder satisfaction throughout the project

D. To analyze project performance over time and identify patterns

Question 72

Given the following information:

- Planned Value (PV): $10,000
- Earned Value (EV): $8,000
- Actual Cost (AC): $9,500

Using the appropriate formula of the Earned Value Method (EVM), what is the value of the Cost Variance (CV)?

A. $2,000

B. −$1,500

C. −$2,000

D. −$500

Question 73

Which of the following is a characteristic of an Agile project life cycle?

A. Sequential and phase-based approach

B. Emphasis on detailed upfront planning

C. Flexibility to accommodate changes throughout the project

D. Emphasis on extensive documentation

Question 74

Which of the following is an Agile framework commonly used for software development?

A. Waterfall

B. Six Sigma

C. Scrum

D. Lean Six Sigma

Question 75

Which framework or model helps in understanding the complexity of a given situation and suggests appropriate management approaches?

A. Cynefin

B. Stacey Matrix

C. Both A and B

D. None of the above

Question 76
Which of the following factors facilitates the use of Adaptive approaches?

A. Hierarchical organizational structure
B. Strict regulatory compliance requirements
C. Empowered and autonomous teams
D. Siloed and departmentalized communication

Question 77
Which of the following is one of the Agile Manifesto values?

A. Predictive planning over adaptability
B. Customer collaboration over contract negotiation
C. Comprehensive documentation over working software
D. Following a detailed process over collaboration

Question 78
Which of the following project life cycles is iterative and incremental in nature?

A. Waterfall
B. Predictive
C. Agile
D. Sequential

Question 79
What is a Release plan?

A. A visual model that outlines the features and functionality of a product
B. The schedule of the features and/or outcomes to release in the several Iterations composing the Release
C. A list of prioritized user stories that define the scope of a project
D. A visual representation of the timeline and milestones for product development

Question 80
What is the purpose of an Iteration Review?

A. To assess the performance and progress of the team
B. To demonstrate the completed work to stakeholders and gather feedback
C. To retrospectively analyze the team's performance and identify areas for improvement
D. To plan and prioritize the work for the next iteration

Question 81
What is the purpose of a Retrospective?

A. To assess the performance and progress of the team
B. To retrospectively analyze the team's performance and identify areas of improvement
C. To plan and prioritize the work for the next iteration
D. To review and validate the completeness of the product backlog

Question 82
What is the purpose of the Iteration Planning meeting?

A. To review and validate the completeness of the product backlog
B. To synchronize and coordinate the work of the development team
C. To plan and prioritize the work for the upcoming iteration
D. To retrospectively analyze the team's performance and identify areas of improvement

Question 83
Which of the following better describe what a User Story is?

A. A test specification
B. A brief description of an outcome for a specific user which is a promise for conversation
C. A detailed requirement specification
D. An issue

Question 84
What is true about Epics?

A. Epics do not fit in one iteration
B. Epics fit in one iteration

C. Epics must not be decomposed

D. User stories are bigger than Epics

Question 85

Velocity is a metric used in Agile to measure:

A. The amount of work completed in a sprint

B. The amount of work remaining in a sprint

C. The number of bugs in the software

D. The overall team performance

Question 86

What is the purpose of a Kanban Board?

A. To visualize and track the progress of work items

B. To estimate the effort required for user stories

C. To facilitate sprint planning meetings

D. To assign tasks to team members

Question 87

In a software development team, the average throughput is eight completed user stories per week. The average cycle time for a user story is four weeks. Based on Little's Law, what is the average work in process (WIP) in the system?

A. 2 user stories

B. 16 user stories

C. 32 user stories

D. 64 user stories

Question 88

A software development team has a total of 100 story points planned for a release. After the first week, they have completed 20 story points. If the release is scheduled for eight weeks, what is the ideal burndown rate per week to complete the release on time?

A. 15 story points per week

B. 10 story points per week

C. 5 story points per week

D. 2.5 story points per week

Question 89
What is the main difference between Cycle Time and Lead Time?

A. Cycle time includes both active and idle time, while lead time only includes active time
B. Cycle time represents the total time taken to complete a work item, while lead time represents the time from request to completion
C. Cycle time focuses on individual tasks within a process, while lead time focuses on the overall process from start to finish
D. Cycle time is used for measuring team productivity, while lead time is used for forecasting project completion

Question 90
What are the Scrum events?

A. Sprint, Sprint planning, Daily scrum, Sprint review, Sprint retrospective
B. Communication, Collaboration, and Commitment
C. Individuals and Interactions, Working Software, Customer Collaboration, and Responding to Change
D. Planning, Execution, and Delivery

Question 91
Which of the following are Kanban principles or properties?

A. Visualize workflow, Limit work in progress, Manage flow, Make process policies explicit
B. Iterative development, Continuous integration, Test-driven development, Pair programming, On-site customer
C. Transparency, Inspection, and Adaptation
D. Plan, Do, Check, Act

Question 92
Which of the following are the eXtreme Programming (XP) practices?

A. Pair programming, Test-driven development (TDD), Continuous integration, Refactoring, Simple design
B. Sprint Planning, Daily Scrum, Sprint Review, Sprint Retrospective
C. User Stories, Tasks, Burndown Chart
D. Product Backlog, Sprint Backlog, Increment

Question 93
Which of the following better describe a Minimum Viable Product (MVP)?

A. MVP is a process
B. MVP is a very large Epic
C. MVP does not necessarily deliver value
D. MVP is the minimum set of features that give value to the customers

Question 94
What is the primary principle behind Test-Driven Development (TDD)?

A. Write tests after writing the code to validate its correctness
B. Write tests before writing the code to guide its implementation
C. Write tests during code refactoring to ensure maintainability
D. Write tests during the code review process to ensure quality

Question 95
Which financial metric is used to measure the profitability of an investment by calculating the present value of future cash flows?

A. Return on Investment (ROI)
B. Net Present Value (NPV)
C. Internal Rate of Return (IRR)
D. Payback Period

Question 96
Which of the following Agile techniques can be used to estimate the effort or size of user stories or backlog items?

A. Planning Poker
B. Value Stream Mapping
C. Control Charts
D. Fishbone Diagrams

Question 97
What is the main difference between the Definition of Ready and the Definition of Done?

A. The Definition of Ready is determined by the Product Owner, while the Definition of Done is determined by the Development Team

B. The Definition of Ready focuses on functional requirements, while the Definition of Done encompasses non-functional requirements and quality standards

C. The Definition of Ready is defined at the beginning of the project, while the Definition of Done is defined for each user story during sprint planning.

D. The Definition of Ready defines the criteria that a user story must meet before it can be included in a sprint, while the Definition of Done specifies the criteria that a user story must meet to be considered complete

Question 98

Which prioritization scheme in Agile projects involves assigning a numerical value to each user story or backlog item to determine its priority?

A. MoSCoW prioritization

B. T-Shirt sizing

C. Cost of Delay (CoD)

D. Kano model

Question 99

What metrics put in relation a Prioritization Matrix?

A. Risks and Time

B. Resource assigned and Effort

C. Effort and Value

D. None of the above

Question 100

You are creating a fictional representation of a user to better understand their needs and behaviors. What is this representation called?

A. Minimum Viable Product

B. Multivoting process

C. Persona

D. Problem solving

Question 101

You are analyzing the sequence of activities and the dependencies between them in a project. What technique are you using?

A. Gantt chart
B. Cause-and-effect diagram
C. Value Stream Mapping
D. Persona

Question 102

You are conducting a workshop to identify and prioritize business requirements. What technique are you using?

A. Minimum Viable Product
B. Brainstorming
C. Verification
D. Wireframes

Question 103

You are analyzing the impact of a proposed change on the project's timeline and resources. What technique are you using?

A. Compliance standard
B. Export Judgment
C. Cost-Benefit Analysis
D. Impact analysis

Question 104

You are conducting interviews with stakeholders to gather their expectations and requirements for a new software application. What is the primary purpose of these interviews?

A. To validate and test a product concept with minimal features
B. To analyze the cost and benefits of the proposed solution
C. To identify and understand stakeholders and their interests
D. To define the project scope

Question 105
You are facilitating a session to identify and evaluate potential solutions to a business problem. What technique are you using?

A. Use case
B. Creative thinking
C. Benchmarking
D. Multivoting process

Question 106
You are conducting a workshop to identify and analyze the potential risks and their impacts on a project. What technique are you using?

A. Force Field Analysis
B. Document Analysis
C. Risk Identification
D. Use case

Question 107
You are creating a visual representation of the flow of activities, inputs, and outputs in a business process. What technique are you using?

A. Context Diagram
B. Cost-Benefit Analysis
C. Persona
D. Traceability

Question 108
You are analyzing the roles, responsibilities, and involvement of stakeholders in a project. What technique are you using?

A. Stakeholder Analysis
B. Verification
C. Value Stream Mapping
D. Business Case

Question 109

You are conducting a session with stakeholders to brainstorm and generate a large number of ideas for a new product feature. What technique are you using?

A. Affinity Diagram
B. Requirement Traceability Matrix
C. Creative thinking
D. Proof of Concept

Question 110

You are documenting the functional and non-functional needs and specifications of a system. What are these called?

A. Stakeholder requirements
B. User stories
C. Business value
D. Requirements

Question 111

You are facilitating a session with stakeholders to prioritize project requirements based on their importance and urgency. What technique are you using?

A. Five Whys technique
B. Minimum Viable Product
C. Multivoting process
D. Product roadmap

Question 112

You are conducting interviews with subject-matter experts to gather detailed information about a specific process. What technique are you using?

A. Problem solving
B. Export Judgment
C. Document Analysis
D. Wireframes

Question 113

You are analyzing the potential causes of a problem by visually mapping out the relationships between different factors. What technique are you using?

A. Cause-and-effect diagram
B. Benchmarking
C. Stakeholder Analysis
D. User Story

Question 114

You are documenting the key features and functionalities that a product should have to meet the needs of the target users. What technique are you using?

A. Value Stream Mapping
B. Persona
C. Use case
D. Requirement

Question 115

You are conducting a session to gather feedback and insights from stakeholders about a proposed solution. What technique are you using?

A. Proof of Concept
B. Compliance standard
C. Validation
D. Epic

Question 116

You are facilitating a session with stakeholders to identify the underlying causes of a problem by repeatedly asking "Why?" What technique are you using?

A. Problem solving
B. Affinity Diagram
C. Five Whys technique
D. Traceability

Question 117
You are creating a visual representation of the interactions between users and a system to achieve specific goals. What technique are you using?

A. Wireframes
B. RACI model
C. Use case
D. Business value

Question 118
You are analyzing the potential risks and opportunities associated with a project by considering both internal and external factors. What technique are you using?

A. Context Diagram
B. SWOT analysis
C. Document Analysis
D. Benchmarking

Question 119
You are conducting interviews with stakeholders to understand their preferences and expectations for a new website design. What technique are you using?

A. Compliance standard
B. Validation
C. Interviews
D. Export Judgment

Question 120
You are analyzing the flow of activities, information, and value delivery in a process to identify areas of waste and improvement. What technique are you using?

A. Persona
B. Value Stream Mapping
C. Creative thinking
D. Product roadmap

Question 121
You are conducting a session with stakeholders to identify and analyze potential risks by considering the likelihood of occurrence and the impact on project objectives. What technique are you using?

A. Cause-and-effect diagram
B. Risk Assessment
C. Export Judgment
D. Minimum Viable Product

Question 122
You are creating a visual representation of the relationships between different requirements and project artifacts. What technique are you using?

A. Stakeholder Analysis
B. Business Case
C. Requirement Traceability Matrix
D. Context Diagram

Question 123
You are conducting interviews with users to gather their preferences, needs, and pain points related to a new mobile application. What technique are you using?

A. Verification
B. Wireframes
C. User Story
D. Interviews

Question 124
You are analyzing the current state of a process to identify areas of improvement and inefficiencies. What technique are you using?

A. Value Stream Mapping
B. Persona
C. Multivoting process
D. Proof of Concept

Question 125

You are conducting a workshop to generate a large number of ideas and potential solutions for a complex business problem. What technique are you using?

A. Benchmarking
B. Brainstorming
C. Requirement Management Plan
D. Validation

Question 126

You are analyzing the potential impact of a proposed change on project scope, schedule, and budget. What technique are you using?

A. Verification
B. Impact analysis
C. Export Judgment
D. Persona

Question 127

You are conducting a session with stakeholders to identify and evaluate potential solutions to a business problem. What technique are you using?

A. Wireframes
B. Problem solving
C. Benchmarking
D. Brainstorming

Question 128

You are analyzing the needs and behaviors of different user groups to ensure that a product meets their specific requirements. What technique are you using?

A. Persona
B. Cost-Benefit Analysis
C. Requirement Traceability Matrix
D. Use case

Question 129

You are reviewing project documentation and deliverables to ensure that they meet the specified quality standards. What technique are you using?

A. Validation
B. Document Analysis
C. Five Whys technique
D. Product roadmap

Question 130

You are conducting interviews with stakeholders to gather their input and requirements for a new system. What technique are you using?

A. Context Diagram
B. Interviews
C. RACI model
D. Export Judgment

Question 131

You are creating a visual representation of the sequence and dependencies of project activities. What technique are you using?

A. Business Case
B. Product roadmap
C. Gantt chart
D. Cost-Benefit Analysis

Question 132

You are analyzing the strengths, weaknesses, opportunities, and threats related to a project or organization. What technique are you using?

A. Brainstorming
B. Compliance standard
C. SWOT analysis
D. Multivoting process

Question 133

You are conducting a session with stakeholders to identify and rank the factors that are driving or restraining change in a project. What technique are you using?

A. Cause-and-effect diagram
B. Problem solving
C. Force Field Analysis
D. Wireframes

Question 134

You are creating a visual representation of the flow of activities, decisions, and information in a process. What technique are you using?

A. Value Stream Mapping
B. Persona
C. Context Diagram
D. Requirement Traceability Matrix

Question 135

You are reviewing project requirements and ensuring that they are clear, concise, and unambiguous. What technique are you using?

A. Validation
B. Document Analysis
C. Definition of Done
D. Stakeholder Analysis

8.2 Full practice exam one – answers

Answer to Question 1: The correct answer is C.
In project management, "issues" refer to current problems or challenges that are impacting the project and need immediate attention. They differ from risks, which are potential future events that might affect the project. Addressing issues promptly is crucial to keep the project on track.

Answer to Question 2: The correct answer is C.
The adaptive approach is a development approach where requirements and solutions evolve through the collaborative effort of cross-functional teams. Unlike the predictive approach, which is linear and fixed, the adaptive approach allows for flexibility and is especially suitable for projects with high levels of uncertainty or where requirements are expected to change.

Answer to Question 3: The correct answer is C.
In project management, a "program" refers to a group of related projects, subprograms, and program activities managed in a coordinated way to obtain benefits not available from managing them individually. Programs are often managed to achieve strategic objectives and can leverage synergies among projects to deliver more value.

Answer to Question 4: The correct answer is C.
"Operations" refer to the day-to-day activities that maintain the ongoing functionality of an organization. While projects are temporary endeavors to create unique outputs, operations involve repetitive tasks that support the business's regular functions.

Answer to Question 5: The correct answer is B.
In project management, "assumptions" represent things that are believed to be true or will become true but have not yet been verified. Assumptions form the basis for planning and decision-making in a project. They need to be documented, and as the project progresses, these assumptions should be validated.

Answer to Question 6: The correct answer is B.
"Issues" are known challenges or problems that are currently impacting the project. They are tangible and need to be addressed promptly. On the other hand, "risks" are uncertain events that, if they occur, might have a positive or negative impact on one or more project objectives.

Answer to Question 7: The correct answer is B.
A "program" is a collection of related projects, subprograms, and program activities managed in a coordinated manner to obtain benefits not available from managing them individually. Programs are designed to achieve strategic objectives and often involve managing interdependencies among the projects within the program. On the other hand, a "project" is a temporary endeavor undertaken to create a unique product, service, or result. Projects have a definite start and end date and are distinct from ongoing operations.

Answer to Question 8: The correct answer is C.
The primary purpose of the "PMI Code of Ethics and Professional Conduct" is to set guidelines and standards for project management professionals in

their professional conduct and interactions. This code ensures that PMI professionals uphold the highest levels of professionalism, honesty, and integrity in their work.

Answer to Question 9: The correct answer is D.
As per the "PMI Code of Ethics and Professional Conduct", the project manager should report the unethical behavior of the team member to the appropriate authority within their organization or the client's organization. Sharing confidential information with a competitor is a serious breach of ethics and could have severe consequences for both the project and the client's business. Project managers are responsible for upholding the highest standards of ethics and integrity, and reporting such misconduct is essential to maintaining trust and protecting the client's interests.

Answer to Question 10: The correct answer is A.
The key characteristic of a "portfolio" in project management is that it consists of a collection of related projects and programs managed together to achieve strategic objectives. Portfolios are designed to align with an organization's strategic goals and priorities.

Answer to Question 11: The correct answer is D.
The project charter is a document that is developed during the project initiation phase, not during the project closure phase. Activities performed during project closure typically include handing over project deliverables to the customer (option A), conducting a final project performance review (option B), and identifying lessons learned for future projects (option C).

Answer to Question 12: The correct answer is C.
The project management plan is a comprehensive document that outlines how the project will be executed, monitored, controlled, and closed. The plan serves as a reference and guide for the project team and stakeholders throughout the project's life cycle. Options A, B, and D are not about the primary purpose of the project management plan.

Answer to Question 13: The correct answer is C.
While Monte Carlo simulation is a powerful technique used in quantitative risk analysis to assess the impact of uncertainties on project outcomes, it is not typically used in the qualitative risk analysis process. In qualitative risk analysis, the focus is on assessing and prioritizing risks based on their probability and impact using techniques such as the probability and impact

matrix (option A), risk probability assessment (option B), and risk categorization (option D).

Answer to Question 14: The correct answer is B.
The project management plan is a comprehensive document that includes various components to guide project execution and control. Among these components, the project schedule is a critical part. It outlines the sequence of project activities, their start and finish dates, and any dependencies between them. The project schedule provides a roadmap for the timely completion of project deliverables.

Answer to Question 15: The correct answer is A.
The project charter provides a high-level overview of the project's objectives, scope, and deliverables. It is a formal document that authorizes the project and gives the project manager the authority to use resources to execute the project. The project charter is typically developed during the project initiation phase and is an essential component of the project management process. The project management plan (option B), the WBS (option C), and the stakeholder registry (option D) do not provide a high-level overview of project's objectives, scope, and deliverables like the project charter.

Answer to Question 16: The correct answer is B.
Stakeholder engagement in a project is crucial for its success. By involving stakeholders in project decision-making processes, project managers can gain valuable insights, receive feedback, and ensure that stakeholders' interests and concerns are considered. Engaging stakeholders throughout the project helps in building strong relationships, promoting buy-in, and fostering a collaborative environment.

Answer to Question 17: The correct answer is B.
The resource management plan defines how project resources will be estimated, acquired, utilized, and managed throughout the project's life cycle. It includes information about the types of resources needed, their quantities, the timeline for acquiring them, and the roles and responsibilities of those involved in resource management. Option A, C, and D do not focus specifically on resource management.

Answer to Question 18: The correct answer is D.
The primary purpose of a work breakdown structure (WBS) in project management is to decompose the project work into smaller, more manageable

components. The WBS breaks down the project deliverables and work into hierarchical levels, providing a clear and organized structure for planning, scheduling, and managing the project. It helps in understanding the project scope, defining tasks, and allocating resources effectively.

Answer to Question 19: The correct answer is D.
In a project schedule, a milestone is a significant point in time that represents the completion of a major project event or deliverable. Milestones are used to track the progress of the project and provide important reference points for project stakeholders.

Answer to Question 20: The correct answer is A.
Brainstorming is a technique used to identify and document project risks by gathering inputs and ideas from team members and subject-matter experts. During a brainstorming session, participants are encouraged to freely share their thoughts and perspectives on potential risks, allowing for a wide range of risks to be considered and documented. Option B, Control Chart, is used to monitor process stability and variation, not for identifying project risks. Option C, Delphi Technique, is a method of obtaining consensus among a group of experts but is not specifically used for risk identification. Option D, Pareto Chart, is used to prioritize issues based on their significance, not for identifying project risks.

Answer to Question 21: The correct answer is C.
EQ plays a significant role in managing stakeholder expectations and team dynamics. Emotional intelligence enables project managers to recognize their own, and other people's emotions, to differentiate between different feelings and label them appropriately, to use this emotional information to guide thinking and behavior, and to manage and adjust emotions to adapt environments or achieve one's goal. This is particularly crucial when working with diverse teams and stakeholders where understanding and managing emotions can greatly impact communication, trust, and overall project success.

Answer to Question 22: The correct answer is C.
The project manager attentively listens to all stakeholders, understanding their needs and concerns, and uses this information to guide project direction. Active listening is a critical skill for a project manager. It allows them to truly understand the requirements, needs, and concerns of stakeholders,

enabling more effective communication, better decision-making, and increased stakeholder engagement.

Answer to Question 23: The correct answer is B.
The project manager is responsible for the execution of the project while the project sponsor acts as a key supporter and decision-maker, especially when strategic direction or resources are concerned. In many organizational structures, the project manager leads the day-to-day operations of the project, ensuring that tasks are completed, and objectives are met, while the project sponsor, usually a senior executive, champions the project at a higher level, ensures it aligns with the organization's strategic goals, and makes critical business decisions related to the project.

Answer to Question 24: The correct answer is C.
EQ enhances a project manager's ability to understand, communicate with, and manage the emotions of themselves and others. This leads to better team dynamics, improved stakeholder relationships, and a more effective management approach. Emotional intelligence is particularly crucial in project management, where collaboration, negotiation, and relationship-building are key.

Answer to Question 25: The correct answer is B.
The project team is responsible for executing tasks, producing deliverables, and providing expertise to ensure the project meets its objectives. The team plays a central role in ensuring that the project progresses as planned and achieves its goals.

Answer to Question 26: The correct answer is C.
Leadership involves setting a vision, inspiring the team, and driving change, whereas management pertains to planning, organizing, and controlling processes to achieve specific objectives. While both leadership and management are essential in project management, they serve distinct objectives and require different sets of skills.

Answer to Question 27: The correct answer is C.
The project team specializes in executing tasks, producing deliverables, and handling the technical nuances of the project. In contrast, the project sponsor champions the project at higher organizational levels, ensuring that it aligns with overarching strategic goals, and makes pivotal business decisions.

Answer to Question 28: The correct answer is D.

While project managers have numerous roles and responsibilities, acting as a "Financial Auditor" is typically not one of them. Auditing is generally a specialized function and is often performed by internal or external auditors or specialized financial professionals.

Answer to Question 29: The correct answer is C.

As a leader, a project manager is tasked with motivating, influencing, and driving change to guide the team toward a shared vision. On the other hand, in their role as a manager, they focus on planning, organizing, and ensuring tasks are executed efficiently to achieve project objectives.

Answer to Question 30: The correct answer is A.

The Project Sponsor is typically responsible for securing necessary resources, advocating for the project within the organization, and making high-level decisions. They play a vital role in providing direction, ensuring alignment with strategic goals, and securing necessary approvals.

Answer to Question 31: The correct answer is C.

Communication management in project management involves a systematic approach to managing and controlling project-related communications. It encompasses planning, executing, and monitoring communication activities to ensure that the right information is delivered to the right stakeholders at the right time.

Answer to Question 32: The correct answer is A.

In an Agile project, conducting a retrospective is an appropriate response to unexpected technical challenges. A retrospective is a regular and essential practice in Agile methodologies where the team reflects on their work and identifies opportunities for improvement. It provides a structured way to examine what went well, what didn't go well, and how the team can enhance their processes moving forward.

Answer to Question 33: The correct answer is D.

The main objective of benefit realization in a project is to ensure that the project delivers the intended benefits and value to the organization. Benefit realization is a crucial aspect of project management, focusing on the ultimate outcome and value the project is expected to bring to the organization's strategic objectives. Throughout the project's life cycle, project managers and stakeholders continuously monitor and assess the progress of benefit realization. This helps in identifying any deviations from the expected outcomes and enables them to take corrective actions to maximize the project's value.

Answer to Question 34: The correct answer is C.
The main purpose of a project charter is to define the project objectives, scope, and authorization. The project charter is a formal document that authorizes the existence of the project and provides the project manager with the authority to allocate resources and use organizational assets for project activities. In addition to authorizing the project, the project charter outlines the high-level objectives and goals of the project, as well as the key deliverables and milestones. It also defines the project's boundaries, including the scope, constraints, and assumptions.

Answer to Question 35: The correct answer is A.
The Project Charter formally authorizes the existence of a project and provides the project manager with the authority to apply organizational resources to project activities. The project charter outlines the project's purpose, objectives, stakeholders, and other important details to set the direction for the project. This is an essential document in the project initiation phase.

Answer to Question 36: The correct answer is C.
Transfer is the risk response strategy where the impact of a potential risk is shifted to a third party. This is often done through mechanisms such as insurance, performance bonds, warranties, or guarantees. When a team purchases insurance or enters a partnership to share a risk, they are employing the "Transfer" risk response strategy.

Answer to Question 37: The correct answer is B.
Re-evaluating and adjusting the communication management plan is the most appropriate action. Effective communication is essential for project success. If it's determined that the current communication strategy isn't effectively reaching all stakeholders, it's crucial to revisit the communication management plan and make necessary adjustments to ensure that all stakeholders are adequately informed.

Answer to Question 38: The correct answer is C.
Managing changes to the project scope is a key responsibility of the project manager during project execution. As the project progresses, changes

may occur, and it is the project manager's responsibility to evaluate these changes, assess their impact on the project, and determine whether they should be approved or rejected. Effective scope change management helps ensure that the project stays on track and meets its objectives.

Answer to Question 39: The correct answer is C.
Project initiation is the initial phase of the project where the project's purpose, scope, and objectives are defined. It sets the foundation for the project and establishes its boundaries. On the other hand, benefit planning involves determining the expected value and benefits the project will deliver to the organization or stakeholders. It focuses on understanding the project's outcomes and how they align with the organization's strategic objectives.

Answer to Question 40: The correct answer is B.
The project team conducts regular status meetings and provides stakeholders with relevant and timely project updates. In a planned communication strategy, it is essential to consider stakeholders' communication preferences and needs. Regular status meetings and timely updates provide stakeholders with the necessary information to stay informed about the project's progress, challenges, and upcoming activities. This promotes transparency and ensures that stakeholders are engaged throughout the project life cycle.

Answer to Question 41: The correct answer is C.
Stand-up meetings, often referred to as "Daily Standups" or "Daily Scrums", are short, daily meetings used in Agile frameworks, especially Scrum. They provide teams an opportunity to synchronize activities, discuss progress, and highlight any impediments. The main aim is to keep the team aligned and address any challenges quickly.

Answer to Question 42: The correct answer is D.
Brainstorming is a technique designed to generate a large number of ideas for the solution to a problem. It encourages participants to come up with thoughts and ideas spontaneously. The key principle of brainstorming is that no idea is criticized, which ensures free flow of ideas without the fear of judgment.

Answer to Question 43: The correct answer is D.
A focus group is a qualitative research method used to gather data on opinions, perceptions, and beliefs from a selected group of individuals. It's an

interactive group setting where participants are free to talk with other group members. They are commonly used in market research and other areas where understanding perceptions and opinions are critical.

Answer to Question 44: The correct answer is D.
A retrospective meeting, commonly used in Agile frameworks, is a meeting held at the end of an iteration to reflect on the process. The team discusses what went well, what could be improved, and how to make those improvements in the next iteration. It promotes continuous improvement and team alignment.

Answer to Question 45: The correct answer is C.
A Fishbone diagram, also known as an Ishikawa diagram or cause-and-effect diagram, is a visual tool used to identify, explore, and depict the potential causes of a specific problem or quality issue. It assists teams in brainstorming and categorizing the various potential causes of a problem to identify its root causes.

Answer to Question 46: The correct answer is B.
The Sprint Review is an event in Scrum and other Agile methodologies where the Scrum Team and stakeholders inspect what was done during the sprint and adapt the product backlog if necessary. This event offers a platform for feedback and adaptation based on the work from the last sprint. It allows stakeholders to see the progress and provides an opportunity for the team to adjust based on feedback.

Answer to Question 47: The correct answer is D.
A scatter plot (or scatter diagram) is a graphical representation where individual data points are plotted on a two-dimensional chart using Cartesian coordinates. By examining the pattern of the plotted points, one can determine if a correlation exists between two variables. It does not necessarily imply causation but helps in visualizing potential relationships.

Answer to Question 48: The correct answer is B.
In Agile methodologies, particularly Scrum, a Sprint or Iteration is a set time period (typically between one and four weeks) where specific work is to be completed and made ready for review. During this time, the team aims to convert a set of user stories or product backlog items into potentially shippable product increments.

Answer to Question 49: The correct answer is C.
A focus group is a tool in which stakeholders and subject-matter experts discuss specific topics. Facilitated by a moderator, focus groups offer a more detailed understanding of stakeholders' feelings, attitudes, and perceptions about the discussed topic. It is especially useful when seeking feedback about project requirements, products, or potential issues.

Answer to Question 50: The correct answer is C.
Well-documented historical project data is an enabling factor for using a predictive plan-based approach in projects. Historical project data includes information on past projects, such as schedules, costs, resource utilization, and lessons learned. This data can be used as a reference for estimating, planning, and executing similar future projects.

Answer to Question 51: The correct answer is D.
Reviewing and Evaluating is not a Process Group in project management. The five Process Groups are Initiating, Planning, Executing, Monitoring and Controlling, and Closing.

Answer to Question 52: The correct answer is A.
Phase Gates in project management are checkpoints or decision points that determine whether a project can proceed to the next phase. They are used to evaluate the project's performance, deliverables, and alignment with business objectives before allowing progression to the next phase.

Answer to Question 53: The correct answer is C.
In a functional organization, departments are organized based on specialized functions, such as marketing, finance, operations, and human resources. Each department operates independently and focuses on its specific area of expertise.

Answer to Question 54: The correct answer is C.
A predictive plan-based approach is suitable when the project has a well-defined scope and operates in a stable environment. This means that the project requirements are well-understood and unlikely to change significantly, allowing for detailed planning and a sequential execution of project activities.

Answer to Question 55: The correct answer is D.
A project schedule network diagram is a graphical representation of the project activities and their logical relationships. It illustrates the sequence

of activities and the dependencies between them, helping to determine the order in which activities should be performed. The network diagram assists in identifying the critical path and it is an essential tool for project scheduling.

Answer to Question 56: The correct answer is B.
A project budget determination technique is used to establish the estimated costs for a project. It involves identifying and estimating the costs associated with various project activities, resources, materials, and other expenses. The budget serves as a baseline for tracking and controlling project costs throughout its execution. By comparing the actual costs incurred against the budgeted amounts, project managers can monitor financial performance, identify variances, and take appropriate actions to control costs and ensure that the project remains within budget.

Answer to Question 57: The correct answer is A.
The types of estimation techniques commonly used for determining project duration and costs are as follows: Analogous Estimating, Parametric Estimating, Three-Point Estimating, Bottom-Up Estimating.

Answer to Question 58: The correct answer is A.
Crashing is a schedule compression technique in project management where additional resources are allocated to critical path activities to reduce the project duration. By adding more resources, such as manpower or equipment, to these activities, their completion time is shortened, allowing for a compressed project schedule.

Answer to Question 59: The correct answer is B.
A Gantt chart is a popular project management tool used to visually represent the project schedule, task dependencies, and progress. It provides a timeline view of the project, illustrating when tasks start and end, as well as their interdependencies. It helps in visualizing the overall project schedule, allowing stakeholders to have a clear understanding of how different tasks and activities are related and how they contribute to the project's timeline.

Answer to Question 60: The correct answer is B.
In earned value analysis, Schedule Variance (SV) is a measure that compares the planned value (PV) of work scheduled to be completed with the earned value (EV) of work completed at a given point in time. A negative SV

indicates that the project is behind schedule, meaning that the actual progress is less than what was planned at that specific point in time.

Answer to Question 61: The correct answer is A.
The primary purpose of creating a Work Breakdown Structure (WBS) in project management is to define the project deliverables and organize the project work into manageable components. A WBS breaks down the project scope into smaller, more manageable work packages, which can then be further decomposed into tasks.

Answer to Question 62: The correct answer is B.
To calculate Schedule Variance (SV), we need to compare the earned value (EV) with the planned value (PV). Given: Planned duration = 10 weeks, and Planned cost = 50,000 Euro, and Actual cost at Week 6 = 30,000 Euro, and Work completed = 60% of the planned work, then: Planned value (PV) = Planned cost = 50,000 Euro, Earned value (EV) = Work completed % * Planned value (PV) = 60% * 50,000 Euro = 30,000 Euro, Schedule Variance (SV) = Earned value (EV) − Planned value (PV), SV = $30,000 − $50,000 = −20,000 Euro. Therefore, the Schedule Variance (SV) for the project is −20,000 Euro.

Answer to Question 63: The correct answer is D.
To calculate the total duration of the critical path, we need to identify the longest sequence of dependent activities. Given the activity durations and dependencies, there are the following two paths:

- F (3 days) -> G (5 days) -> I (4 days) -> L (6 days) => Total Path duration = 18 days
- F (3 days) -> H (2 Days) -> I (4 days) -> L (6 days) => Total path duration = 15 days

The Critical Path is the path determining the end date of the project, that is, the Critical Path is the one with the higher Total path duration. In the above two paths, the higher path duration is 18 days. Therefore, the correct answer is D: 18 days.

Answer to Question 64: The correct answer is A.
A Quality Management Plan in project management is a document that outlines the approach, activities, and resources needed to ensure that the

project meets the required quality standards. It defines the processes, procedures, and methodologies that will be used to achieve and maintain project quality throughout its life cycle. The Quality Management Plan includes activities such as quality planning, quality assurance, and quality control.

Answer to Question 65: The correct answer is C.
The term "percentage of completion" in project management refers to the measure of progress made on a project. It represents the portion or percentage of work that has been completed relative to the total work required for the project. By tracking the percentage of completion, project managers can assess the project's progress and compare it against the planned schedule.

Answer to Question 66: The correct answer is B.
Estimates at Completion (EAC) is calculated by adding the Actual Cost (AC) of the project to the Estimate to Complete (ETC). EAC represents the projected total cost of the project based on the actual cost incurred and the estimated cost to complete the remaining work.

Answer to Question 67: The correct answer is D.
Control charts are statistical tools primarily used to monitor and analyze process variations in terms of quality performance. They help identify common cause variations (random variations inherent in the process) and special cause variations (unusual or unexpected events). Control charts are not specifically used to monitor cost or schedule performance, although they can be adapted for other performance monitoring purposes in project.

Answer to Question 68: The correct answer is C.
Root Cause Analysis is a systematic and structured approach used to identify the underlying or primary causes of project issues or problems. It goes beyond addressing the symptoms and aims to identify the fundamental reasons behind the occurrence of the problem. By identifying and addressing the root causes, project managers can implement effective corrective actions to prevent similar issues from recurring in the future.

Answer to Question 69: The correct answer is D.
Variance analysis in project management involves comparing the planned values (such as planned costs, schedule, or scope) with the actual values to identify the variances. It helps project managers understand and analyze the differences between what was planned and what has been achieved. By

examining these variances, project managers can take appropriate actions to control and manage project performance effectively.

Answer to Question 70: The correct answer is D.
Status reports in project management serve as a means of communication between the project team and stakeholders. They provide updates on project progress, including completed tasks, milestones achieved, risks identified, issues encountered, and other pertinent information. Status reports are shared with stakeholders to keep them informed about the project's status and facilitate decision-making.

Answer to Question 71: The correct answer is D.
Trend analysis in project management involves analyzing project performance data over time to identify patterns, trends, and deviations from the expected trajectory. By conducting trend analysis, project managers can gain insights into the project's performance dynamics, forecast future performance, and make informed decisions to keep the project on track.

Answer to Question 72: The correct answer is B.
To calculate the Cost Variance (CV), we use the formula: $CV = EV - AC$. Given: $EV = \$8,000$, and $AC = \$9,500$, then: $CV = \$8,000 - \$9,500 = -\$1,500$. A negative value indicates that the project is over budget, meaning the actual costs (AC) exceeded the earned value (EV).

Answer to Question 73: The correct answer is C.
One of the characteristics of an Agile project life cycle is its ability to adapt and accommodate changes throughout the project. Unlike sequential and phase-based approaches, Agile projects embrace change and allow for flexibility in responding to customer needs and evolving requirements.

Answer to Question 74: The correct answer is C.
Scrum is a popular Agile framework commonly used for software development. It emphasizes iterative and incremental development, cross-functional teams, and regular feedback loops. Scrum promotes collaboration, transparency, and adaptability to deliver value to customers.

Answer to Question 75: The correct answer is C.
Both Cynefin and Stacey Matrix are frameworks/models that help in understanding the complexity of a given situation and provide guidance on appropriate management approaches.

Answer to Question 76: The correct answer is C.
Empowered and autonomous teams facilitate the use of Adaptive approaches in projects. Agile and Lean methodologies emphasize the importance of self-organizing teams with the authority to make decisions and take ownership of their work. Hierarchical organizational structures, strict regulatory compliance requirements, and siloed communication are factors that can create obstacles to Agile or Lean adoption.

Answer to Question 77: The correct answer is B.
One of the values of the Agile Manifesto is "Customer collaboration over contract negotiation". The other values of the Agile Manifesto include valuing individuals and interactions over processes and tools, working software over comprehensive documentation, and responding to change over following a plan.

Answer to Question 78: The correct answer is C.
Agile project life cycles are iterative and incremental in nature. Agile approaches, such as Scrum and XP, promote the delivery of value in short iterations. The project progresses through a series of iterations, with each iteration producing potentially usable and valuable increment of product.

Answer to Question 79: The correct answer is B.
The Release Plan sets expectations for the dates, features, and/or outcomes expected to be delivered over the course of multiple iterations.

Answer to Question 80: The correct answer is B.
The Iteration Review, also known as the Sprint Review in Scrum, is a collaborative meeting where the development team showcases the completed work to stakeholders. The purpose of the Iteration Review is to gather feedback, validate the work, and make any necessary adjustments or course corrections. It provides an opportunity for stakeholders to provide input, ask questions, and ensure that the product is on the right track.

Answer to Question 81: The correct answer is B.
The Retrospective is a meeting held at the end of each iteration, where the team reflects on their performance and identifies opportunities for improvement. The purpose of the retrospective is to review what went well, what didn't go well, and what actions can be taken to enhance the team's effectiveness and productivity in future iterations.

Answer to Question 82: The correct answer is C.

The purpose of the Iteration Planning meeting, also known as Sprint Planning in Scrum, is to plan and prioritize the work that will be undertaken in the upcoming iteration. During this meeting, the development team collaborates with the product owner to review the product backlog and select the items that will be included in the iteration.

Answer to Question 83: The correct answer is B.

A User Story is a brief description of an outcome for a specific user, which is a promise for conversation to clarify details.

Answer to Question 84: The correct answer is A.

An Epic is a logical container for large user story that are too big to complete within an iteration.

Answer to Question 85: The correct answer is A.

Velocity in Agile refers to the measure of the amount of work completed by a team during an iteration. It represents the rate at which the team is delivering user stories or product backlog items. It is usually measured in story points or the number of completed user stories. Velocity helps the team in planning and forecasting future sprints based on their historical performance.

Answer to Question 86: The correct answer is A.

A Kanban Board is a visual tool used in Agile to visualize and track the progress of work items within a project or team. It typically consists of columns representing different stages of the workflow, such as "To Do", "In Progress", and "Done". Work items, represented by cards or sticky notes, are moved across the board as they progress through the workflow, allowing the team to have a clear visual representation of the work-in-progress and the overall flow of work.

Answer to Question 87: The correct answer is C.

According to Little's Law, the average work in process (WIP) can be calculated by multiplying the average throughput by the average cycle time. In this case, the average throughput is 8 completed user stories per week, and the average cycle time is 4 weeks. WIP = Throughput × Cycle Time, WIP = 8 user stories/week × 4 weeks = 32 user stories. Therefore, the average work in process (WIP) in the system is 32 user stories.

Answer to Question 88: The correct answer is B.

To calculate the ideal burndown rate per week, we need to divide the remaining story points by the number of weeks remaining in the release.

Total story points planned for the release is 100 story points, Story points completed after the first week is 20 story points, Remaining story points is 100 − 20 = 80 story points, Number of weeks remaining is 8 weeks. Ideal burndown rate per week = Remaining story points / Number of weeks remaining = 80 story points / 8 weeks = 10 story points per week. Therefore, the ideal burndown rate per week to complete the release on time is 10 story points per week.

Answer to Question 89: The correct answer is B.
Cycle time refers to the total time taken to complete a work item, starting from the moment work begins on the item until it is considered done. It measures the actual time spent actively working on the item, excluding any idle or waiting time. On the other hand, Lead Time represents the time from the moment a work item is requested or initiated until it is completed and delivered.

Answer to Question 90: The correct answer is A.
The Scrum events are Sprint, Sprint planning, Daily Scrum, Sprint review, Sprint Retrospective.

Answer to Question 91: The correct answer is A.
The Kanban method is based on several principles or properties: Visualize workflow, Limit work in progress (WIP), Manage flow, Make process policies explicit, Improve collaboratively, Implement feedback loops.

Answer to Question 92: The correct answer is A.
eXtreme Programming (XP) is an Agile software development methodology that emphasizes a set of practices to improve software quality and responsiveness. The key practices of XP are as follows: Whole Team, Planning game, Small Releases, On-site customer, Collective code ownership, Coding standard, Sustainable pace, Metaphor, Continuous Integration, Simple design, Pair Programming, Test-driven Development, Refactoring.

Answer to Question 93: The correct answer is D.
MVP is the minimum set of features that give value to the customers.

Answer to Question 94: The correct answer is B.
The primary principle behind Test-Driven Development (TDD) is to write tests before writing the code. In TDD, developers start by writing a test case that defines the expected behavior of the code they are going to write. This test case is initially expected to fail since the code hasn't been implemented

yet. The developer then proceeds to write the minimum amount of code necessary to pass the test case. Once the code is written, it is then executed against the test case. The tests serve as a specification for the code.

Answer to Question 95: The correct answer is B.
Net Present Value (NPV) is the financial metric used to measure the profitability of an investment by calculating the present value of future cash flows. It considers the time value of money by discounting future cash flows to their present value. A positive NPV indicates a potentially profitable investment, while a negative NPV suggests a potential loss.

Answer to Question 96: The correct answer is A.
Planning Poker is an Agile estimation technique commonly used to estimate the effort or size of user stories or backlog items. It involves a collaborative process where team members assign relative sizes or effort points to each item. The team discusses and debates the complexity, risks, and dependencies associated with the item before reaching a consensus on the estimation.

Answer to Question 97: The correct answer is D.
The Definition of Ready (DoR) is a set of criteria that a user story must meet before it is considered ready to be included in a sprint. The DoR ensures that user stories are adequately prepared and understood before they are taken up by the development team. On the other hand, the Definition of Done (DoD) specifies the criteria that a user story must meet to be considered complete and potentially shippable. It outlines the standards, quality measures, and expectations that the development team must meet for each user story.

Answer to Question 98: The correct answer is C.
Cost of Delay (CoD) is a prioritization approach that considers the potential impact of delaying the delivery of a user story or backlog item. It considers factors such as the expected value, urgency, market opportunity, and potential consequences of delay. By assigning a numerical value to these factors, the items can be ranked based on their relative cost of delay, and priorities can be determined accordingly. MoSCoW prioritization (option A), is a prioritization scheme that categorizes items into must-have, should-have, could-have, and won't-have categories based on their importance and necessity. T-Shirt sizing (option B), is a relative sizing technique that assigns

sizes (such as XS, S, M, L, XL) to user stories or backlog items to represent their relative effort or complexity. The Kano model (option D), helps categorize customer needs based on satisfaction and dissatisfaction, determining if a feature or requirement is a basic expectation, a satisfier, or a delighter.

Answer to Question 99: The correct answer is C.
A Prioritization Matrix is a scatter diagram that plots effort against value so as to classify items by priority

Answer to Question 100: The correct answer is C.
Persona. A persona is a fictional representation of a user that helps in understanding user needs, goals, and behaviors.

Answer to Question 101: The correct answer is A.
A Gantt chart is specifically used to analyze the sequence of activities and their dependencies in a project. Incorrect Answers: Cause-and-effect diagrams (option B), also known as fishbone diagrams, are used to identify and analyze the causes of a problem. Value Stream Mapping (option C) is used to visualize and analyze the flow of activities and information in a process to identify areas of waste and improvement. Personas (option D) are fictional representations of users used to understand their needs and behaviors in the context of designing products or services.

Answer to Question 102: The correct answer is B.
Brainstorming is a technique used to generate many ideas and potential solutions through group creativity and free thinking. Minimum Viable Product (MVP – option A) refers to the development of a product with minimal features to test its viability and gather user feedback. Verification (option C) is the process of checking that project deliverables meet specified requirements. Wireframes (option D) are visual representations of the layout and structure of a user interface or website.

Answer to Question 103: The correct answer is D.
Impact analysis is a technique used to assess the potential impact of a proposed change on a project's timeline, resources, and other project elements. Compliance standards (option A) refer to regulations or guidelines that organizations must adhere to. Export judgment (option B) is not a recognized technique in business analysis. Cost-Benefit Analysis (option C) is used to compare the costs and benefits of a proposed solution.

Answer to Question 104: The correct answer is C.
The primary purpose of conducting interviews with stakeholders is to gather their expectations, requirements, and understand their interests in relation to the project. Validating and testing a product concept with minimal features (option A) typically involves prototyping or conducting user testing. Analyzing costs and benefits (option B) is part of a cost-benefit analysis, which is a separate technique. Defining the project scope (option D) involves gathering requirements and establishing the project's boundaries and objectives.

Answer to Question 105: The correct answer is B.
The technique used in this scenario is creative thinking, which involves generating innovative and unconventional ideas to solve business problems. Use cases (option A) are used to describe interactions between users and a system to achieve specific goals. Benchmarking (option C) is the process of comparing an organization's performance or processes with industry best practices. Multivoting (option D) is a technique used to prioritize options or ideas through a voting process.

Answer to Question 106: The correct answer is C.
Risk identification is the technique used to identify risks on a project. Force Field Analysis (option A) is a technique used to analyze the forces that drive and restrain change in a project or organization. Document Analysis (option B) involves reviewing existing documents and materials to extract requirements and insights. Use cases (option D) are used to describe interactions between users and a system to achieve specific goals.

Answer to Question 107: The correct answer is A.
A context diagram is a visual representation of the flow of activities, inputs, and outputs in a business process. Cost-Benefit Analysis (option B) is a technique used to compare the costs and benefits of a proposed solution. Personas (option C) are fictional representations of users used to understand their needs and behaviors. Traceability (option D) refers to the ability to trace and track requirements and their relationships throughout a project.

Answer to Question 108: The correct answer is A.
Stakeholder Analysis is the technique used to analyze the roles, responsibilities, and involvement of stakeholders in a project.

Answer to Question 109: The correct answer is C.
Creative thinking is the technique used to generate a large number of ideas through brainstorming for a new product feature. Affinity Diagram (option A) is a technique used to group related ideas and requirements together. Requirement Traceability Matrix (option B) is used to track the relationships between requirements and other project artifacts. Proof of Concept (option D) involves conducting a small-scale test to validate the feasibility of a proposed solution.

Answer to Question 110: The correct answer is D.
The functional and non-functional needs and specifications of a system are called requirements. Stakeholder requirements (option A) refer to the needs and expectations of stakeholders. User stories (option B) are short descriptions of desired functionality or features from the end user's perspective. Business value (option C) refers to the benefits and value that a project or solution brings to the organization.

Answer to Question 111: The correct answer is C.
The Multivoting process is used to prioritize project requirements based on their importance and urgency through participant voting. The Five Whys technique (option A) is used to identify the root cause of a problem by repeatedly asking "Why?". Minimum Viable Product (MVP – option B) refers to the development of a product with minimal features to test its viability and gather user feedback. A product roadmap (option D) is a visual representation of the planned release schedule and key milestones for a product.

Answer to Question 112: The correct answer is C.
Document Analysis involves reviewing existing documents and materials to gather detailed information about a specific process or topic. Problem solving (option A) is a general approach to identifying, analyzing, and solving problems. Export Judgment (option B) is not a recognized technique in business analysis. Wireframes (option D) are visual representations of the layout and structure of a user interface or website.

Answer to Question 113: The correct answer is A.
Cause-and-effect diagram, also known as a fishbone diagram, is used to visually map out the relationships between different factors contributing to a problem.

Answer to Question 114: The correct answer is D.
Requirements involve documenting the key features and functionalities that a product should have to meet the needs of the target users.

Answer to Question 115: The correct answer is C.
Validation is the process of gathering feedback and insights from stakeholders to confirm that a proposed solution meets their needs and requirements. Proof of Concept (option A) involves conducting a small-scale test to evaluate the feasibility and potential success of a proposed solution. Compliance standards (option B) refer to regulations or guidelines that organizations must adhere to. An epic (option D) is a high-level description of a desired functionality or feature, often used in Agile.

Answer to Question 116: The correct answer is C.
The Five Whys technique is used to identify the underlying causes of a problem by repeatedly asking "Why?" to uncover deeper issues. Incorrect Answers: Problem solving (option A) is a general approach to identifying, analyzing, and solving problems. Affinity Diagram (option B) is a technique used to group related ideas and requirements together. Traceability (option D) refers to the ability to trace and track requirements and their relationships throughout a project.

Answer to Question 117: The correct answer is C.
Use cases are used to create a visual representation of the interactions between users and a system to achieve specific goals. Wireframes (option A) are visual representations of the layout and structure of a user interface or website. The RACI model (option B) is used to identify and document the roles and responsibilities of individuals and groups involved in a project. Business value (option D) refers to the benefits and value that a project or solution brings to the organization.

Answer to Question 118: The correct answer is B.
SWOT analysis is used to analyze the potential risks and opportunities associated with a project by considering both internal and external factors.

Answer to Question 119: The correct answer is C.
Interviews are conducted with stakeholders to understand their preferences and expectations for a new website design.

Answer to Question 120: The correct answer is B.
Value Stream Mapping is used to analyze the flow of activities, information, and value delivery in a process to identify areas of waste and improvement. A persona (option A) is a fictional representation of a user that helps in understanding user needs, goals, and behaviors. Creative thinking (option C) is a technique used to generate innovative and unconventional ideas to solve business problems. A product roadmap (option D) is a visual representation of the planned release schedule and key milestones for a product.

Answer to Question 121: The correct answer is B.
Risk Assessment is used to identify and analyze potential risks by considering their likelihood of occurrence and impact on project objectives.

Answer to Question 122: The correct answer is C.
A Requirement Traceability Matrix is used to create a visual representation of the relationships between different requirements and project artifacts.

Answer to Question 123: The correct answer is D.
Interviews are conducted with users to gather their preferences, needs, and pain points related to a new mobile application.

Answer to Question 124: The correct answer is A.
Value Stream Mapping is used to analyze the current state of a process, identify areas of improvement, and uncover inefficiencies.

Answer to Question 125: The correct answer is B.
Brainstorming is used to generate a large number of ideas and potential solutions for a complex business problem through group creativity and free thinking. Benchmarking (option A) is the process of comparing performance or practices against industry standards or best practices. A Requirement Management Plan (option C) describes the purpose, objectives, and approach for managing requirements throughout a project. Validation (option D) is the process of confirming that a deliverable or product meets the specified requirements and satisfies customer needs.

Answer to Question 126: The correct answer is B.
Impact analysis is used to assess the potential impact of a proposed change on project scope, schedule, and budget.

Answer to Question 127: The correct answer is D.
Brainstorming is used to generate many ideas and potential solutions for a business problem through group creativity and free thinking.

Answer to Question 128: The correct answer is A.
Personas are used to analyze the needs and behaviors of different user groups to ensure that a product meets their specific requirements.

Answer to Question 129: The correct answer is B.
Document Analysis involves reviewing project documentation and deliverables to ensure that they meet the specified quality standards.

Answer to Question 130: The correct answer is B.
Interviews are conducted with stakeholders to gather their input and requirements for a new system.

Answer to Question 131: The correct answer is C.
A Gantt chart is used to create a visual representation of the sequence and dependencies of project activities.

Answer to Question 132: The correct answer is C.
SWOT analysis is used to analyze the strengths, weaknesses, opportunities, and threats related to a project or organization.

Answer to Question 133: The correct answer is C.
Force Field Analysis is used to identify and rank the factors that are driving or restraining change in a project.

Answer to Question 134: The correct answer is A.
Value Stream Mapping is used to create a visual representation of the flow of activities, decisions, and information in a process.

Answer to Question 135: The correct answer is C.
Definition of Done. Explanation: The Definition of Done ensures that project requirements are clear, concise, and unambiguous.

Chapter 9

Full practice exam two

The CAPM® full practice exam consists of 135 questions which should be completed in no more than 3 hours in total. The PMI exam does contain 150 questions; however, 15 questions are not scored. Table 9.1 gives an overview of the CAPM® exam breakdown, which you should use if you need to go back and revisit the chapter and as a confirmation that all content has been covered, understood, and mastered.

Table 9.1 CAPM® practice exam one breakdown

Domain	Split	Questions	Test questions
Project management fundamentals and core concepts	36%	49	1–49
Predictive, plan-based methodologies	17%	23	50–72
Agile frameworks/methodologies	20%	27	73–99
Business analysis frameworks	27%	36	100–135
Summary	**100%**	**135**	**1–135**

Section 9.1 contains questions and space for answering the questions. Each question includes four possible answers; however, only one is correct. Section 9.2 includes all the answers and explanations. At this stage you should have at least 95 correct questions before moving on to the actual certification exam.

Do not attempt to take the full practice exams before you are ready. You will not get the full benefits and retaking the exam may result in flawed results. These are the last practice exams you should take before getting above average on the actual PMI exam.

Some of the questions you find below could not be relatable to topics discussed explicitly in this book, but in the answers, you'll always find the references to the external books in the CAPM® reference list, to motivate the correct answers. So, the practice exams of this book are to verify your learning by this book and to learn something else useful for taking the CAPM® exam.

9.1 Full practice exam two – questions

Question 1

What is the primary distinction between predictive and adaptive approaches in project management?

- A. Predictive approach uses a flexible plan, while the adaptive approach uses a fixed plan
- B. Predictive approach is mostly used for software projects, while adaptive approach is for manufacturing
- C. Predictive approach focuses on detailed planning at the beginning, while adaptive approach allows changes to the plan based on feedback and learning
- D. Adaptive approach is an older methodology, while predictive is a newer one

Question 2

Explain how a project can be a vehicle for change.

- A. Projects always change the organizational structure
- B. Projects are undertaken to maintain the status quo
- C. Projects result in a new or modified product, service, or process, leading to change
- D. Projects have no relation to change as they focus on keeping things the same

Question 3

You are a project manager for a software development project. You've noticed that certain elements of the project scope are continuously being modified due to evolving client requirements. Given this situation, which project management approach would be most suitable?

A. Predictive approach, as it would allow for a detailed plan to be established from the outset
B. Hybrid approach, combining elements of predictive and adaptive approaches
C. Adaptive approach, to cater to the evolving requirements and facilitate flexibility
D. Operations approach, focusing on the ongoing needs of the organization

Question 4

You are overseeing a large infrastructure project. During the project meetings, team members frequently use terms such as issues, risks, assumptions, and constraints. As the project manager, you need to ensure that everyone has a clear understanding of these terms. Which of the following statements accurately distinguishes between these terms?

A. Assumptions are uncertain events that can affect the project for good or bad, while constraints are limitations imposed on the project
B. Issues are known problems that have occurred, risks are uncertain events that might affect the project, assumptions are beliefs considered true without proof, and constraints limit the project's options
C. Risks are known problems, issues are potential problems, assumptions are factors considered for project planning, and constraints are guidelines to follow
D. Assumptions are known problems, risks are challenges faced by team members, constraints are beliefs considered true, and issues are limitations imposed on the project

Question 5

Consider a scenario where Sarah, a project manager, is faced with an ethical dilemma. A key stakeholder is pressuring her to cut corners in order to meet the project deadline, even if it compromises the quality of the deliverable. According to the PMI Code of Ethics and Professional Conduct, which of the following actions should Sarah take?

A. Sarah should comply with the stakeholder's request since the stakeholder is key to the project's success

B. Sarah should assess the impact on the project's quality, and if minimal, she can proceed with the stakeholder's request
C. Sarah should prioritize the integrity and professionalism of her work, declining the request and explaining her commitment to quality and ethics
D. Sarah should document the request and submit it to higher management, letting them decide the right course of action

Question 6

In the context of project management, which of the following best describes a program?

A. A temporary effort to create a unique product, service, or result
B. The systematic series of activities directed toward causing an end result
C. A group of related projects managed in a coordinated way to obtain benefits and control which are not available from managing them individually
D. A collection of projects, programs, subsidiary portfolios, and operations managed as a group to achieve strategic objectives

Question 7

During the initial stages of a project, the project team identifies certain events or conditions that, if they occur, could have a positive or negative impact on the project. What are these events or conditions called in project management terminology?

A. Assumptions
B. Risks
C. Constraints
D. Issues

Question 8

You are managing a project that involves developing a new software application for a client. The client has requested changes to the project scope, which would require additional work not initially planned. What is the most appropriate action as a project manager in this situation?

A. Politely decline the client's request to avoid scope creep
B. Immediately incorporate the changes without evaluating their impact

C. Assess the changes and their impact on the project and communicate the potential consequences to the client

D. Inform the client that scope changes are not allowed in the project

Question 9

In project management, which of the following is an example of an assumption?

A. The project team assumes that the required raw materials will be delivered on time by the supplier

B. The project manager assumes that the project will be completed ahead of schedule

C. The project team assumes that there will be no changes to the project scope

D. The project manager assumes that the project budget will not be exceeded

Question 10

You are managing a project that involves building a new office building for a company. The project is expected to take 18 months to complete, and during this time, the organization will need to continue its day-to-day operations. How would you distinguish between this project and the ongoing operations of the company?

A. The project involves constructing a unique product (the office building) with a specific start and end date, while operations are ongoing and repetitive activities that sustain the organization's business

B. The project involves maintaining the organization's status quo, while operations focus on introducing changes and improvements

C. The project is constrained by time, while operations are not bound by time limitations

D. The project is a series of interconnected activities, while operations consist of a single activity

Question 11

You are the project manager of a software development project, and you need to define the work that must be accomplished to deliver the project successfully. Which document should you create to capture the work scope, schedule, cost estimates, and resource requirements?

    A. Risk Management Plan
    B. Product Management Plan
    C. Stakeholder Register
    D. Project Management Plan

Question 12

As a project manager, you are tasked with identifying potential risks that may impact the project. Which of the following best represents a tool or technique that can help you systematically identify risks by gathering inputs from relevant stakeholders?

    A. Risk Register
    B. Risk Breakdown Structure (RBS)
    C. Resource Management Plan
    D. Schedule Management Plan

Question 13

You are the project manager for a construction project, and your team has identified several potential risks that could affect the project's success. Which of the following actions should you take to effectively manage these risks?

    A. Record the risks in a Risk Register and regularly review and update it throughout the project
    B. Immediately implement risk response strategies for all identified risks to mitigate their impact
    C. Ignore the risks if their probability of occurrence is low and focus on other project activities
    D. Delegate the responsibility of risk management to individual team members

Question 14

As a project manager, you need to develop a comprehensive document that outlines how the project will be executed, monitored, and controlled. Which of the following documents should you create for this purpose, and what are the typical components it may include?

    A. Cost Management Plan; it includes project budget, cost baseline, and cost control measures
    B. Risk Management Plan; it includes risk identification, risk analysis, and risk response strategies

C. Project Management Plan; it includes project scope, schedule, cost estimates, risk management approach, and other essential elements
D. Stakeholder Management Plan; it includes stakeholder identification, stakeholder engagement strategies, and communication plans

Question 15

As a project manager, you need to ensure that the project's end product meets the desired quality standards and fulfills the customer's requirements. Which document should you create to outline how the product will be designed, developed, and delivered to meet these objectives?

A. Project Management Plan
B. Risk Management Plan
C. Quality Management Plan
D. Product Management Plan

Question 16

In project management, milestones play a significant role in tracking progress and evaluating the project's success. What is the primary purpose of a milestone in a project?

A. To identify potential risks and uncertainties in the project
B. To represent significant points in the project schedule for monitoring progress
C. To allocate resources and define their roles in the project
D. To document the detailed requirements of the project deliverables

Question 17

As a project manager, you have successfully completed a construction project, and it's time to formally close the project. What are the main activities involved in the project closure phase, and why is it essential to go through this phase?

A. Handing over the deliverables to the customer and celebrating project success; it marks the end of the project and ensures a smooth transition to ongoing operations or new projects
B. Holding a final team meeting and preparing a detailed lessons learned report; it provides an opportunity to reflect on the project's outcomes and identify areas for improvement in future projects

C. Releasing project team members from their roles and responsibilities; it allows team members to move on to new assignments or projects
D. Initiating a new project and developing a new Project Management Plan; it sets the foundation for the next project in the organization

Question 18

You are managing a marketing project for a new product launch, and you have identified several stakeholders with different levels of interest and influence. Some stakeholders are supportive, while others are resistant to the project's success. What should you do to effectively manage these stakeholders?

A. Record the stakeholder information in a Stakeholder Register and regularly review and update it throughout the project
B. Ignore the stakeholders who are resistant and focus only on the supportive ones
C. Delegate the responsibility of stakeholder management to a dedicated team member
D. Develop a new project schedule to accommodate the interests of the supportive stakeholders

Question 19

In project management, there are two important documents that provide guidance on different aspects of the project. What is the primary difference between the project management plan and the project scope statement?

A. The project management plan outlines how the project will be executed, monitored, and controlled, while the project scope statement defines the work that needs to be accomplished
B. The project management plan is a comprehensive document that includes all project information, while the project scope statement focuses only on the project's objectives and deliverables
C. The project management plan is prepared by the project team, while the project scope statement is developed by the project stakeholders
D. The project management plan is updated throughout the project lifecycle, while the project scope statement remains fixed once it is finalized

Question 20

As a project manager, you are leading a large project with multiple team members, stakeholders, and external partners. Effective communication is crucial for project success. What is the primary purpose of a communication management plan in project management?

A. To identify potential risks and uncertainties related to project communication
B. To allocate resources and define their roles in project communication
C. To provide guidance on how project communication will be planned, executed, and controlled
D. To ensure that project communication is aligned with the organizational communication strategy

Question 21

Which of the following best describes the primary role of a project sponsor in a project?

A. Responsible for the day-to-day management of the project tasks
B. Provides funding and resources for the project
C. Directly involved in technical problem-solving
D. Responsible for the project's user acceptance testing

Question 22

As a project manager, understanding emotional intelligence (EQ) is essential. Which of the following best describes how EQ impacts project management?

A. EQ allows a project manager to allocate resources more efficiently
B. EQ helps a project manager in understanding and managing their own emotions and those of others, leading to better team dynamics
C. EQ ensures that a project is completed within its scope, time, and budget constraints
D. EQ provides a technical roadmap for project execution

Question 23

In a project environment, which statement best differentiates leadership from management?

A. Leadership is about setting a direction or vision, while management is about executing the plan
B. Leadership deals with the technical aspects, while management focuses on people

C. Leaders are responsible for project success, while managers handle failures
D. Management is an innate trait, while leadership can be learned

Question 24

Imagine you are managing a project team composed of professionals from various departments and levels of the organization. One member, Sarah, is a top-performing expert in her field but struggles with understanding how her work fits into the broader project objectives. This often leads to misaligned work products and delays. Based on the roles described, who should be primarily responsible for ensuring Sarah understands the project's objectives and her role within the team?

A. The Project Manager
B. The Project Sponsor
C. The other team members
D. Sarah herself

Question 25

Which of the following best describes the importance of the role the project manager plays as a "listener" within a project team?

A. The project manager ensures that all technical problems are solved promptly
B. The project manager listens to team members to dictate the project's direction based on their feedback
C. By actively listening, the project manager can identify underlying issues, concerns, or ideas that may not be explicitly stated
D. The project manager listens only to prioritize tasks and delegate responsibilities

Question 26

Within a project environment, the role of a project manager is multifaceted. As a 'coach', which of the following best describes the project manager's responsibility?

A. To define the project scope and objectives
B. To handle all technical issues that arise during the project

C. To guide, mentor, and support team members in their personal and professional development

D. To provide regular updates to the project stakeholders about progress

Question 27

As a project manager of a newly formed team, you find that there are conflicts arising frequently between team members. You believe that by fostering better understanding and collaboration, these conflicts can be reduced. Which of the following project management roles emphasizes understanding team dynamics, mediating disputes, and fostering a collaborative environment?

A. Initiator

B. Negotiator

C. Facilitator

D. Working member

Question 28

In a project, who is primarily responsible for ensuring that the project aligns with the strategic objectives of the organization and for making critical decisions regarding the project's direction, especially when challenges or roadblocks arise?

A. The project manager

B. The project sponsor

C. The project team

D. The stakeholders

Question 29

Imagine you're working on a project with a tight deadline. As the project manager, you have multiple roles to play. In a high-pressure situation, which aspect of emotional intelligence (EQ) would be most beneficial for maintaining team morale and ensuring collaboration among team members?

A. Understanding the technical intricacies of the project

B. Focusing solely on the project timeline and tasks

C. Demonstrating empathy and understanding toward team members' concerns and emotions

D. Assigning additional overtime to ensure tasks are completed

Question 30

You are managing a project where you have to interact with multiple departments and stakeholders. Which role primarily requires the project manager to ensure open communication lines, manage stakeholders' expectations, and resolve any misalignments between stakeholders and the project goals?

A. Technical lead
B. Listener
C. Facilitator
D. Initiator

Question 31

Which of the following best describes the primary purpose of project initiation?

A. Allocating the budget and resources for the project
B. Defining the project scope and identifying stakeholders
C. Creating the project schedule and assigning tasks
D. Closing out the project and ensuring all deliverables are met

Question 32

In which process group would you typically find the creation of the project communication management plan?

A. Initiating
B. Planning
C. Executing
D. Monitoring and controlling

Question 33

During the project execution phase, a key stakeholder requests a change to the project scope that will add additional features to the final product. What should the project manager do first?

A. Accept the change request and immediately implement it
B. Analyze the impact of the change on the project's schedule and budget
C. Inform the stakeholder that changes are not allowed during the execution phase
D. Request approval from the project sponsor before taking any action

Question 34

During the project, a team member identifies a potential quality issue with a deliverable. What should the project manager do first?

A. Review the team member's findings and determine if the issue is valid
B. Immediately inform the project sponsor about the quality concern
C. Ignore the issue as it may not have a significant impact on the project
D. Escalate the concern to the project team for resolution

Question 35

Which process is responsible for identifying, analyzing, and planning responses to project risks?

A. Plan risk responses
B. Identify risks
C. Perform qualitative risk analysis
D. Control risks

Question 36

During the project execution phase, a team member notifies the project manager about a conflict between two stakeholders. What should the project manager do first?

A. Ignore the conflict and let the stakeholders resolve it themselves
B. Address the conflict immediately and take necessary actions to resolve it
C. Document the conflict and add it to the project risk register
D. Gather more information about the conflict before taking any action

Question 37

During the project, the project team identifies a new opportunity that could significantly enhance the project's outcomes without affecting the project's critical path. What should the project manager do first?

A. Immediately implement the opportunity to maximize project benefits
B. Analyze the impact of the opportunity on the project's objectives
C. Document the opportunity and inform the project sponsor
D. Seek approval from the stakeholders before taking any action

Question 38

During the project execution phase, the project manager notices that the team is facing communication challenges. Some team members are not receiving important project updates and are feeling left out. What should the project manager do first?

A. Schedule a team meeting to address the communication issues
B. Assign blame to the team members who are not staying informed
C. Review the project communication plan and update it as necessary
D. Ignore the communication issues as they may resolve on their own

Question 39

During the project execution phase, a stakeholder raises concerns about potential environmental impacts resulting from the project activities. What should the project manager do first?

A. Assure the stakeholder that environmental impacts will be considered later
B. Ignore the concerns as they are not critical to the project's success
C. Initiate an environmental impact assessment to understand the potential effects
D. Report the stakeholder's concerns to the project sponsor

Question 40

During the project, the project manager is identifying and documenting project stakeholders. Which of the following should the project manager consider while identifying stakeholders?

A. Their social media activity related to the project
B. Their influence, interest, and potential impact on the project
C. Their availability to attend project meetings
D. Their willingness to promote the project publicly

Question 41

Which of the following tools is used to generate, organize, and prioritize ideas in a structured manner?

A. Decision tree analysis
B. Affinity diagram

C. Scatter diagram

D. Control chart

Question 42

In a project meeting, the team members are discussing the progress of their tasks, and a few members seem to dominate the conversation while others remain silent, even though they have valuable inputs. As a project manager, what should you do to encourage equal participation from all team members?

A. Interrupt the dominating members and ask the quieter ones to speak up

B. Let the meeting flow naturally, as some team members may prefer not to speak

C. Conduct a separate meeting with the quieter members to gather their inputs

D. Disband the current team and form a new team with better communication skills

Question 43

During the project planning, the project manager wants to gather insights and opinions from a diverse group of stakeholders about a new product's features. Which of the following techniques is most suitable for this purpose?

A. Brainstorming

B. Focus groups

C. Standup meetings

D. Risk analysis

Question 44

You are managing a project, and your team is facing a complex issue with multiple interrelated factors. You want to identify the root cause of the problem systematically. Which problem-solving tool would be the most appropriate for this scenario?

A. Ishikawa diagram (Fishbone diagram)

B. Control chart

C. Critical path method (CPM)

D. Pareto chart

Question 45

Your project team is working on a software development project with tight deadlines. During the development phase, the team wants to encourage creativity, generate new ideas, and come up with innovative solutions to a technical challenge. Which of the following techniques would be most suitable for this purpose?

A. Focus groups
B. Stand-up meetings
C. Brainstorming sessions
D. Virtual meetings

Question 46

Your project team is facing a critical issue that requires immediate resolution. As the project manager, you decide to conduct a meeting with all key stakeholders to analyze the problem, discuss potential solutions, and make decisions quickly. Which meeting type would be most appropriate for this scenario?

A. Focus groups
B. Kick-off meetings
C. Crisis meetings
D. Brainstorming sessions

Question 47

As a project manager, you are leading a large infrastructure project with multiple stakeholders. The project is at a critical juncture, and you need to ensure all stakeholders are updated on the project's status and address any concerns promptly. Which type of meeting would be most suitable for this purpose?

A. Kick-off meetings
B. Virtual meetings
C. Status review meetings
D. Brainstorming sessions

Question 48

Your project team has been working on a complex project for several months, and progress is not meeting the initial expectations. As a project manager, you decide to gather the team to assess the current situation, identify potential bottlenecks, and develop corrective actions. Which type of meeting would be most suitable for this purpose?

A. Focus groups
B. Lessons learned meetings
C. Risk review meetings
D. Root cause analysis meetings

Question 49

Your project team is working on a critical software development project. As the project manager, you decide to conduct daily stand-up meetings with the team. However, you notice that the meetings are taking longer than the allocated time, and some team members tend to go into unnecessary details. What action would be most appropriate to address this issue?

A. Increase the frequency of stand-up meetings to ensure all topics are covered
B. Allow team members to discuss technical details during stand-up meetings
C. Set strict time limits for each team member's update and encourage focusing on progress and impediments
D. Conduct the stand-up meetings less frequently to save time

Question 50

Which of the following Enterprise Environmental Factors most affects the decision to adopt a predictive approach in project management?

A. Competitor analysis and market conditions
B. Regulatory requirements and legal constraints
C. Organizational culture and governance framework
D. Stakeholder communication and engagement strategies

Question 51

What is the primary role of project management in a project executed within a functional organizational structure?

A. To coordinate and integrate the efforts of functional departments
B. To directly manage and supervise the project team members.

C. To establish and enforce organizational policies and procedures

D. To report project progress to senior management and stakeholders

Question 52

What is the purpose of the Plan Schedule Management process in project management?

A. To define and document the project schedule

B. To estimate the duration of project activities

C. To determine the scheduling method and tools to be used

D. To monitor and control the project schedule

Question 53

What is the primary difference between contingency reserve and management reserve?

A. Contingency reserve is used to address identified risks, while management reserve is used to address unknown risks

B. Contingency reserve is set aside for scope changes, while management reserve is set aside for unforeseen events

C. Contingency reserve is controlled by the project manager, while management reserve is controlled by the project sponsor

D. Contingency reserve is part of the project budget, while management reserve is part of the organizational budget

Question 54

Which of the following factors most affects the decision to not adopt a predictive approach in project management?

A. High project complexity and uncertainty

B. Regulatory requirements and compliance

C. Availability of historical project data

D. Limited project resources and time constraints

Question 55

What does lag time represent in a project schedule network?

A. The amount of time an activity can be delayed without impacting the project schedule

B. The amount of time required to complete an activity
C. The time between the start of one activity and the start of its successor activity
D. The time between the completion of one activity and the start of its successor activity

Question 56

Which of the following is the correct sequence of project management processes leading to the development of a project schedule?

A. Define activities, estimate activity durations, sequence activities, develop schedule
B. Sequence activities, define activities, estimate activity durations, develop schedule
C. Define activities, sequence activities, estimate activity durations, develop schedule
D. Estimate activity durations, define activities, sequence activities, develop schedule

Question 57

What is the best practice for managing change requests in a predictive project?

A. Implement a formal change control process
B. Immediately accommodate all change requests
C. Reject all change requests to maintain project stability
D. Handle change requests informally without documentation

Question 58

Consider the following project activities with their durations:

■ Activity A: 4 days; Activity B: 5 days; Activity C: 3 days; Activity D: 6 days; Activity E: 2 days;

and the following finish-to-start dependencies between activities:

■ A -> B; A -> C; B -> D; C -> E; D -> E;

what is the Critical Path of the above project schedule network?

A. Critical Path: A-B-C-E
B. Critical Path: A-C-E

C. Critical Path: A-B-D-E
D. Critical Path: A-B-E

Question 59

Consider the following project activities with their durations:

■ Activity A: 5 days; Activity B: 7 days; Activity C: 4 days; Activity D: 6 days; Activity E: 8 days

and the following dependencies:

■ A -> B; A -> C; B -> D; C -> D; D -> E

What is the Float of Activity C in the above schedule network?

A. Float: 0 days
B. Float: 1 days
C. Float: 2 days
D. Float: 3 days

Question 60

A project has a planned value (PV) of $50,000, an earned value (EV) of $45,000, and an actual cost (AC) of $55,000. Calculate the schedule variance (SV) and the schedule performance index (SPI) for the project.

A. SV = 5,000 euro, SPI = 0.9
B. SV = −5,000 euro, SPI = 0.9
C. SV = −5,000 euro, SPI = 0.82
D. SV = 5,000 euro, SPI = 1.1

Question 61

Which of the following is NOT typically included in a Quality Management Plan?

A. Quality objectives and metrics
B. Roles and responsibilities for quality management
C. Project schedule and milestones
D. Quality assurance and control activities

Question 62

Which of the following statements about the WBS and WBS Dictionary is correct?

A. The WBS is a hierarchical breakdown of project deliverables, while the WBS dictionary provides detailed descriptions and attributes of each work package
B. The WBS is a detailed list of project activities, while the WBS dictionary provides a summary of the project's objectives
C. The WBS is a graphical representation of project dependencies, while the WBS dictionary provides a timeline of project milestones
D. The WBS is a documentation of project risks, while the WBS dictionary provides a list of project stakeholders

Question 63

Consider the following information for a specific activity:

■ Effort required: 40 person-hours
■ Resource availability: 4 persons
■ Work hours per day: 8 hours

Based on the given information, calculate the duration (in days) required to complete the activity, assuming the work feasible using all the resources available.

A. 1.2 days
B. 3.5 days
C. 4.3 days
D. 5.0 days

Question 64

Consider the following information for a project:

■ Planned Value (PV): 50,000 euro
■ Earned Value (EV): 40,000 euro

Based on the given information, calculate the Schedule Variance (SV) for the project and interpret the result.

A. 10,000 euro; the project is ahead of schedule
B. –10,000 euro; the project is behind schedule
C. 50,000 euro; the project is ahead of schedule
D. –50,000 euro; the project is behind schedule

Question 65

Which of the following statements correctly describes a difference between the project charter and the project management plan?

A. The project charter outlines the project objectives, while the project management plan details the project scope
B. The project charter defines the project organization, while the project management plan outlines the project schedule
C. The project charter is created during the initiating process group, while the project management plan is created during the executing process group
D. The project charter is a high-level document, while the project management plan provides detailed information about project execution

Question 66

Control charts are graphical tools used in project management to monitor and analyze process performance over time. Which of the following is an indicator of an out-of-control process in a control chart?

A. Data points consistently falling within the control limits
B. Data points clustering around the mean value
C. Data points crossing the control limits or exhibiting non-random patterns
D. Data points showing a consistent upward or downward trend

Question 67

Given the following information:

- Budget at Completion (BAC): 100,000 euro
- Planned Value (PV): 60,000 euro
- Earned Value (EV): 50,000 euro
- Actual Cost (AC): 70,000 euro
- Cost Performance Index (CPI): 0.714

Calculate the Estimate To Complete (ETC) using the appropriate formula of the Earned Value Method.

A. 120,000 euro
B. 70,000 euro
C. 150,000 euro
D. 200,000 euro

Question 68

Given the following information:

- Earned Value (EV): 50,000 euro
- Actual Cost (AC): 60,000 euro

Calculate the Cost Variance (CV) using the appropriate formula.

A. 10,000 euro
B. –10,000 euro
C. –50,000 euro
D. –60,000 euro

Question 69

Which of the following activities is associated with the Perform Integrated Change Control process in a predictive project?

A. Creating the project charter
B. Developing the project schedule
C. Assessing and approving change requests
D. Identifying project stakeholders

Question 70

In project management, leading indicators and lagging indicators are used to measure and monitor project performance. Which of the following statements best describes the difference between leading indicators and lagging indicators?

A. Leading indicators are backward-looking, while lagging indicators are forward-looking
B. Leading indicators are quantitative, while lagging indicators are qualitative

C. Leading indicators are predictive, while lagging indicators are historical
D. Leading indicators measure project outcomes, while lagging indicators measure project inputs

Question 71

In a construction project, the project team has identified that the project is behind schedule due to unforeseen delays in the delivery of construction materials. The project manager wants to take corrective actions to re-align the project schedule. Which of the following corrective actions would be most appropriate in this scenario?

A. Increasing the working hours of the construction team
B. Negotiating with suppliers for expedited delivery of materials
C. Modifying the project scope to accommodate the delays
D. Ignoring the delays and continuing with the existing schedule

Question 72

A status report is a crucial communication tool used in predictive project management to provide stakeholders with an update on the project's progress. Which of the following components is typically included in a status report?

A. Project budget forecast
B. Stakeholder analysis
C. Detailed project schedule
D. Summary of completed tasks

Question 73

Which of the following is an Enterprise Environmental Factor that can facilitate the use of Agile or Lean approaches to projects?

A. Hierarchical organizational structure
B. Strict regulatory compliance requirements
C. Siloed communication channels
D. Supportive and collaborative culture

Question 74

Which of the following organizational structures is most conducive to Adaptive approaches to projects?

A. Functional organization
B. Matrix organization
C. Project-based organization
D. Hierarchical organization

Question 75
Which of the following is a characteristic of a high performing team?

A. Rigid adherence to a detailed project plan
B. Individual task ownership and siloed work
C. Emphasis on hierarchy and top-down decision-making
D. Collaboration and empowerment

Question 76
Which of the following is a characteristic of Servant Leadership?

A. Command and control management style
B. Decision-making without consulting team members
C. Putting the needs of the team first
D. Micro-management of team tasks

Question 77
Which of the following is NOT one of the Disciplined Agile Tactical Scaling Factors?

A. Geographic distribution
B. Organizational complexity
C. Team size
D. Regulatory compliance

Question 78
Which of the following statements best describes the relationship between cross-functional teams and "T-Shaped" people?

A. Cross-functional teams are formed exclusively with "T-Shaped" people
B. "T-Shaped" people possess expertise in a single functional area within a cross-functional team
C. Cross-functional teams benefit from the presence of "T-Shaped" people who possess both depth and breadth of skills

D. "T-Shaped" people are not suitable for cross-functional teams as they lack specialization

Question 79

What is the purpose of the Iteration Review in Agile projects?

A. To demonstrate the completed functionality to stakeholders and gather feedback
B. To conduct a retrospective analysis of the team's performance and identify areas for improvement
C. To review and adjust the iteration backlog based on changing priorities or requirements
D. To plan and prioritize the work for the upcoming iteration or sprint

Question 80

What is the purpose of Product Backlog Refinement in Agile projects?

A. To create a prioritized list of features and user stories for the product backlog
B. To estimate the effort and complexity of each item in the product backlog
C. To review and update the product backlog based on changing priorities or requirements
D. To assign tasks and responsibilities to team members for upcoming iterations or sprints

Question 81

What is the purpose of the Definition of Done (DoD) in Agile projects?

A. To create a detailed description of each user story or feature
B. To specify the acceptance criteria for each user story or feature
C. To define the criteria that must be met for a user story or feature to be considered complete
D. To assign tasks and responsibilities to team members for upcoming iterations or sprints

Question 82

What is a most common reason why the project team might not be able to insert certain User Stories or Features all at a higher priority in the Product Backlog, into the Iteration Backlog during the Iteration Planning?

A. Insufficient clarity or understanding of the requirements
B. Lack of clear acceptance criteria for the User Stories or Features
C. Limited availability of resources or capacity
D. Inadequate communication among team members

Question 83
How can dependencies between Agile teams be effectively resolved?

A. Establishing clear communication channels and regular coordination meetings
B. Creating cross-functional teams that include members from different teams
C. Implementing a dependency management process to identify, track, and address dependencies
D. All the above

Question 84
What is the most appropriate option for the project team when the Product Owner, during an Iteration Planning meeting, asks the team to put a feature in the Iteration Backlog of the next iteration, but the project team has already fulfilled their capacity?

A. Negotiate with the Product Owner to reprioritize existing User Stories or Features
B. Increase the team's capacity by adding more resources to accommodate the new feature
C. Ignore the capacity limitations and include the new feature in the Iteration Backlog
D. Defer the new feature to a future iteration or release

Question 85
What is the Work In Process (WIP) Limit also known as Work In Progress (WIP) Limit?

A. The maximum number of tasks that can be worked on simultaneously
B. The minimum number of tasks that should be completed in a sprint
C. The maximum amount of time a task can stay in the "In Progress" stage
D. The minimum amount of time a task should be allocated for completion

Question 86

In a software development project, the cycle time for completing a task is 4 days, and the lead time for delivering the task from the time it is requested is 6 days. What is the wait time in this case?

A. 2 days
B. 4 days
C. 6 days
D. 10 days

Question 87

A project team is using relative estimations to estimate the size or effort of user stories. They want to establish a baseline by selecting a user story as the reference point for 1 story point. Which of the following practices can they use to determine the user story for this purpose?

A. Select a user story that represents the highest complexity in the project
B. Select a user story that represents the lowest complexity in the project
C. Select a user story that the team is most familiar with and has recently completed
D. Select a user story that is of average complexity and represents a typical task in the project

Question 88

The project team is analyzing the release burndown chart and notices that the actual burndown line is consistently above the ideal burndown line in the last two iterations. They also observe that the scope of the work in the backlog (total work in backlog) is not increased during the same timeframe. Which of the following options could be a possible cause of this delay?

A. High team morale and productivity leading to faster completion of tasks
B. Insufficient work items in the backlog, resulting in lower completion rate
C. Unexpected technical challenges or dependencies causing delays in task completion
D. Frequent scope changes or additions impacting the planned work

Question 89

The project team is examining a Kanban Board with 5 columns: Backlog, Analysis, Development, Testing, and Done. The team has set the following WIP limits for the three central columns:

- Analysis: WIP limit of four user stories
- Development: WIP limit of three user stories
- Testing: WIP limit of five user stories

They observe the following number of user stories in progress in each of the columns:

- Analysis: Two user stories
- Development: Three user stories
- Testing: Three user stories

Based on the above information, which column is the bottleneck?

A. Analysis
B. Development
C. Testing
D. Backlog

Question 90

Which Adaptive framework is focused on continuous flow, visualizing work, limiting work in progress (WIP), and using explicit policies?

A. Lean startup
B. Scrum
C. Kanban
D. XP (eXtreme Programming)

Question 91

What is a key difference between Scrum and eXtreme Programming (XP)?

A. Scrum focuses on iterative development, while XP emphasizes continuous delivery
B. Scrum places more emphasis on individual developer skills, while XP emphasizes teamwork and collaboration
C. Scrum has defined roles and ceremonies, while XP has specific engineering practices
D. Scrum emphasizes customer collaboration, while XP focuses on technical excellence

Question 92
What is a key difference between Kanban and Scrum?

A. Scrum focuses on time-boxed iterations, while Kanban emphasizes a continuous flow of work
B. Kanban has defined roles and ceremonies, while Scrum emphasizes visual management and limiting work in progress (WIP)
C. Kanban places more emphasis on customer collaboration, while Scrum focuses on optimizing the team's workflow
D. Kanban is a framework for project management, while Scrum is an engineering framework

Question 93
What is the primary responsibility of the Product Owner in Scrum?

A. Writing code and developing the product
B. Facilitating the Scrum events and ensuring the team follows the Scrum framework
C. Representing the stakeholders and managing the Product Backlog
D. Ensuring the team has all the necessary resources and tools for development

Question 94
What is the primary responsibility of the Scrum Master in Scrum?

A. Writing code and developing the product
B. Representing the stakeholders and managing the Product Backlog
C. Facilitating the Scrum events and ensuring the team follows the Scrum framework
D. Ensuring the team has all the necessary resources and tools for development

Question 95
What is the primary purpose of using business value metrics in Agile projects?

A. To measure the financial return on investment (ROI) of the project
B. To assess the satisfaction level of the stakeholders

C. To evaluate the effectiveness and efficiency of the development process

D. To prioritize and make decisions based on the value delivered by the project

Question 96

What is the primary financial metric used to measure the profitability of an investment by considering the time value of money?

A. Return on investment (ROI)

B. Net present value (NPV)

C. Internal rate of return (IRR)

D. Payback period

Question 97

In Agile projects, which type of backlog focuses on delivering a specific product or system?

A. Product backlog

B. Release backlog

C. Sprint backlog

D. Project backlog

Question 98

What is the purpose of a Definition of Done (DoD) in Agile projects?

A. To define the quality criteria and standards that must be met for a user story or backlog item to be considered complete

B. To outline the tasks and activities required to implement a user story or backlog item

C. To capture the acceptance criteria and expectations of stakeholders for a user story or backlog item

D. To prioritize the user stories or backlog items based on their importance and value

Question 99

Which of the following best describes return on investment (ROI) in Agile project management?

A. ROI measures the profitability of an investment by comparing the expected benefits to the costs incurred

B. ROI represents the amount of money a project has generated compared to the initial investment
C. ROI is a metric used to evaluate the team's performance and efficiency in delivering value
D. ROI is a measure of the project's risk exposure and potential impact on the organization

Question 100

You are working as a business analyst for a software development project. The project team is finalizing the requirements and needs to define the criteria that will be used to determine whether the software meets the specified requirements. What is this called?

A. Acceptance criteria
B. Affinity diagram
C. Benchmarking
D. Benefits

Question 101

You are facilitating a session with stakeholders to identify and group related ideas or items together. What technique are you using?

A. Acceptance criteria
B. Affinity diagram
C. Benchmarking
D. Benefits

Question 102

You are analyzing the current performance of your organization and comparing it against industry standards or best practices. What technique are you using?

A. Acceptance criteria
B. Affinity diagram
C. Benchmarking
D. Benefits

Question 103

You are evaluating the positive outcomes or advantages that are expected to result from a project or solution. What are these called?

A. Acceptance criteria
B. Affinity diagram
C. Benchmarking
D. Benefits

Question 104

You are facilitating a brainstorming session to generate innovative ideas for a new product feature. What technique are you using?

A. Acceptance criteria
B. Affinity diagram
C. Benchmarking
D. Benefits

Question 105

You are analyzing the value that a project or solution brings to the organization. What is this called?

A. Acceptance criteria
B. Affinity diagram
C. Benchmarking
D. Benefits

Question 106

You are conducting interviews with stakeholders to gather their requirements and preferences for a new system. What technique are you using?

A. Acceptance criteria
B. Affinity diagram
C. Benchmarking
D. Benefits

Question 107

You are analyzing the cause-and-effect relationships between different factors to identify the root cause of a problem. What technique are you using?

A. Acceptance criteria
B. Affinity diagram
C. Benchmarking
D. Benefits

Question 108
You are creating a visual representation of the inputs and outputs of a system and its external entities. What technique are you using?

A. Acceptance criteria
B. Affinity diagram
C. Benchmarking
D. Benefits

Question 109
You are ensuring that your project adheres to regulations or guidelines set by external authorities. What is this called?

A. Acceptance criteria
B. Affinity diagram
C. Benchmarking
D. Compliance standard

Question 110
You are working on a project to improve the efficiency of a manufacturing process. You are collecting and analyzing data to identify areas of improvement and quantify the potential cost savings. What technique are you using?

A. Export judgment
B. Five Whys technique
C. Benchmarking
D. Cost–benefit analysis

Question 111
You are conducting interviews with key stakeholders to understand their needs, preferences, and expectations for a new product. What technique are you using?

A. Persona
B. Multivoting process
C. Interviews
D. Kano classification

Question 112
You are analyzing the potential risks and uncertainties associated with a project and developing strategies to mitigate or respond to them. What technique are you using?

A. Problem solving
B. Verification
C. Risk management
D. Proof of concept

Question 113
You are creating a visual representation of the sequence and dependencies of project activities in a time-based manner. What technique are you using?

A. Value stream mapping
B. Use case
C. Gantt chart
D. User story

Question 114
You are identifying and documenting the roles and responsibilities of project team members to ensure clear accountability. What technique are you using?

A. Stakeholder analysis
B. RACI model
C. Wireframes
D. Requirements documentation

Question 115
You are facilitating a workshop with stakeholders to generate innovative ideas and solutions for a complex problem. What technique are you using?

A. Creative thinking
B. Requirement management plan
C. Force field analysis
D. Compliance standard

Question 116
You are documenting the desired behaviors, characteristics, and goals of a specific type of user for a software application. What is this called?

A. Minimum viable product
B. Problem solving
C. Persona
D. Product roadmap

Question 117
You are analyzing the relationships and dependencies between different requirements to ensure that all are addressed and no gaps exist. What technique are you using?

A. Traceability
B. Definition of done
C. Elicitation
D. Affinity diagram

Question 118
You are conducting a thorough review of project documents, requirements, and deliverables to ensure completeness and accuracy. What technique are you using?

A. Validation
B. Compliance standard
C. Document analysis
D. Context diagram

Question 119
You are analyzing the internal strengths, weaknesses, external opportunities, and threats of an organization or project. What technique are you using?

A. SWOT analysis
B. Export judgment
C. Use case
D. Requirement traceability matrix

Question 120
You are conducting a workshop with stakeholders to prioritize features and requirements based on their relative importance. What technique are you using?

A. Stakeholder analysis
B. Multivoting process
C. Value stream mapping
D. Use case

Question 121

You are creating a visual representation of the flow of activities, information, and materials in a process to identify areas of waste and inefficiency. What technique are you using?

A. Five Whys technique
B. Export judgment
C. Business value
D. Value stream mapping

Question 122

You are analyzing the potential impacts and consequences of a proposed change to the project scope. What technique are you using?

A. Verification
B. Compliance standard
C. Impact analysis
D. Problem solving

Question 123

You are working on a project to develop a new mobile application. You are creating a simplified, high-level representation of the app's user interface. What is this called?

A. Persona
B. Export judgment
C. Proof of concept
D. Wireframes

Question 124

You are identifying the key stakeholders for a project and analyzing their interests, influence, and potential impact on the project. What technique are you using?

A. Stakeholder analysis
B. Affinity diagram

C. Product roadmap

D. Requirements documentation

Question 125

You are analyzing the potential risks and uncertainties associated with a project and their likelihood and impact on project objectives. What technique are you using?

A. Risk management

B. Cost–benefit analysis

C. Cause and effect diagram

D. Traceability

Question 126

You are creating a detailed description of a specific user interaction with a system or application. What is this called?

A. User story

B. Definition of done

C. Minimum viable product

D. Problem solving

Question 127

You are conducting a structured and systematic examination of a project's requirements to ensure they are complete, consistent, and feasible. What technique are you using?

A. Validation

B. Compliance standard

C. Document analysis

D. Context diagram

Question 128

You are analyzing the relationships between different requirements, design elements, and test cases to ensure that each requirement is tested. What technique are you using?

A. Affinity diagram

B. Requirement management plan

C. Traceability

D. Creative thinking

Question 129

You are analyzing the internal and external factors that could positively or negatively impact the success of a project or organization. What technique are you using?

A. SWOT analysis

B. Affinity diagram

C. Use case

D. Requirement traceability matrix

Question 130

You are facilitating a session to identify and analyze the underlying causes of a problem by repeatedly asking "why" until the root cause is determined. What technique are you using?

A. Force field analysis

B. Problem solving

C. Five Whys technique

D. Compliance standard

Question 131

You are developing a visual representation of the relationships and dependencies between different requirements, showing how changes to one requirement may impact others. What is this called?

A. Affinity diagram

B. Use case

C. Requirement traceability matrix

D. Document analysis

Question 132

You are conducting a session with stakeholders to elicit requirements by collaboratively creating and refining user scenarios or narratives. What technique are you using?

A. Elicitation

B. Prototype

C. Kano classification
D. Wireframes

Question 133

You are evaluating the feasibility and potential benefits of a proposed project or solution by developing a scaled-down version with limited features or functionality. What is this called?

A. Export judgment
B. Proof of concept
C. Persona
D. Problem solving

Question 134

You are conducting a comprehensive analysis of the strengths, weaknesses, opportunities, and threats associated with a new business venture. What technique are you using?

A. Compliance standard
B. SWOT analysis
C. Cost–benefit analysis
D. Multivoting process

Question 135

You are working on a project to develop a new software application. During the requirements gathering phase, you are creating a detailed description of a specific functionality or feature from the user's perspective. What is this called?

A. Minimum viable product
B. User story
C. Persona
D. Business case

9.2 Full practice exam two – answers

Answer to Question 1: The correct answer is C.
The predictive approach, often called the waterfall model, focuses on detailed upfront planning with the idea that there will be fewer changes to

the plan as the project progresses. The adaptive approach, commonly associated with agile methodologies, embraces changes and iterative development, with the understanding that requirements may evolve over time due to various factors like changing business needs or market conditions.

Answer to Question 2: The correct answer is C.
Projects are typically initiated to create a unique product, service, or result. This often leads to changes, whether it's a change in how an organization operates, a change in the products or services it offers, or a change in its processes.

Answer to Question 3: The correct answer is C.
Given the evolving client requirements and frequent modifications to the project scope, an adaptive approach, often associated with agile methodologies, would be ideal. This approach is flexible and allows for iterative development, catering to changing requirements over time.

Answer to Question 4: The correct answer is B.
Issues are known problems that need to be addressed. Risks are potential events or conditions that may have a positive or negative effect on the project. Assumptions are factors that, for planning purposes, are considered to be true, real, or certain without empirical evidence. Constraints are restrictions or limitations on the project, such as time, budget, resources, or scope.

Answer to Question 5: The correct answer is C.
According to the PMI Code of Ethics and Professional Conduct, Sarah should prioritize her professional integrity and commitment to quality. While documenting and elevating issues can be beneficial in some scenarios, the primary responsibility for ethical decision-making lies with the individual project manager. Hence, Sarah should decline the request that compromises the quality and explain her commitment to upholding ethical standards and delivering quality work.

Answer to Question 6: The correct answer is C.
A program is a group of related projects managed in a coordinated manner to obtain benefits and control that would not be achievable if these projects were managed individually. Programs are aligned with an organization's strategic objectives and often involve complex interdependencies between projects.

Answer to Question 7: The correct answer is B.
In project management, events or conditions that could have a positive or negative impact on the project are called risks. Risk management is an essential process to identify, assess, and mitigate these potential risks throughout the project's lifecycle.

Answer to Question 8: The correct answer is C.
As a project manager, it's essential to assess the changes requested by the client, evaluate their impact on the project's scope, schedule, and budget, and then communicate the potential consequences to the client. This process ensures that all stakeholders have a clear understanding of the impact of scope changes before any decisions are made.

Answer to Question 9: The correct answer is A.
An assumption is a factor considered to be true, real, or certain for planning purposes without empirical evidence. In this case, the assumption is that the required raw materials will be delivered on time by the supplier.

Answer to Question 10: The correct answer is A.
The project to build a new office building is a temporary endeavor with a specific start and end date, aiming to create a unique product. On the other hand, the ongoing operations of the company involve repetitive activities that sustain the organization's day-to-day business.

Answer to Question 11: The correct answer is D.
The Project Management Plan is a comprehensive document that defines how the project will be executed, monitored, controlled, and closed. It includes various components such as the project scope, schedule, cost estimates, resource requirements, risk management approach, communication plan, and other essential elements needed to manage the project effectively.

Answer to Question 12: The correct answer is A.
The Risk Register is a document used to systematically capture and maintain information about identified risks throughout the project lifecycle. It includes details about each risk, such as its description, potential impact, probability of occurrence, risk response strategies, and assigned ownership. The Risk Register is an essential tool for risk management as it allows the project manager to monitor and control risks effectively.

Answer to Question 13: The correct answer is A.
To effectively manage risks in a project, it is essential to record all identified risks in a Risk Register. The Risk Register contains detailed information about each risk, including its description, potential impact, probability of occurrence, risk response strategies, and assigned ownership. Regularly reviewing and updating the Risk Register throughout the project allows the project manager and the team to stay vigilant about potential risks and take appropriate actions to address them.

Answer to Question 14: The correct answer is C.
Project Management Plan; it includes project scope, schedule, cost estimates, risk management approach, and other essential elements. The Project Management Plan is a comprehensive document that provides guidance on how the project will be executed, monitored, controlled, and closed.

Answer to Question 15: The correct answer is C.
The Quality Management Plan is a document that outlines how the project's quality objectives will be achieved and how the end product will meet the desired quality standards. It includes processes and methodologies for quality planning, quality assurance, and quality control. The plan defines the quality metrics, acceptance criteria, and quality review processes to ensure that the deliverables meet the customer's requirements and expectations.

Answer to Question 16: The correct answer is B.
In project management, milestones are specific points in time that represent significant events or achievements in the project. They serve as important reference points for tracking progress and measuring the project's performance against the planned schedule. Milestones help the project manager and stakeholders understand how well the project is progressing and if it is on track to meet its objectives within the defined timeframes.

Answer to Question 17: The correct answer is A.
The main activities involved in the project closure phase include formally handing over the project deliverables to the customer or relevant stakeholders, verifying that all project objectives have been met, and celebrating the success of the project. Additionally, project closure involves conducting lessons learned sessions to identify strengths, weaknesses, and areas for improvement in future projects. Project closure is essential because it marks the official end of the project and ensures that all deliverables are transferred to the customer, ensuring their acceptance and satisfaction.

Answer to Question 18: The correct answer is A.
To effectively manage stakeholders with different levels of interest and influence in a marketing project, it is essential to document their information in a Stakeholder Register. The Stakeholder Register contains details about each stakeholder, their interests, concerns, level of support, and potential impact on the project.

Answer to Question 19: The correct answer is A.
The project management plan outlines how the project will be executed, monitored, and controlled, while the project scope statement defines the work that needs to be accomplished. The project management plan is a comprehensive document that provides guidance on how the project will be executed, monitored, controlled, and closed. It includes various components such as project scope, schedule, cost estimates, risk management approach, quality management approach, resource management approach, communication plan, and more. The primary difference is that the project management plan addresses the overall project management approach, while the project scope statement specifically focuses on what work needs to be done and the project's objectives.

Answer to Question 20: The correct answer is C.
The Communication Management Plan is a document that outlines how project communication will be planned, executed, monitored, and controlled. It defines the communication objectives, stakeholders' information needs, communication methods, frequency, and the responsible parties for communication activities.

Answer to Question 21: The correct answer is B.
A project sponsor typically provides funding and resources for the project. They play a crucial role in the initial stages by giving direction and making decisions that affect the project's scope, budget, and timeline. The sponsor also helps to overcome obstacles by leveraging organizational resources and influence. Their primary responsibility is not the day-to-day management of project tasks, which is the project manager's role.

Answer to Question 22: The correct answer is B.
Emotional intelligence (EQ) is the ability to identify, understand, and manage our own emotions as well as the emotions of others. For a project manager, having a high EQ can help in understanding team dynamics, resolving conflicts, motivating team members, and building a positive work environment.

While EQ can indirectly influence aspects like resource allocation or project execution, its primary impact is on interpersonal relationships and team dynamics.

Answer to Question 23: The correct answer is A.
Leadership primarily focuses on setting a vision, inspiring, and motivating the team, whereas management concentrates on planning, organizing, and ensuring the execution of tasks according to the plan. Leaders provide direction and purpose, while managers ensure that projects and tasks are carried out efficiently and effectively.

Answer to Question 24: The correct answer is A.
The project manager is responsible for ensuring that all team members, including experts like Sarah, understand the project's objectives and how their individual roles fit into the broader project. Effective communication, guidance, and support are fundamental responsibilities of the project manager to ensure the project progresses smoothly and that every member is aligned with the project goals.

Answer to Question 25: The correct answer is C.
By actively listening, the project manager can discern not just the spoken words but also the underlying issues, concerns, or ideas that might not be overtly expressed. Active listening is a key communication skill that allows project managers to understand team members better, build trust, and address potential issues before they escalate.

Answer to Question 26: The correct answer is C.
As a "coach", the project manager's role is to guide, mentor, and support team members in both their personal and professional development. This helps in building a more cohesive, skilled, and motivated team, which in turn can positively impact project outcomes.

Answer to Question 27: The correct answer is C.
A facilitator is someone who makes a process easy or easier. In the context of project management, a facilitator would be responsible for understanding team dynamics, mediating disputes, and fostering a collaborative environment. They would guide discussions, ensure every team member's voice is heard, and work toward a consensus. An initiator, on the other hand, is typically someone who begins or introduces a process or activity.

Answer to Question 28: The correct answer is B.
The Project Sponsor is primarily responsible for ensuring that the project aligns with the organization's strategic objectives. They also play a crucial role in making critical decisions related to the project's direction, particularly when there are challenges or significant issues.

Answer to Question 29: The correct answer is C.
In high-pressure situations, demonstrating empathy and understanding toward team members' concerns and emotions is vital. It not only helps maintain team morale but also fosters a collaborative environment where team members feel valued and understood, ultimately leading to better project outcomes.

Answer to Question 30: The correct answer is C.
As a facilitator, a project manager would focus on ensuring open communication, understanding and managing stakeholders' expectations, and guiding discussions to ensure alignment between stakeholders and project goals.

Answer to Question 31: The correct answer is B.
The primary purpose of project initiation is to formally start the project and involves defining the project scope, objectives, and stakeholders. It ensures that the project has a clear direction and purpose from the beginning. This phase also ensures that all stakeholders are identified and have a shared understanding of the project's objectives and deliverables.

Answer to Question 32: The correct answer is B.
The creation of the project communication management plan is typically done during the planning process group. In this phase, the project manager and team develop a comprehensive plan that outlines how communication will be managed throughout the project, including the stakeholders' communication needs, frequency, methods, and distribution of information.

Answer to Question 33: The correct answer is B.
When a key stakeholder requests a change to the project scope during the project execution phase, the project manager should first analyze the impact of the change on the project's schedule and budget. This analysis is necessary to understand how the change will affect the project's overall objectives and constraints. Based on this analysis, the project manager can then determine the feasibility and implications of implementing the change and present the findings to the project sponsor for approval.

Answer to Question 34: The correct answer is A.

When a team member identifies a potential quality issue with a deliverable during the project execution phase, the project manager should first review the team member's findings and determine if the issue is valid. It is essential to assess the validity and severity of the quality concern before taking any further actions. If the issue is valid and could impact the project's objectives, the project manager can then work with the project team to develop a plan to address and resolve the quality concern.

Answer to Question 35: The correct answer is A.

The process responsible for identifying, analyzing, and planning responses to project risks is "Plan Risk Responses". In this process, the project team, with inputs from stakeholders, determines appropriate strategies to address potential risks identified during risk analysis. These strategies can include risk avoidance, risk mitigation, risk transfer, or risk acceptance. The goal is to develop a comprehensive plan to manage and respond to the identified risks effectively.

Answer to Question 36: The correct answer is D.

When a project manager is notified about a conflict between two stakeholders during the project execution phase, the first step should be to gather more information about the conflict before taking any action. Understanding the root cause, concerns, and perspectives of the involved stakeholders will help the project manager make informed decisions on how to address the conflict effectively. Jumping into immediate action without understanding the context may escalate the situation further.

Answer to Question 37: The correct answer is B.

When the project team identifies a new opportunity during the project execution phase that could significantly enhance the project's outcomes without affecting the critical path, the project manager should first analyze the impact of the opportunity on the project's objectives. This analysis is essential to understand the potential benefits and risks associated with implementing the opportunity. Once the analysis is complete, the project manager can then decide whether to proceed with the opportunity or seek approval from stakeholders, depending on its impact and alignment with the project's goals.

Answer to Question 38: The correct answer is C.

When the project manager notices communication challenges during the project execution phase, the first step should be to review the project communication plan and update it as necessary. The communication plan outlines how communication is managed in the project, including the stakeholders' communication needs, methods, and frequency. By reviewing and updating the communication plan, the project manager can ensure that all team members receive the necessary project updates and are kept informed, thus addressing the communication challenges effectively.

Answer to Question 39: The correct answer is C.
When a stakeholder raises concerns about potential environmental impacts resulting from project activities during the project execution phase, the project manager should first initiate an environmental impact assessment to understand the potential effects. This assessment will help in identifying any environmental risks associated with the project and allow the project manager to develop appropriate mitigation measures to address those concerns. It demonstrates the project's commitment to environmental sustainability and responsible project management.

Answer to Question 40: The correct answer is B.
While identifying stakeholders during the project planning phase, the project manager should consider their influence, interest, and potential impact on the project. Identifying stakeholders based on their level of influence and interest helps prioritize communication and engagement efforts. It allows the project manager to tailor communication strategies and involve stakeholders in a way that aligns with their needs and expectations, thereby increasing the project's chances of success.

Answer to Question 41: The correct answer is B.
An affinity diagram, also known as an affinity chart or KJ method, is a problem-solving tool used to generate, organize, and prioritize ideas in a structured manner. It helps teams categorize and understand large amounts of data, ideas, or issues and find meaningful patterns or relationships among them.

Answer to Question 42: The correct answer is B.
As a project manager, it is essential to create a conducive environment where all team members feel comfortable sharing their inputs and ideas. However, some team members may naturally be more reserved or introverted, and they may prefer not to speak up in a large group setting. It is not appropriate to interrupt the dominating members or force the quieter ones to speak. As a project manager, you can encourage equal participation by letting the meeting flow naturally and providing opportunities for all

team members to contribute in their preferred way. You can follow up with quieter team members individually after the meeting to gather their inputs if needed.

Answer to Question 43: The correct answer is B.
Focus groups are most suitable for gathering insights and opinions from a diverse group of stakeholders, especially during the project planning. In focus groups, a small group of participants, typically 5 to 10 individuals, is brought together to discuss and provide feedback on a specific topic, product, or service. The facilitator guides the discussion to gather valuable insights, opinions, and perceptions from the participants. During the focus group session, stakeholders can express their thoughts openly, listen to others' perspectives, and collaborate in a controlled and structured environment.

Answer to Question 44: The correct answer is A.
The Ishikawa Diagram, also known as the Fishbone Diagram or Cause-and-Effect Diagram, is a problem-solving tool used to identify the root cause of complex issues with multiple interrelated factors. It helps visually represent the potential causes contributing to a specific problem, allowing the project team to systematically explore various categories of causes, such as people, process, equipment, materials, and environment. By using the Ishikawa Diagram, the project team can conduct a structured analysis and identify the primary factors leading to the problem.

Answer to Question 45: The correct answer is C.
Brainstorming sessions are most suitable for encouraging creativity, generating new ideas, and coming up with innovative solutions to a technical challenge. During a brainstorming session, team members openly and freely share their thoughts, suggestions, and ideas related to the specific problem or challenge. The focus is on quantity rather than quality at the initial stage, allowing diverse and unconventional ideas to emerge. Brainstorming creates a collaborative and non-judgmental environment, which can spark creativity and lead to breakthrough solutions.

Answer to Question 46: The correct answer is C.
Crisis Meetings would be most appropriate for the scenario described. Crisis Meetings are convened to address critical issues or urgent situations that require immediate attention and resolution. In this case, since your project team is facing a critical issue that needs quick decisions and actions, a Crisis Meeting allows all key stakeholders to come together, analyze the problem,

discuss potential solutions, and make timely decisions. Crisis Meetings are characterized by their urgency, focus on problem-solving, and the involvement of relevant decision-makers.

Answer to Question 47: The correct answer is C.
Status Review Meetings would be most suitable for the purpose of updating all stakeholders on the project's status and addressing any concerns promptly. These meetings are designed to provide project updates, discuss progress, and review the current status of the project. They play a crucial role in keeping stakeholders informed, ensuring transparency, and facilitating communication among all involved parties. In a large infrastructure project with multiple stakeholders, holding regular status review meetings allows everyone to stay informed about the project's progress, identify any potential issues or risks, and make informed decisions to keep the project on track. The project manager can use this platform to report achievements, discuss challenges, and provide an opportunity for stakeholders to ask questions or raise concerns.

Answer to Question 48: The correct answer is D.
Root Cause Analysis Meetings would be most suitable for assessing the current situation, identifying potential bottlenecks, and developing corrective actions when the project progress is not meeting the initial expectations. In a Root Cause Analysis Meeting, the project team collaboratively investigates the factors contributing to the project's challenges and identifies the root cause or causes. Root Cause Analysis Meetings are essential for continuous improvement and ensuring that recurring issues are addressed at their source, rather than just treating the symptoms.

Answer to Question 49: The correct answer is C.
To address the issue of stand-up meetings taking longer than allocated time and team members going into unnecessary details, setting strict time limits for each team member's update and encouraging a focus on progress and impediments would be the most appropriate action. Daily stand-up meetings are meant to be time-boxed and short, typically lasting around 15 minutes. By enforcing time limits for each team member's update, the project manager can ensure that the meeting remains focused and efficient.

Answer to Question 50: The correct answer is B.
Among the given options, regulatory requirements and legal constraints are the Enterprise Environmental Factors that most affect the decision to adopt a

predictive approach in project management. Industries and projects subject to strict regulations or legal frameworks often require a predictive approach to ensure compliance and meet specific requirements. Adhering to these regulations and constraints necessitates detailed planning, documentation, and adherence to predefined processes, which align with the characteristics of a predictive approach.

Answer to Question 51: The correct answer is A.
In a project executed within a functional organizational structure, the primary role of project management is to coordinate and integrate the efforts of various functional departments involved in the project. Project managers act as liaisons between different departments, ensuring effective communication, collaboration, and alignment of goals. Their role includes facilitating cross-functional coordination, resolving conflicts, and integrating the work of individual team members to achieve project objectives. While project managers may have some supervisory authority over the project team members, their primary focus is on managing the project's overall coordination, rather than directly supervising the functional team members.

Answer to Question 52: The correct answer is C.
The purpose of the Plan Schedule Management process in project management is to determine the scheduling method and tools to be used throughout the project. This process involves establishing the policies, procedures, and documentation for developing, managing, executing, and controlling the project schedule. It defines the approach to be taken, such as whether to use a critical path method (CPM), agile methodologies, or other scheduling techniques. It also identifies the tools and software that will be utilized to create and maintain the project schedule.

Answer to Question 53: The correct answer is D.
The primary difference between contingency reserve and management reserve in project management lies in their budgetary allocation. Contingency reserve is a portion of the project budget that is specifically set aside to address identified risks or uncertainties within the project. On the other hand, management reserve is a portion of the organizational budget that is allocated for unforeseen events or situations that may arise during the project. It is not specifically tied to any identified risks but serves as a buffer to handle unexpected issues or opportunities that may arise. Contingency reserve is project-specific and managed by the project manager, while

management reserve is typically controlled by the project sponsor or higher-level management.

Answer to Question 54: The correct answer is A.
Among the given options, high project complexity and uncertainty are the factors that most affect the decision to not adopt a predictive approach in project management. When a project is characterized by a high degree of complexity and uncertainty, it becomes challenging to accurately predict and plan all aspects of the project in advance. In such cases, a more adaptive or iterative approach, such as Agile or hybrid methodologies, may be preferred over a predictive approach. These approaches allow for flexibility and continuous adaptation to changing project conditions, enabling better management of complex and uncertain projects.

Answer to Question 55: The correct answer is D.
Lag time in a project schedule network represents the time between the completion of one activity and the start of its successor activity. It represents a delay or waiting period that occurs between the two activities. Lag time is added to the project schedule to account for dependencies, resource availability, or other factors that require a delay before the start of the next activity. For example, if Activity A must be completed before Activity B can start, and there is a two-day lag time between the completion of Activity A and the start of Activity B, it means that two days will elapse after Activity A finishes before Activity B can begin.

Answer to Question 56: The correct answer is C.
The correct sequence of project management processes leading to the development of a project schedule is as follows: Define Activities, Sequence Activities, Estimate Activity Durations, Develop Schedule.

Answer to Question 57: The correct answer is A.
The best practice for managing change requests in a predictive project is to implement a formal change control process. A formal change control process provides a structured approach for evaluating, reviewing, and deciding on change requests. By implementing a formal change control process, the project team can ensure that change requests are properly assessed for their impact on the project's scope, schedule, budget, and other constraints. This process involves documenting and analyzing change requests, evaluating their feasibility, assessing the potential risks and benefits, and making informed decisions based on the project's objectives and priorities.

Answer to Question 58: The correct answer is C.
To calculate the Critical Path we need to determine the longest path in the project schedule network diagram. In the given project schedule network, we have the following two paths:

- A -> B -> D-> E
- A -> C -> E

The path A -> B -> D-> E has total duration equal to 17=4+5+6+2 days. The path A -> C -> E has total duration equal to 9=4+3+2 days. Therefore, the Critical Path is A -> B -> D-> E.

Answer to Question 59: The correct answer is B.
Float represents the amount of time an activity can be delayed without affecting the project's overall duration. To calculate the float and total float for Activity C, we need to analyze the project schedule and identify the critical path. We have a path of activities A->B->D->E with total duration of 24 days=5+7+6+8 days, and a path of activities A->C->D->E with total duration 23 days=5+4+6+8 days. So, the Critical Path is A->B->D->E and the only activity in the project schedule that is not critical is Activity C. Activity C can be delayed of 1 day before affecting the total duration of the project (1=24-23 days). Therefore, the correct answer is B. Float: 1 days

Answer to Question 60: The correct answer is B.
In Earned Value Analysis, Schedule Variance (SV) is calculated by subtracting the Planned Value (PV) from the Earned Value (EV), and Schedule Performance Index (SPI) is calculated by dividing the EV by the PV. Given: PV = 50,000 euro, EV = 45,000 euro, AC = 55,000 euro, then SV = EV − PV = 45,000 euro − 50,000 euro = −5,000 euro (negative indicates behind schedule), SPI = EV/PV = 45,000 euro/50,000 euro = 0.9 (less than 1 indicates behind schedule). Therefore, the correct answer is B. SV = −5,000 euro, SPI = 0.9.

Answer to Question 61: The correct answer is C.
A Quality Management Plan typically includes various components related to quality assurance and control. These components ensure that the project meets the defined quality standards. However, the project schedule and milestones are not typically included in a Quality Management Plan.

Answer to Question 62: The correct answer is A.

The work breakdown structure (WBS) is a hierarchical breakdown of the project's deliverables and work packages. It organizes the project scope into manageable and logical components, allowing for easier planning, execution, and control. On the other hand, the WBS Dictionary is a companion document to the WBS that provides detailed descriptions, attributes, and information about each work package within the WBS. It includes additional information such as work package descriptions, responsible parties, milestones, dependencies, required resources, and any relevant technical information.

Answer to Question 63: The correct answer is A.

To calculate the duration required to complete the activity, we need to consider the available resources and the effort required. To find the duration, we divide the required effort by the total available resources.

- Duration in hours = Effort required/resource availability
- Duration in hours = 40 person-hours/4 persons = 10 hours
- Duration in days = Duration in hours/work hours per day
- Duration in days = 10 hours/8 hours per day = 1.25 days

The duration required to complete the activity is approximately 1.25 days; therefore, the correct answer is A. 1.25 days.

Answer to Question 64: The correct answer is B.

To calculate the Schedule Variance (SV) in the Earned Value Method, we need to find the difference between the Earned Value (EV) and the Planned Value (PV). Schedule Variance (SV) = EV − PV = 40,000 euro − 50,000 euro = −$10,000. Since the Schedule Variance (SV) is negative (−10,000 euro), it indicates that the project is behind schedule. Therefore, the correct answer is B. −10,000 euro; The project is behind schedule.

Answer to Question 65: The correct answer is D.

The project charter and the project management plan serve different purposes and contain different levels of detail. The project charter is a high-level document that is created during the initiating process group of the project. It provides an overview of the project, including the project objectives, high-level requirements, key stakeholders, and initial project authorization. On the other hand, the project management plan is a comprehensive document that provides detailed information about how the project will be executed, monitored, and controlled. The project management plan is developed during the planning process group of the project and serves as a roadmap for project execution.

Answer to Question 66: The correct answer is C.
In a control chart, if the data points consistently cross the control limits or exhibit non-random patterns such as trends, cycles, or unusually high or low values, it indicates an out-of-control process. Crossing the control limits suggests that the process is not performing within the expected range of variation, and non-random patterns may indicate the presence of special causes that need to be investigated and addressed.

Answer to Question 67: The correct answer is B.
To calculate the Estimate To Complete (ETC) using the Earned Value Method, considering the past costs performance of the project, we can use the formula: ETC = (BAC − EV)/CPI. Given: BAC = 100,000 euro, EV = 50,000 euro, CPI = 0.714, then ETC = (100,000 euro - 50,000 euro)/0.714 = 70,028 euro. Therefore, the correct answer is B.

Answer to Question 68: The correct answer is B.
To calculate the Cost Variance (CV) using the Earned Value Method, we use the formula: CV = EV − AC. Given: EV = 50,000 euro, AC = 60,000 euro, then CV = 50,000 euro − 60,000 euro = −10,000 euro. A negative value for the Cost Variance (CV) indicates that the project is over budget, meaning the actual costs (AC) have exceeded the earned value (EV).

Answer to Question 69: The correct answer is C.
The Perform Integrated Change Control process in a predictive project involves evaluating and making decisions regarding proposed changes to the project. This includes assessing the potential impacts of the change, considering the project's objectives and constraints, and determining whether to approve or reject the change request. It is an essential process for maintaining control over project changes and ensuring that they align with the project's overall objectives and requirements.

Answer to Question 70: The correct answer is C.
Leading indicators are metrics or measures that provide insights into future performance or trends. They help project managers anticipate potential issues or opportunities before they occur. Leading indicators focus on

predictive factors and are used to monitor and manage ongoing project activities. On the other hand, lagging indicators are based on historical data and measure past performance or outcomes. They provide an assessment of what has already occurred in the project. Lagging indicators are used to evaluate project success or failure after the completion of activities or milestones.

Answer to Question 71: The correct answer is C.
In the given scenario, where the project is behind schedule due to delays in material delivery, modifying the project scope to accommodate the delays would be the most appropriate corrective action. By revisiting the project scope, the project manager can assess which deliverables or tasks can be adjusted, removed, or rescheduled to account for the delays. Increasing the working hours of the construction team may put undue strain on the team and may not address the root cause of the delay. Negotiating with suppliers for expedited delivery of materials is a valid option to improve the process of supply to avoid future delays caused by the same root-cause, but it not recovers the current delays. Ignoring the delays and continuing with the existing schedule would only worsen the situation and could lead to further schedule slippage.

Answer to Question 72: The correct answer is D.
A status report typically includes a summary of completed tasks as one of its components. This section highlights the tasks or activities that have been successfully accomplished since the last reporting period. It provides stakeholders with an overview of the progress made in terms of task completion and serves as an indicator of the project's overall advancement. While components like the project budget forecast, stakeholder analysis, and detailed project schedule are important aspects of project management, they may not be included in a standard status report. However, they can be part of other project management documents or reports.

Answer to Question 73: The correct answer is D.
A supportive and collaborative culture is an Enterprise Environmental Factor that can facilitate the use of Agile or Lean approaches to projects. Agile and Lean methodologies rely on teamwork, collaboration, and open communication. A culture that encourages these values and behaviors provides a conducive environment for the successful implementation of Agile or Lean practices. On the other hand, hierarchical organizational structures, strict

regulatory compliance requirements, and siloed communication channels can create barriers to Agile or Lean adoption by inhibiting collaboration, flexibility, and open communication.

Answer to Question 74: The correct answer is C.
A project-based organizational structure is most conducive to Agile or Lean approaches to projects. In a project-based organization, teams are formed specifically for each project, allowing for greater flexibility, collaboration, and alignment with Agile or Lean principles. This structure promotes cross-functional teams, close collaboration between team members, and a focus on delivering value and outcomes. While matrix organizations can support Agile or Lean approaches, they may introduce additional complexity and potential conflicts. Hierarchical organizations have a strict top-down command and control structure, which may limit autonomy, adaptability, and the ability to embrace Agile or Lean practices.

Answer to Question 75: The correct answer is D.
Collaboration and empowerment are key characteristics of a high performing team. Agile and Lean teams collaborate and are empowered by the organization to take decisions on the way of working to adopt in the project. Rigid adherence to a detailed project plan goes against the Agile principles of embracing change and responding to customer needs. Individual task ownership and siloed work are not encouraged in Agile. Agile teams promote cross-functionality and collective responsibility, where team members collaborate and work together toward shared goals. Emphasis on hierarchy and top-down decision-making contradicts the Agile value of empowering teams and distributing decision-making authority.

Answer to Question 76: The correct answer is C.
Putting the needs of the team first is a characteristic of Servant Leadership. Servant Leadership is a leadership approach that focuses on serving and supporting the needs of the team members, enabling their growth, and fostering a collaborative and empowered work environment. A servant leader prioritizes the well-being and development of their team, and they actively seek to remove obstacles and provide support to help the team succeed.

Answer to Question 77: The correct answer is B.
"Organizational complexity" is not one of the Disciplined Agile Tactical Scaling Factors, while "Organizational distribution" is. The Disciplined Agile toolkit focuses on providing guidance and options for scaling Agile practices

in various contexts. The Tactical Scaling Factors identified in Disciplined Agile are Team size, Geographic distribution, Organizational distribution, Skill availability, Compliance, Solution complexity, Domain complexity.

Answer to Question 78: The correct answer is C.
In the context of cross-functional teams, "T-Shaped" people refer to individuals who have expertise in a specific area (represented by the vertical bar of the "T") but also possess a broad range of knowledge and skills across different disciplines (represented by the horizontal bar of the "T"). These individuals can contribute to cross-functional teams by bringing their deep expertise in a specific domain while also being able to collaborate effectively and understand multiple perspectives. Option A is incorrect because cross-functional teams are not formed exclusively with "T-Shaped" people. Cross-functional teams can have individuals with various skill sets and expertise, including both "T-Shaped" people and specialists in specific areas. Option B is incorrect because "T-Shaped" people possess expertise beyond a single functional area, rather than being limited to a single functional area within a cross-functional team. Option D is incorrect because "T-Shaped" people, with their combination of depth and breadth of skills, can contribute effectively to cross-functional teams by bridging gaps, fostering collaboration, and providing a holistic perspective.

Answer to Question 79: The correct answer is A.
The purpose of the Iteration Review, also known as the Sprint Review in the Scrum framework, in Agile projects is to demonstrate the completed functionality to stakeholders and gather their feedback. It is an opportunity for the development team to showcase the work that has been accomplished during the iteration or sprint. During the Iteration Review, the team presents the features and user stories that have been completed and demonstrates their functionality. Stakeholders, including product owners, customers, and other relevant parties, can provide feedback, ask questions, and suggest improvements.

Answer to Question 80: The correct answer is C.
The purpose of Product Backlog Refinement in Agile projects is to review and update the product backlog based on changing priorities or requirements. It is an ongoing activity that involves the mainly the product owner supported by the development team, and other relevant stakeholders. During Product Backlog Refinement, the team collaboratively reviews the items in the product backlog, ensures they are well-defined, and adjusts their

priorities as needed. The team may add, remove, or modify items based on new insights, feedback, or changes in business needs. The goal is to maintain a product backlog that is up to date, prioritized, and aligned with the overall vision and goals of the project.

Answer to Question 81: The correct answer is C.
The purpose of the Definition of Done (DoD) in Agile projects is to define the criteria that must be met for a user story, or feature, or an increment of product to be considered complete. It serves as a shared understanding and agreement within the development team on the level of quality and completeness expected for each deliverable. The Definition of Done typically includes criteria related to functionality, quality, and other aspects of the product.

Answer to Question 82: The correct answer is C.
A common reason why the project team might not be able to insert certain User Stories or Features at a higher priority within the Iteration Backlog during the Iteration Planning is limited availability of resources or capacity. This refers to situations where the team does not have enough resources or capacity to take on additional work or prioritize certain User Stories or Features over others. While insufficient clarity or understanding of the requirements (option A), lack of clear acceptance criteria (option B), and inadequate communication among team members (option D) should usually be resolved during the Iteration Planning meeting talking with the stakeholders to clarify the User Stories, or Features also about their acceptance criteria, and to solve any communication issue between team members.

Answer to Question 83: The correct answer is D.
To effectively resolve dependencies between Agile teams, multiple approaches can be employed. Clear and open communication is essential to identify and address dependencies. Teams should establish channels for sharing information, updates, and concerns. Regular coordination meetings facilitate discussions, synchronization, and problem-solving. By forming cross-functional teams, organizations can bring together individuals with diverse skills and knowledge from multiple teams. A formalized dependency management process helps teams proactively identify, document, and track dependencies between teams. This process may involve visualizing dependencies on a shared board, maintaining a dependency register, and regularly reviewing and addressing dependencies during planning and retrospectives.

Answer to Question 84: The correct answer is A.
When the project team has already fulfilled their capacity for the next iteration and the Product Owner requests the inclusion of a new feature, the most appropriate option is to negotiate with the Product Owner to reprioritize existing User Stories or Features. By engaging in a discussion about the relative importance and urgency of the new feature compared to the prioritized features, the team can collaborate with the Product Owner to determine which items should be reprioritized or potentially removed from the current iteration to make room for the new feature. Increasing the team's capacity by adding more resources (option B) may not be feasible or practical in the short term and ignoring the capacity limitations and including the new feature (option C) can lead to overcommitment and negatively impact the team's ability to deliver on their commitments. Deferring the new feature to a future iteration or release (option D) will create a conflict between the Product Owner and the project team that could be resolved using option A.

Answer to Question 85: The correct answer is A.
The Work in process (WIP) limit refers to the maximum number of tasks or work items that a team can work on simultaneously within a specific stage or phase of the workflow. It helps to prevent overloading the team with too much work and promotes a smooth flow of work through the process. By setting WIP limits, teams can visualize and control the amount of work in progress, identify bottlenecks, and maintain a balanced workflow. It encourages teams to focus on completing tasks before starting new ones, reducing multitasking, and improving overall productivity.

Answer to Question 86: The correct answer is A.
To calculate the wait time, we subtract the cycle time from the lead time. In this case, the cycle time is 4 days, and the lead time is 6 days. Wait time = Lead time − Cycle time = 6 days − 4 days = 2 days

Answer to Question 87: The correct answer is C.
When establishing a baseline for relative estimations, it is recommended to select a user story that the team is familiar with and has recently completed. This practice allows the team to have a clear understanding of the effort and complexity involved in that user story. By choosing a user story that is well-known and fresh in the team's memory, it becomes easier to compare the relative effort of other user stories to this reference point. It provides a consistent frame of reference for estimating the size or effort of subsequent user stories.

Answer to Question 88: The correct answer is C.
When analyzing the release burndown chart and observing that the actual burndown line is consistently above the ideal burndown line in the last two iterations, along with no increase in the scope of work in the backlog, a possible cause of the delay could be unexpected technical challenges or dependencies. These challenges or dependencies may arise during the execution of tasks, causing delays in their completion. They could include unforeseen technical complexities, integration issues, or external dependencies that impact the team's ability to finish tasks within the expected time frame.

Answer to Question 89: The correct answer is B.
In the given scenario, the team is examining the Kanban Board and observing the number of user stories in progress in each column, along with the specified WIP limits. Based on the information provided, the "Development" column is the bottleneck. The Development column has reached its WIP limit of three user stories, indicating that the team cannot accommodate any more tasks for development now. This suggests a constraint or limitation in the development process, which can lead to a slowdown in the overall workflow.

Answer to Question 90: The correct answer is C.
Kanban is an Agile framework that focuses on continuous flow, visualizing work, limiting work in progress (WIP), and using explicit policies. Kanban boards are often used to visualize the flow of work, and teams use WIP limits to prevent overloading and promote smooth workflow. Kanban emphasizes transparency, efficiency, and incremental improvement. Lean Startup is a methodology for developing new products and services, Scrum is a framework for iterative software development, and Extreme Programming (XP) is an Agile software development methodology. While they may incorporate certain principles of flow and visualization, they do not specifically focus on continuous flow, limiting WIP, and explicit policies like Kanban does.

Answer to Question 91: The correct answer is C.
One of the key differences between Scrum and Extreme Programming (XP) lies in their respective focus areas. While both Scrum and XP are Agile methodologies, they have distinct characteristics. Scrum is characterized by its defined roles, such as Product Owner, Scrum Master, and Development Team, and its ceremonies, including Sprint Planning, Daily Scrum, Sprint

Review, and Sprint Retrospective. Scrum places a strong emphasis on project management and collaboration, providing a framework for iterative development, transparency, and regular inspection and adaptation. On the other hand, XP places more emphasis on specific engineering practices. XP emphasizes practices such as Test-Driven Development (TDD), Continuous Integration, Pair Programming, and Refactoring. These practices aim to improve code quality, promote collaboration, and enable the delivery of high-quality software in a sustainable manner. While Scrum focuses on project management and collaboration, XP focuses on technical excellence and engineering practices to drive software development.

Answer to Question 92: The correct answer is A.
One of the key differences between Kanban and Scrum lies in their approach to work management and flow. Kanban focuses on visualizing and optimizing the flow of work, allowing for a continuous and steady stream of work items. In Kanban, there are no predefined time-boxed iterations like in Scrum. Instead, work items are pulled from a backlog and progress through the workflow as capacity allows. On the other hand, Scrum follows a time-boxed iteration known as a Sprint, typically lasting 1–4 weeks. During the Sprint, the team commits to a set of User Stories from the Product Backlog and works toward completing them within the Sprint time frame.

Answer to Question 93: The correct answer is C.
The primary responsibility of the Product Owner in Scrum is to represent the stakeholders and manage the Product Backlog. The Product Owner collaborates with stakeholders to understand their needs, gather requirements, and prioritize the features or items in the Product Backlog. The Product Owner continuously evaluates the trade-offs between different features, business goals, and stakeholder needs to maximize the value delivered by the product. The Product Owner works closely with the Development Team to clarify requirements, answer questions, and provide necessary information for the successful implementation of the Product Backlog items.

Answer to Question 94: The correct answer is C.
The primary responsibility of the Scrum Master in Scrum is to facilitate the Scrum events and ensure that the team follows the Scrum framework. The Scrum Master plays a crucial role in supporting the Scrum Team and promoting the effective implementation of Scrum principles and practices. The Scrum Master identifies and removes any obstacles or impediments that may

hinder the team's progress. They work closely with the team and stakeholders to address issues, promote a productive work environment, and enable the team to deliver value.

Answer to Question 95: The correct answer is D.
The primary purpose of using business value metrics in Agile projects is to prioritize and make decisions based on the value delivered by the project. Business value metrics help assess the relative importance or value of different features, user stories, or backlog items. By understanding the business value associated with each item, teams can prioritize their work and focus on delivering the most valuable features or functionality first.

Answer to Question 96: The correct answer is B.
Net present value (NPV) is the primary financial metric used to measure the profitability of an investment by considering the time value of money. NPV calculates the present value of future cash flows associated with an investment, considering the discount rate. It helps determine whether an investment will generate positive or negative value over its lifecycle. A positive NPV indicates a potentially profitable investment, while a negative NPV suggests a potential loss. Option A, Return on Investment (ROI), measures the return or profitability of an investment as a percentage, without explicitly considering the time value of money. Option C, Internal Rate of Return (IRR), is the discount rate that makes the NPV of cash inflows equal to the initial investment. It is a complementary metric used alongside NPV. Option D, Payback Period, measures the time it takes for an investment to recover its initial cost but does not consider the profitability beyond that point.

Answer to Question 97: The correct answer is A.
In Agile projects, the Product Backlog focuses on delivering a specific product or system. It is a prioritized list of user stories, features, and other deliverables that represent the requirements and desired functionality of the product. The Product Backlog evolves throughout the project as new insights are gained and priorities change. Option B, Release Backlog, represents a subset of the Product Backlog containing the user stories and features planned for a specific release or iteration. Option C, Sprint Backlog, is a subset of the Product Backlog that contains the user stories and tasks selected for a specific sprint or iteration. Option D, Project Backlog is not a commonly used term in Agile projects.

Answer to Question 98: The correct answer is A.

The purpose of a Definition of Done (DoD) in Agile projects is to establish the quality criteria and standards that must be met for a user story or backlog item to be considered complete. It sets clear expectations for the team regarding the level of quality, functionality, and completeness required for each item. Option B, outlining tasks and activities, is not the primary purpose of the DoD. It is typically captured in the team's Agile process or Sprint plan. Option C, capturing acceptance criteria and stakeholder expectations, is important but is typically specified within the user story itself, rather than being part of the DoD. Option D, prioritizing user stories or backlog items, is not the purpose of the DoD. Prioritization is typically done through other means, such as backlog refinement or prioritization techniques.

Answer to Question 99: The correct answer is A.

Return on Investment (ROI) in Agile project management refers to the measurement of the profitability or financial viability of an investment. It assesses the value generated by comparing the expected benefits or returns to the costs incurred in executing the project. ROI helps stakeholders evaluate the financial feasibility and effectiveness of an investment decision. Option B is incorrect because ROI does not solely represent the amount of money generated in comparison to the initial investment. It considers the ratio of benefits to costs. Option C is incorrect because ROI is not a metric to evaluate team performance or efficiency. Option D is incorrect because ROI is not a measure of project risk exposure or potential impact.

Answer to Question 100: The correct answer is A.

In the given scenario, the team is finalizing the requirements and needs to define the criteria that will be used to determine whether the software meets the specified requirements. This is known as acceptance criteria. Acceptance criteria are a set of conditions or criteria that must be satisfied for the product, system, or feature to be accepted by the stakeholders.

Answer to Question 101: The correct answer is B.

In the given scenario, you are facilitating a session with stakeholders to identify and group related ideas or items together. The technique used for this purpose is called an Affinity Diagram. It is a method that helps in organizing and categorizing large amounts of information or ideas into meaningful groups.

Answer to Question 102: The correct answer is C.
In the given scenario, you are analyzing the current performance of your organization and comparing it against industry standards or best practices. This technique is known as Benchmarking. Benchmarking involves measuring an organization's processes, performance, or practices against those of competitors or industry leaders to identify areas for improvement.

Answer to Question 103: The correct answer is D.
In the given scenario, you are evaluating the positive outcomes or advantages that are expected to result from a project or solution. These positive outcomes or advantages are referred to as benefits. Evaluating the benefits helps in assessing the value and potential return on investment of a project or solution.

Answer to Question 104: The correct answer is B.
In the given scenario, you are facilitating a brainstorming session to generate innovative ideas for a new product feature. The technique used to organize and group related ideas is an Affinity Diagram. This technique allows for the visual clustering of ideas to identify patterns, themes, or commonalities among them.

Answer to Question 105: The correct answer is D.
In the given scenario, you are analyzing the value that a project or solution brings to the organization. This analysis of value is centered around the benefits that the project or solution provides. Understanding and quantifying the benefits helps in assessing the viability and value proposition of the project or solution.

Answer to Question 106: The correct answer is A.
In the given scenario, you are conducting interviews with stakeholders to gather their requirements and preferences for a new system. The technique used to define the criteria for accepting the system is known as acceptance criteria. Acceptance criteria are used to establish the standards and expectations that the system must meet to be considered acceptable by the stakeholders.

Answer to Question 107: The correct answer is C.
In the given scenario, you are analyzing the cause-and-effect relationships between different factors to identify the root cause of a problem. The technique used for this purpose is called a Cause and Effect Diagram, also

known as a Fishbone Diagram. It helps in visually mapping out the potential causes and effects of a problem to identify the root cause.

Answer to Question 108: The correct answer is C.
In the given scenario, you are creating a visual representation of the inputs and outputs of a system and its external entities. The technique used for this purpose is called a Context Diagram. It helps in understanding the interactions between the system and its external entities, providing a high-level overview of the system's boundaries and interfaces.

Answer to Question 109: The correct answer is D.
In the given scenario, you are ensuring that your project adheres to regulations or guidelines set by external authorities. This process involves following a Compliance standard. Compliance standards are established by external entities to ensure that organizations meet legal, regulatory, or industry-specific requirements.

Answer to Question 110: The correct answer is D.
In the given scenario, you are collecting and analyzing data to identify areas of improvement and quantify the potential cost savings. The technique used for this purpose is Cost-Benefit Analysis. Cost-Benefit Analysis is a systematic approach to comparing the costs and benefits of a project, investment, or decision to determine its overall value and feasibility.

Answer to Question 111: The correct answer is C.
In the given scenario, you are conducting interviews with key stakeholders to understand their needs, preferences, and expectations for a new product. Interviews are a valuable technique for gathering firsthand information and insights from stakeholders, allowing for a deeper understanding of their requirements and perspectives.

Answer to Question 112: The correct answer is C.
In the given scenario, you are analyzing potential risks and uncertainties associated with a project and developing strategies to mitigate or respond to them. This process is known as risk management. Risk management involves identifying, assessing, and prioritizing risks, as well as developing and implementing risk response plans to minimize their impact on the project.

Answer to Question 113: The correct answer is C.
In the given scenario, you are creating a visual representation of the sequence and dependencies of project activities in a time-based manner.

The technique used for this purpose is a Gantt chart. A Gantt chart is a bar chart that illustrates the project schedule, including the start and end dates of activities, dependencies, and milestones.

Answer to Question 114: The correct answer is B.
In the given scenario, you are identifying and documenting the roles and responsibilities of project team members to ensure clear accountability. The technique used for this purpose is the RACI model. The RACI model is a matrix that defines the roles and responsibilities of individuals involved in a project, indicating who is responsible, accountable, consulted, and informed for each task or decision.

Answer to Question 115: The correct answer is A.
In the given scenario, you are facilitating a workshop with stakeholders to generate innovative ideas and solutions for a complex problem. The technique used for this purpose is creative thinking. Creative thinking techniques, such as brainstorming, mind mapping, and analogies, stimulate the generation of new and unconventional ideas to solve problems and drive innovation.

Answer to Question 116: The correct answer is C.
In the given scenario, you are documenting the desired behaviors, characteristics, and goals of a specific type of user for a software application. This documentation is called a persona. A persona is a fictional representation of a user archetype, providing insights into their needs, goals, behaviors, and preferences to guide the design and development of user-centric solutions.

Answer to Question 117: The correct answer is A.
In the given scenario, you are analyzing the relationships and dependencies between different requirements to ensure that all are addressed and no gaps exist. The technique used for this purpose is traceability. Traceability ensures that requirements are linked to their sources, such as stakeholder needs or business objectives, and that changes to requirements are managed and communicated effectively.

Answer to Question 118: The correct answer is C.
In the given scenario, you are conducting a thorough review of project documents, requirements, and deliverables to ensure completeness and accuracy. The technique used for this purpose is document analysis. Document analysis involves a systematic examination of project artifacts, such as

requirements documents, specifications, and reports, to gather insights, validate information, and identify any discrepancies or gaps.

Answer to Question 119: The correct answer is A.
In the given scenario, you are analyzing the internal strengths, weaknesses, external opportunities, and threats of an organization or project. This analysis is known as SWOT analysis. SWOT analysis is a strategic planning technique that helps identify and evaluate the internal and external factors that can impact the success of a project or organization. It provides a holistic view of the current situation and helps in developing strategies to leverage strengths, address weaknesses, exploit opportunities, and mitigate threats.

Answer to Question 120: The correct answer is B.
In the given scenario, you are conducting a workshop with stakeholders to prioritize features and requirements based on their relative importance. The technique used for this purpose is the multivoting process. Multivoting is a group decision-making technique where participants select their preferred options from a larger set of choices, helping to identify the most important or popular items through a voting process.

Answer to Question 121: The correct answer is D.
In the given scenario, you are creating a visual representation of the flow of activities, information, and materials in a process to identify areas of waste and inefficiency. This technique is called Value Stream Mapping. Value Stream Mapping helps in identifying and analyzing the value-added and non-value-added activities in a process, facilitating process improvement and streamlining efforts.

Answer to Question 122: The correct answer is C.
In the given scenario, you are analyzing the potential impacts and consequences of a proposed change to the project scope. This analysis is known as impact analysis. Impact analysis helps in understanding the potential effects of a change on various aspects of a project, such as costs, timeline, resources, and stakeholders, enabling informed decision-making and risk management.

Answer to Question 123: The correct answer is D.
In the given scenario, you are working on a project to develop a new mobile application and creating a simplified, high-level representation of the app's user interface. This representation is called wireframes. Wireframes are

visual representations that outline the structure, layout, and functionality of a user interface, providing a blueprint for design and development.

Answer to Question 124: The correct answer is A.
In the given scenario, you are identifying the key stakeholders for a project and analyzing their interests, influence, and potential impact on the project. This technique is called stakeholder analysis. Stakeholder analysis helps in understanding the stakeholders' perspectives, needs, and expectations, enabling effective communication, engagement, and stakeholder management throughout the project lifecycle.

Answer to Question 125: The correct answer is A.
In the given scenario, you are analyzing the potential risks and uncertainties associated with a project and their likelihood and impact on project objectives. This analysis is part of the risk management process. Risk management involves identifying, assessing, and managing risks to minimize their impact and maximize opportunities, ensuring the successful completion of a project.

Answer to Question 126: The correct answer is A.
In the given scenario, you are creating a detailed description of a specific user interaction with a system or application. This description is called a user story. User stories are concise, written statements that capture a user's perspective and requirements, focusing on the value delivered by the system and serving as a basis for development and testing.

Answer to Question 127: The correct answer is C.
In the given scenario, you are conducting a structured and systematic examination of a project's requirements to ensure they are complete, consistent, and feasible. This examination is called document analysis. Document analysis involves reviewing and analyzing project documents, such as requirements specifications, design documents, and business cases, to validate and verify their content, quality, and alignment with project objectives.

Answer to Question 128: The correct answer is C.
In the given scenario, you are analyzing the relationships between different requirements, design elements, and test cases to ensure that each requirement is tested. This analysis is part of traceability management. Traceability management involves establishing and maintaining traceability links between project artifacts, ensuring that each requirement is traced to its

origins, stakeholders, and related artifacts, facilitating impact analysis, change management, and overall project understanding.

Answer to Question 129: The correct answer is A.
In the given scenario, you are analyzing the internal and external factors that could positively or negatively impact the success of a project or organization. This analysis is called SWOT analysis. SWOT analysis involves evaluating the strengths, weaknesses, opportunities, and threats of an entity, providing insights into its current state, competitive advantages, potential growth areas, and potential risks.

Answer to Question 130: The correct answer is C.
In the given scenario, you are facilitating a session to identify and analyze the underlying causes of a problem by repeatedly asking "why" until the root cause is determined. This technique is known as the Five Whys technique. It helps in digging deeper into a problem by asking "why" multiple times to uncover the root cause rather than addressing only the symptoms.

Answer to Question 131: The correct answer is C.
Explanation: In the given scenario, you are developing a visual representation of the relationships and dependencies between different requirements, showing how changes to one requirement may impact others. This visual representation is called a Requirement Traceability Matrix. A Requirement Traceability Matrix is a table that links requirements to their sources, stakeholders, associated test cases, and other project artifacts, enabling effective tracking, impact analysis, and change management.

Answer to Question 132: The correct answer is B.
In the given scenario, you are conducting a session with stakeholders to elicit requirements by collaboratively creating and refining user scenarios or narratives. The technique used for this purpose is prototyping. Prototyping involves creating a tangible representation or model of a system or product to gather feedback, validate requirements, and refine the design based on stakeholder input.

Answer to Question 133: The correct answer is B.
In the given scenario, you are evaluating the feasibility and potential benefits of a proposed project or solution by developing a scaled-down version with limited features or functionality. This is known as a Proof of Concept. A Proof of Concept is a small-scale implementation or demonstration of

a concept or idea to test its viability, validate assumptions, and assess its potential before committing resources to full-scale development.

Answer to Question 134: The correct answer is B.
In the given scenario, you are conducting a comprehensive analysis of the strengths, weaknesses, opportunities, and threats associated with a new business venture. This analysis is called SWOT analysis. SWOT analysis helps in assessing the internal and external factors that can impact the success of a venture, providing insights into its competitive advantages, challenges, potential growth areas, and potential risks.

Answer to Question 135: The correct answer is B.
In the given scenario, during the requirements gathering phase of a project to develop a new software application, you are creating a detailed description of a specific functionality or feature from the user's perspective. This description is called a User Story. A User Story is a concise, user-centered statement that captures a specific requirement or desired functionality of the system, focusing on the value it delivers to the end user. User Stories are commonly used in Agile methodologies to capture requirements in an easily understandable and manageable format.

Appendix A: Introduction to the *PMBOK® Guide* 7th Edition

The *PMBOK® Guide* 7th Edition including *The Standard for Project Management* has been published by the Project Management Institute in August 2021. It is currently the last edition of the *PMBOK® Guide*. It introduces a huge transformation in contents compared with the previous edition of the guide until the 6th edition.

The main changes in the *PMBOK® Guide* 7th Edition including *The Standard for Project Management* compared against the previous editions until the 6th edition are as follows:

- The *PMBOK® Guide* 7th Edition embraces Adaptive, and Hybrid approaches (Project life cycles), in addition to the Predictive approach as it was for the previous editions of the guide
- The *Standard for Project Management* in the 7th Edition of the *PMBOK® Guide* is based on 12 Principles for project management, while the previous editions of the Guide and Standard until the 6th edition were based on 49 Processes grouped in 5 Process Groups
- The *PMBOK® Guide* 7th Edition describes 8 Performance Domains of project management compliant with the 12 Principles of project management defined in the *Standard for Project Management*, while the previous editions of the Guide and Standard until the 6th edition described 10 Knowledge Areas intersecting the Processes of project management.
- The *PMBOK® Guide* 7th Edition has one principle and a whole chapter dedicated to tailoring the practices of project management on the basis of the context of the project

■ The *PMBOK® Guide* 7th Edition defines a set of Models, Methods, and Artifacts usable as support to the activities of the project management performance domain, while the previous edition of the Guide and Standard until the 6th edition described the Input, Tools, Techniques, and Output (ITTO) for the execution of the project management processes.

In Table A.1, you will find a mapping of the main concepts of the *PMBOK® Guide* 7th Edition including the *Standard for Project Management*, with the concepts of the *PMBOK® Guide* 6th Edition including the *Standard for Project Management.*

Table A.1   Mapping *PMBOK® Guide* 7th Edition and *Standard for Project Management*, with *PMBOK® Guide* 6th and the *Standard for Project Management*

The Standard for Project Management in PMBOK® Guide *6th Edition*	*The Standard for Project Management in* PMBOK® Guide *7th Edition*
• Process Groups: Initiating, Planning, Executing, Monitoring and Control, Closing	• Introduction • System for Value Delivery • Project Management Principles: Stewardship, Tailoring, Team, Quality, Stakeholder, Complexity, Value, Risk, System Thinking, Adaptability and Resilience, Leadership, Change
PMBOK® Guide 6th Edition	**PMBOK® Guide 7th Edition**
• Introduction, Project environment, and role of the Project Manager • Knowledge Areas: Integration, Scope, Schedule, Cost, Quality, Resources, Communications, Risk, Procurement, Stakeholders	• Project Performance Domains: Stakeholders, Planning, Team, Project work, Development, Delivery, Approach and life cycle, Measurement, Uncertainty • Tailoring • Models, Methods, and Artifacts

A.1 A system for value delivery

A system for value delivery is the environment you usually can find within the enterprises hosting the projects. A system is a set of components and interactions between them. The interacting components of a system for value delivery within the enterprise system are Portfolios, Programs, Projects, Products, and Operations.

A **Portfolio** is a set of Programs, Projects, and Operations. Portfolio Management is the set of activities to plan a long-term strategy to realize value for the enterprise using Programs, Projects, Products, and Operations. With Portfolio Management, executives take decisions on what Initiatives (potentially Programs, Products, or Projects) to start to generate value for the enterprise, on the basis of Business Value metrics such as ROI, NPV, IRR, Cash-flow.

A **Program** is a set of Projects and Operations to realize Products to put them in Operation. Program Management is the set of activities to coordinate and integrate Projects that share some common resources, objectives, and outcomes to generate the expected value and benefits defined at Portfolio scale. Depending on the size of the enterprise, or the size of the product to realize, Programs could not exist, that is, Programs are useful if needed.

A **Project** is a temporary endeavor undertaken to create a unique product, service, or result. Projects can stand alone or be part of a Portfolio or Program.

A **Product** is an artifact that is produced, is quantifiable, and can be either an end item in itself or a component item.

An **Outcome** is a result or consequence of a process.

Value is the worth, importance, or usefulness of something. Value is subjective and is perceived in different ways by the different stakeholders of a project. Part of Value is the Business Value that is a financial metric such as the benefits less the costs to realize those benefits.

The **Information flows** through the several components of the System for Value Delivery, from the strategy to the operations, in a structure nested feedback loops between Portfolios, Programs, and Projects. The shorter in time are the feedbacks, the highest is the probability to realize the expected value by the system.

A.2 Project management principles

The 12 Principles of Project Management defined in the *Standard for Project Management* included in the *PMBOK® Guide* 7th Edition are as follows:

Be a diligent, respectful, and caring steward. Stewards conscientiously execute tasks with honesty, diligence, and reliability, adhering to both internal and external guidelines. They exhibit a strong dedication to considering the financial, social, and environmental effects of the projects they engage with. .

Create a collaborative project team environment. Project Team is the most important stakeholder to take care of because project outcomes are delivered by them. Creating a collaborative environment in the project team takes to development and self-development of the teammates, optimal contribution to deliver desired outcomes, and alignment with organizational culture and guidelines, having at the same time the opportunity to create their own "local" culture.

Effectively engage with stakeholders. Having the project stakeholders continuously aligned with the project information and involved in the project progress is the most important way to get to the success of a project. Any stakeholder is different from the other and they have their own interest and impact in the project outcomes, so it's important to have a common shared understanding of the project goals.

Focus on value. Value can be realized through the project, at the end of the project, or after the project is complete. Value is the most important metric to evaluate the success of the project. It can be easily measured like in case of Business Value or hard to measure like in the case of impacts of the project in long term in the society and external environment. We always must be focused on frequently assessing and measuring the value metrics during the project to align the project itself to the dynamics of the internal and external project environment.

Recognize, evaluate, and respond to system interactions. The System for value Delivery introduced before is the system where the project is a component of. The project as a component of the System for Value Delivery interacts with all the other components of the system. So, it's important to recognize, and evaluate the solicitations of any component of the system to promptly respond to such solicitations, adapting with resilience the behavior of the project.

Demonstrate leadership behaviors. Tailoring is not only about adapting the way of working within the project but also adapting the leadership style to what the context requires. The project team characteristics can require different types of leadership to adopt. Stakeholders often need to be led implicitly or explicitly. Within a project the leadership behaviors can come from anyone of the project team and from any of the stakeholders. It is important to promote and enable the emergency of leadership.

Tailor based on context. A project creates a unique product, service, or result. That is, a project is unique. Any project has always some difference with the others, such differences could be minimal, but they exist. That's why the way of working within a project cannot be the same as done in the past projects. That's why we need to tailor project performance domains, models, methods, artifacts on the basis of the Enterprise Environmental Factors and Organizational Process Assets.

Build quality into processes and deliverables. Quality metrics measures the compliancy of a deliverable and process to quality requirements. If we consider all quality requirements as product/deliverable requirements, then the high quality of both product and process comes automatically. That is, if we are effective in creating a qualitative product, then we also are efficient in the processes that realize such product. And the contrary is not always true.

Navigate complexity. The higher the number of relations between the components composing a system, the higher is the system complexity. A high complexity takes to high uncertainty, because the dynamics of the interacting components of the system become less predictable than in less complex systems. The interactions by the components of the System for Value Delivery where the project is a component of, are mainly human interactions, and they are not fully predictable by nature. So, what we need to do is to continuously assess the complexity and uncertainty of the project environment and be ready to respond to the system interactions.

Optimize risk responses. Risks are probable future events that impacts the outcomes of the project. Risk Management starts with identifying risks, doing a quantitative and qualitative analysis of the risk, planning the risks mitigation strategies, and implementing the response actions to decrease the probability of the risk or their impact on the projects. Optimizing the risk responses is to balance the costs and the benefits from the implementation of a mitigation strategy.

Embrace adaptability and resiliency. This principle is at the base of most of the ideas contained in the principles "Recognize, Evaluate, and Respond to System Interactions", "Tailor Based on Context", "Navigate Complexity", and "Optimize Risk Responses". Adaptability is the ability to adapt the project to the changing conditions of the context, mitigating the risks of having negative impacts. Resiliency is the ability to absorb impacts and to recover quickly from a setback or failure, especially on raising of issues not plannable in advance as risks. It's important to build a culture of adaptability and resilience into the organization's and project team's to help to accommodate changes, recover from setbacks, and advance the work of the projects.

Enable change to achieve the envisioned future state. This principle is the complement of the Tailor Based on Context principle. Indeed, while we tailor the project to the context, we also must adapt the context to the project outcomes. That is, projects are "agent of changes" within the organization, and we must enable the organization to receive the changes the project will provide.

A.3 Project performance domains

A project performance domain is a group of related activities that are critical for the effective delivery of project outcomes. We can see the Project Performance Domain as a possible implementation of the Project Management Principles defined in the *Standard for Project Management*. The eight Project Performance Domains described in the *PMBOK® Guide* 7th Edition are as follows:

Stakeholder. This performance domain implements the principles Effectively Engage with Stakeholder and Demonstrate leadership behavior. The activities executed by the project team within the Stakeholder Performance domain results in producing a productive working relationship with stakeholders, and adapting the engagement type to the interest and impact of the stakeholder to the project.

Team. This mainly implements the Create a Collaborative Project Team Environment, and Be a Diligent, Respectful, and Caring Steward principles. Important outcomes of the Team performance domain are creating a shared ownership of the project results with the project team, developing the team to a High-Performing team, promote and enable emergent leadership in teammates.

Development approach and life cycle. This is mainly the implementation of the Tailoring Based on Context principle. Here, the project team takes decision on what approach is given to the project: Predictive, Hybrid, Adaptive, what delivery cadence, what type of project life cycle; for instance, if predictive, then takes decision about what phases and how many phases; if Agile, then which time-box for the iterations, etc.

Planning. This performance domain is the implementation of most of the project management principles. Plan and re-plan to organize and coordinate at the start of the project and during the project, deciding frequency and items to plan and re-plan, what to plan, how to plan, when to plan. Spend the appropriate effort in planning, not too much, not too little, but the right for the context.

Project work. Also, this one implements most of the project management principles. Here is where the work of the project is executed. Outcomes of this performance domain are efficiency of the processes and effectiveness of the project results, execution of the tailored processes appropriate for the project, physical resources rightly managed, effectively communicate with stakeholders, management of procurement, team development due to continuous learning and processes improvement.

Delivery. The Delivery Performance Domain is composed of activities and functions to deliver the scope and quality that the project expects. This is the implementation of several project management principles, but mainly the implementation of the Build Quality into Processes and Deliverables, Focus on Value, and Enable Change to Achieve the Envisioned Future State principles. The execution of the Delivery activities results in full understanding of the vision and project requirements of the project team, the project outcome realization as expected, the benefits realization as expected, and the stakeholder acceptance and satisfaction of the project deliverables.

Measurement. This is mainly the implementation of the Build Quality into Processes and Deliverables, and Focus on Value principles. The Measurement performance domain is composed of the activities of project performance assessment, and the corrective and improvement actions to re-align the performance. Outcomes of this performance domain could be the understanding of the project status, data gathering to facilitate decisions, corrective actions to apply to the project, monitoring and adaptation of the business value metrics.

Uncertainty. Here we have all the activities to effectively implement the following principles: Recognize, Evaluate, and Respond to System Interactions, Navigate Complexity, and Optimize Risk Responses. It addresses risks (threats and opportunities we could know in advance), and uncertainty (threats and opportunities we have no knowledge of it in advance). Important outcomes of this performance domain are the setting of risks responses when risks are identifiable in advance and plannable for mitigation, and the promptness to react to events that are manifesting with no alerting signals, in a way to reduce the negative impacts on the project variables, or exploiting the positive impacts.

A.4 Tailoring

In this chapter of the *PMBOK® Guide* 7th Edition, there are details about a possible tailoring process. The chapter answers questions such as "Why to tailor?", "What to Tailor?", "How to tailor?". The tailoring exemplificative process description described in the chapter can be summarized as follows:

1. Select the initial development approach for the project;
2. Tailor based on the organizational processes;
3. Tailor based on project requirements such as size and criticality; and
4. Implement ongoing improvements.

A.5 Model, methods, artifacts

In this chapter of the *PMBOK® Guide* 7th Edition, some possible Model, Methods and Artifacts, useful in the project, are defined and in some cases also described. These are the definitions of the three concepts:

- A **Model** is a thinking strategy to explain a process, framework, or a phenomenon.
- A **Method** is the means for achieving an outcome, output, result, or project deliverable.
- An **Artifact** can be a template, document, output, or a project deliverable.

Models, Methods, and Artifacts are grouped by the performance Domains where they could be used more effectively. For instance, the Process Group model is related to Planning, Project Work, Delivery and Measurement performance domains; the Cynefin model is related to several performance domains including the Development Approach and life-cycle performance domain; the Backlog Refinement method is related to Stakeholders, Planning, Project Work and Delivery performance domain; the Risk registry artifact is related to uncertainty performance domain, etc.

There are hundreds of Models, Methods, and Artifacts referenced or described in the *PMBOK® Guide* 7th Edition, but this is not a comprehensive list. It does not want to be a comprehensive list, because Project

Management is a dynamic discipline and new Methods, Models, and Artifacts could come up from the experience on the fields, or innovations on the field. That's why the *PMBOK® Guide* 7th Edition is also annexed with a Digital Resource, that is a Web Site, where contents about Performance Domains, Models, Methods, and Artifacts are frequently updated; this is the "Standards Plus" PMI website.

Appendix B: Introduction to the *Agile Practice Guide*

As mentioned in the introduction to Chapter 4 of this book, in 2017 PMI published the *PMBOK® Guide* 6th Edition, which added references to the Agile mindset and Agile approaches in the body of the document to the previous version.

To better understand these additions, and to supplement the knowledge of project managers who knew little about agility, the *PMBOK® Guide* 6th Edition was delivered with a complementary book: The *Agile Practice Guide*. It helps bridge the gap between traditional and Agile approaches and is the result of collaboration between the Project Management Institute and the Agile Alliance.

The Agile Alliance is a nonprofit association founded following the publication of the Manifesto for Agile Software Development in 2001. Its overriding aim is to promote Agile values, principles, and practices among people and organizations. To achieve this, it provides a global set of resources, events, and communities. In 2023, it had over 72,000 members worldwide.

The content of the *Agile Practice Guide* is largely covered in Chapter 6 of this book. Therefore, the aim of this appendix is not to provide details, but to give the general structure and main ideas. This will enable you to identify where in the guide you may wish to go for further information on a particular subject. In view of its quality and moderate length, we recommend that you read the entire *Agile Practice Guide* anyway, whether in preparation for your certification or to improve your knowledge of agility.

B.1 Introduction

Agile is an iterative and incremental approach to delivering value to customers. It promotes adaptive planning, evolutionary development, and rapid and flexible response to change, all with a focus on customer collaboration and feedback.

The Agile manifesto

The foundation of Agile lies in the Agile Manifesto, emphasizing:

■ Individuals and Interactions over Processes and Tools,
■ Working Software over Comprehensive Documentation,
■ Customer Collaboration over Contract Negotiation,
■ Responding to Change over Following a Plan.

Underpinning these four values are twelve guiding principles. These principles, ranging from satisfying the customer through early and continuous delivery to maintaining a sustainable pace of work, are the compass by which Agile navigates.

From the vocabulary used, we can see that the initial field of application of the Agile manifesto was software development. In fact, the full name of the document was Manifesto for Agile Software Development. However, experience shows that, since its creation in 2001, the Agile mindset embodied by the four values and twelve principles has spread widely across all industries.

Several methodologies or frameworks fall under the so-called agile umbrella, including Scrum, Kanban, Lean, XP (Extreme Programming), and more. Each offers its own approach, but all adhere to the core Agile values and principles.

B.2 Life cycle selection

Different projects require different approaches (or life cycles). Factors affecting this choice include organizational culture, project size, and complexity.

The four main life cycles are the following:

- **Predictive life cycle:** It assumes the project's requirements are well-understood and stable. It is composed of sequential project phases (e.g., Analyze, Design, Build, Test, Deliver). There is a single delivery at the end of the project. The priority is to minimize cost by doing each activity once.
- **Iterative life cycle:** Allows to revisit any project phase multiple times as long as necessary, before moving to the next phase. There is a single delivery at the end of the project. The priority is to maximize the quality.
- **Incremental life cycle:** Provides successive partial solutions until the final product, each activity being performed once for each of the multiple deliveries. The priority is to deliver fast and frequently.
- **Agile life cycle:** Combines iterative and incremental processes to quickly deliver smaller, usable portions of a final product. The priority is to deliver value frequently thanks to the regular feedback received from the customer.

Factors to consider when selecting a life cycle include:

- Level of clarity regarding the solution;
- Stability of the project's scope;
- Frequency of changes; and
- Level of stakeholder involvement.

An hybrid approach consists in combining predictive, iterative, incremental, and/or agile approaches, according to the context of the project.

Different agile approaches can also be blended in the same project, such as Scrum, Kanban, and XP.

B.3 Implementing agile: Creating an agile environment

To implement agility in a team, it is crucial that its leader adopts a servant leader posture.

The servant leader creates an environment in which the team has a clear vision, is respected and recognized, as are the individuals who compose it, and can thrive to create Value.

The servant leader does not use hierarchical power but is a facilitator who puts himself at the service of the team to create the healthiest possible working environment, and to clear the way when it encounters external obstacles. The servant leader listens to and supports the team and raises stakeholder awareness so that everyone is aligned with the vision and the creation of Value.

Roles in an Agile team are generally divided between three main roles.

Team members (also called developers) are expected to bring together all the skills needed to be autonomous over the entire "product manufacturing chain", from idea to delivery to the end user (cross-functionality). As far as possible, the team is stable, dedicated, and co-located to foster collaboration.

The **Product owner** is empowered to prioritize the job to be done in order to maximize value while minimizing time and effort, relentlessly communicating with stakeholders and inside the Agile team.

The **Team facilitator** acts as a servant leader for the team

B.4 Implementing agile: Delivering in an agile environment

In an Agile environment, delivery is an ongoing process of incremental progress and value delivery.

In particular, this involves the use of practices such as backlog management, iteration planning, daily stand-ups, reviews and retrospectives.

Engineering practices such as continuous integration, ongoing testing, ATDD (Acceptance Test Driven Development), TDD (Test-Driven Development), and BDD (Behavior-Driven Development) can further enhance the quality of the team's work.

For example, with Test-Driven Development (TDD), developers first write tests for a new feature before crafting the code. This "test first" approach ensures the software functions as intended and reduces post-development defects.

Measuring agile project performance

Velocity is used predominantly in Scrum. It measures the amount of work a team completes in an iteration. By tracking velocity over time, teams can forecast future performance and make necessary adjustments.

Burn-Down and Burn-Up Charts are graphical representations providing insights into work progress. While a Burn-Down chart showcases the remaining work, a Burn-Up chart displays the completed work, offering a visual representation of the project's trajectory.

A Cumulative Flow Diagram visualizes the contents of a Kanban board, highlighting the evolution of the number of items in each column of the board, and the associated metrics (lead time, cycle time).

The metrics traditionally used in project management, organized around the notion of Earn Value Management, can also be transposed to an Agile context.

B.5 Organizational considerations for project agility

Running Agile projects in a traditional organization will generate changes and sometimes difficulties. Agile projects will be more effective and faster if they evolve in an organization that embraces agility as a whole. Such organizations also have the capacity to thrive in an increasingly uncertain world.

Whether for projects or, even more so, for organizations, moving toward greater agility represents a change that needs to be understood and piloted from a number of perspectives.

Fast and frequent deliveries and agile approaches may challenge the current way of working of the organization. Consequently, it's important to assess from the very start which existing factors are favorable to embrace agility (openness to change, budgeting cycle, etc.) as well as those which could constitute impediments (organizational silos, procurement management, etc.).

In the same way, the culture of the organization can be assessed through different possible models to identify the drivers that could be used as a priority, such as the level of appetence for exploration, speed, quality, flexibility, etc.

Procurement management is also required to evolve to enable the organization to enter into agility-compatible contracts with service providers. The evolution can concern several aspects, such as considering the value produced rather than the deliverables supplied, subdividing a monolithic global commitment into numerous smaller commitments that are easier to control, introducing a dynamic scope clause, etc.

In the most widespread Agile frameworks, such as Scrum, agility is approached for a team of around three to ten people. Sometimes, the amount of work to be done requires several agile teams to work together coherently. In this case, coordination can be ensured using scaled agility frameworks, such as SAFe (Scaled Agile Framework), LeSS (Large Scale Scrum), and DA (Disciplined Agile).

Still with the idea of coordinating work and teams in a relevant way, the notion of PMO (Project Management Office) can be adapted to agility with a logic focused on value creation and support.

Finally, the organization's evolution toward agility is a journey that will be even better supported and visualized if it also makes use of Agile tools and practices.

B.6 Annexes and appendices

You can find at the end of the *Agile Practice Guide* a useful annex describing the main Agile and Lean approaches and frameworks: Scrum, Kanban, XP, Crystal, Scrumban, FDD, DSDM, AUP, SoS, SAFe, LeSS, Enterprise Scrum, and Disciplined Agile.

An appendix also provides a visual model enabling decision-making about the Agile suitability of a project. This radar chart focuses on three main areas: Team, culture, and project. Before starting a project, it enables to see to which degree it could use a predictive, Agile, or hybrid approach.

Appendix C: Introduction to the *Business Analysis for Practitioners: A Practice Guide*

The *Business Analysis for Practitioners: A Practice Guide* (2015) is important to read as it contains a lot of the content you need to pass Domain 4: *Business Analysis Frameworks (27%)* for the CAPM® exam. Harvard Business Review (Hillman, 2013) calls the position of business analyst or data scientist the "sexiest job of the 21st century", so you better start reading. Also, it's a great read and relevant for other PMI certifications such as the PMI Project Management Ready and the PMI Professional in Business Analysis (PMI-PBA) certification. You can download the book for free (PDF version) at the global PMI website, if you have a PMI membership.

The book has the following structure which is very much aligned with the PMI-PBA Examination Content Outline.

- Chapter 1 – Introduction, page 1–10
- Chapter 2 – Need Assessment, page 11–36
- Chapter 3 – Business analysis planning, page 37–68
- Chapter 4 – Requirements elicitation and analysis, Page 69–136
- Chapter 5 – Traceability and Monitoring, page 137–156
- Chapter 6 – Solution evaluation, page 157–176
- Appendix x1, page 177–178
- Appendix x2, page 179–182
- Glossary, page 183–198
- Index, page 199–227

Table C.1 aligns the structure of the *Business Analysis for Practitioners: A Practice Guide* and the required reading for the CAPM® exam. You don't have to read chapter 1, but it is highly recommended, and chapters 2–6 is mandatory. If you have limited time, then read chapters 2 and 4. Appendices are of little use, but Glossary might be relevant for checking key terms.

Table C.1   Business analysis frameworks readings

Task #	*Domain 4:* Business Analysis Frameworks (27%)	*PMI* Business Analysis for Practitioners: A Practice Guide *(2015)*	
		Pages	*Chapter*
Task 1	Demonstrate an understanding of business analysis (BA) roles and responsibilities	11–36, 72	2 (4)
Task 2	Determine how to conduct stakeholder communication	132, 144	(5)
Task 3	Determine how to gather requirements	7, 11–36, 69–136, 137, 145, 157–176	4
Task 4	Demonstrate an understanding of product roadmaps	37–38, 72–75, 77–86, 151–154	(3) (4) (5)
Task 5	Determine how project methodologies influence business analysis processes		(2)
Task 6	Validate requirements through product delivery	111–117, 146–147, 157–-158, 169	(4) (5) (6)

Appendix D: Introduction to *The PMI Guide to Business Analysis*

The PMI Guide to Business Analysis is a great guide for Business Analysis work and relevant for the CAPM® exam in terms of Domain 4: *Business Analysis Frameworks (27%).* You can download the book for free at the global PMI website. However, much of the content is somewhat like the content found in the PMI *Business Analysis for Practitioners: A Practice Guide* (2015). The outline of *The PMI Guide to Business Analysis* is described below.

- Chapter 1 – Introduction, page 3–30
- Chapter 2 – The Environment in which Business Analysis is Conducted, page 32–42
- Chapter 3 – The Role of the Business Analyst, page 43–54
- Chapter 4 – Need assessment, page 55–108
- Chapter 5 – Stakeholder engagement, page 109–152
- Chapter 6 – Elicitation, page 153–174
- Chapter 7 – Analysis, page 175–250
- Chapter 8 – Traceability and Monitoring, page 251–276
- Chapter 9 – Solution Evaluation, page 277–300
- The standard for Business Analysis, page 303–346
- Appendix x1, page 351–356
- Appendix x2, page 357
- Appendix x3, page 367–380

As you can see-, chapters 4–9 is like chapters 2–6 in the PMI *Business Analysis for Practitioners: A Practice Guide.* But most of the CAPM® exam relevant content is found in chapters 5 and 7, which should be your focus if you want to limit your reading. Alternatively read the first 300 pages. One of the strengths of the book is the ten pages of Appendix x2 which describes the tools and techniques categorized in both books and Appendix x3 which highlights the Business analysis competencies required. Both appendices are extremely relevant for the overview of the CAPM® exam content for this domain. The reading mapped with the Examination Content Outline is documented in Table D.1.

Table D.1   Business analysis frameworks readings

Task #	*Domain 4:* Business Analysis Frameworks (27%)	The PMI Guide to Business Analysis *(December 2017)*	
		Pages	*Chapter*
Task 1	Demonstrate an understanding of business analysis (BA) roles and responsibilities	229–236	7
Task 2	Determine how to conduct stakeholder communication	109–152, 223, 232–235, 368	5
Task 3	Determine how to gather requirements	112, 159–163, 212–215, 251–276, 277–300	5, 8
Task 4	Demonstrate an understanding of product roadmaps	92–95, 182–207, 281–282	7, 9
Task 5	Determine how project methodologies influence business analysis processes		
Task 6	Validate requirements through product delivery	66–72, 175–250	7

Appendix E: PMI Code of Ethics and Professional Conduct

The concept of a professional Code of Ethics and Professional Conduct has been common throughout history, as evidenced by the early use of the Hippocratic oath within health care. Ethics has been defined as involving the systematic application of moral, rules, standards, or principles to concrete problems. Ethics involves learning what is right or wrong and then doing the right thing.

Aside from the obvious, the reasons for ethical behaviors are many. One is the retention of high-quality employees. Another, according to respected leaders, is that it is a requirement for long-term success and media exposure. Ethics and project management are closely related and are part of the day-to-day project management activities, whether that be dealing with the objectives of the project, stakeholders, risks, or the project team.

We live with the assumption that *"the modern day, well-educated and responsible project manager must possess the knowledge and skills to be able to discern and debate ethical issues"* (Helgadóttir, 2007). This is where the PMI Code of Ethics and Professional Conduct springs into action. *"Codes of ethics are valuable as they both raise awareness of ethical issues and dilemmas that professionals may potentially face and serve to enhance the public profile of the profession. Furthermore, codes of ethics may provide clarifications about the conduct deemed acceptable in client-professional relationships"* (Davison, 2000).

In general ethics can be outcome or process oriented. The PMI Code of Ethics & Professional Conduct seems to be inspired by the outcome-oriented virtues in terms of virtue ethics, the mark of the profession and utilitarianism where we conduct our tasks as project managers or Agile team member for the benefit of as many people as possible. The process-oriented ethics of deontology and egoism are at bay while preserving the natural rights of others and being respectful of their duties come to the fore. Table E.1 illustrates the nature of ethics (Wood-Harper et al., 2010).

Table E.1 Nature of ethics

Label	Beneficiary	Objective	Good
Deontological	Not considered	Follow the rules	Follow the rules
Individual consequentiality (egoist ethic)	Individual	Maximize good for individual	Happiness well-being, fame, riches
Group consequentiality	Group (social group, organization nation)	Maximize good for group	Survival, autonomy, ascendancy
Utilitarian	Society as a whole	Maximize good for human race or all sentient beings	Life, liberty, standard, or living

PMI developed the PMI Code of Ethics and Professional Conduct to provide some guidance to all PMI members and credential holders to adhere to a high standard of ethical behavior. Ethical behavior is important in satisfying basic human needs as many professionals have a need to work in an ethically sound way. Some academics argue that ethical behavior creates credibility which can help during the project to make things work. Unethical behavior is a strong force for conflict in projects, while ethical behavior can unite people and help create a strong basis for a good project execution.

Ethical behavior is also a robust basis for decision-making. IBM's global CEO study Leading through Connections 2012 based upon interviews with 1709 CEOs in 64 countries and 18 industries reveals that when it comes to the organizational attributes that engage employees to draw out the best in their workforces, CEOs are most focused on ethics and value. Ethical behavior has a wide range of long-term gains, while the lack of ethical behavior can cause its own wide range of distress for most projects and participants. Table E.2 (Wood-Harper et al., 2010) illustrates how the ethical approaches of different stakeholders affect their decision-making and behavior.

Table E.2 Ethical approaches of different stakeholders

Stakeholder	Ethics	Example
Government	Group consequentiality	Triage rules and other service trade-offs
CHS	Deontological egoist	Legal compliance and continued funding
Business manager	Egoist group consequentiality	Salary increase and group harmony
Nurse	Deontological	Follow management directives
Client/patient	Egoist	Increase good health

An article by Aiken (Aiken et al., 2004) entitled Using Codes of Conduct to Resolve Legal Disputes highlighted another key aspect of the application of Code of Conducts: as court evidence. The customer would expect and state in most types of contracts that their vendor follow best practice and code of conduct within the industry. If things go bad in the project and in the negotiations following, the project may end up in court where the code of conduct may be applied against the vendor.

Vision

PMI created a vision for ethical behavior:

> *As practitioners of project management, we are committed to doing what is right and honorable. We set high standards for ourselves and we aspire to meet these standards in all aspects of our lives – at work, at home, and in service to our profession.*

This Code of Ethics and Professional Conduct describes the expectations that we have of ourselves and our fellow practitioners in the global project management community. It articulates the ideals to which we aspire as well as the behaviors that are mandatory in our professional and volunteer roles (PMI, 2012).

Purpose

The code of PMI enhances the profession and helps us become better professionals.

The purpose of this Code is to instill confidence in the project management profession and to help an individual become a better practitioner. We do this by establishing a profession-wide understanding of appropriate behavior. We believe that the credibility and reputation of the project management profession is shaped by the collective conduct of individual practitioners. We believe that we can advance our profession, both individually and collectively, by embracing this Code of Ethics and Professional Conduct. We also believe that this Code will assist us in making wise decisions, particularly when faced with difficult situations where we may be asked to compromise our integrity or our values. Our hope that this Code of Ethics and Professional Conduct will serve as a catalyst for others to study, deliberate, and write about ethics and values. Further, we hope that this Code will ultimately be used to build upon and evolve our profession.

(PMI, 2012)

It would be great if the code could apply to all Agile practitioners and professionals in project management, but that is hardly the case, as most outside the PMI world are unfamiliar with the code. This means that the code of ethics and professional conduct only applies to PMI members and individuals who are not members of PMI but meet one or more of the following criteria:

■ Non-members who hold a PMI certification.
■ Non-members who apply to commence a PMI certification process.
■ Non-members who serve PMI in a volunteer capacity.

(PMI.org, 2012)

Those who do not follow the code miss the opportunity to give something back to the project management profession and improve themselves as practitioners. At a formal level, failure to follow the code may also mean that PMI members can be expelled, but that is another story.

Structure

The Code of Ethics & Professional Conduct is divided into sections that contain standards of conduct which are aligned with the four values.

These values were identified as most important to the project management community:

- Responsibility
- Respect
- Fairness
- Honesty

(PMI, 2012)

Each section of the Code of Ethics and Professional Conduct includes both aspirational standards and mandatory standards. The aspirational standards describe the conduct that we strive to uphold as practitioners.

Although adherence to the aspirational standards is not easily measured, conducting ourselves in accordance with these is an expectation that we have of ourselves as professionals – it is not optional.

The mandatory standards establish firm requirements and, in some cases, limit or prohibit practitioner behavior. Practitioners who do not conduct themselves in accordance with these standards will be subject to disciplinary procedures before PMI's Ethics Review Committee.

(PMI, 2012)

Responsibility

The first of the four general values is responsibility. It is a basic standard for ethical behavior and is spelled out by several mandatory and aspirational standards. Hopefully, most Agile practitioners should be able to recognize and commit to the mandatory values without having to make too many changes in their life. The aspirational standards falling under the category of responsibility may be slightly more abstract, but they, too, contain many good concepts to bear in mind. Included in the standard of responsibility are several mandatory standards of responsibility.

Mandatory Standards of Responsibility:

- We inform ourselves and uphold the policies, rules, regulations, and laws that govern our work, professional, and volunteer activities.
- We report unethical or illegal conduct to appropriate management and, if necessary, to those affected by the conduct.
- We bring violations of this Code to the attention of the appropriate body for resolution.

- We only file ethics complaints when they are substantiated by facts.
- We pursue disciplinary action against an individual who retaliates against a person raising ethics concerns.

Aspirational Standards of Responsibility:

- We make decisions and take actions based on the best interests of society, public safety, and the environment.
- We accept only those assignments that are consistent with our background, experience, skills, and qualifications.
- We fulfill the commitments that we undertake – we do what we say we will do.
- When we make errors or omissions, we take ownership and make corrections promptly. When we discover errors or omissions caused by others, we communicate them to the appropriate body as soon as they are discovered. We accept accountability for any issues resulting from our errors or omissions and any resulting consequences.
- We protect proprietary or confidential information that has been entrusted to us.
- We uphold this Code and hold each other accountable to it.

In an Agile context, the value of responsibility lies in making ethical decisions and reporting unethical behaviors. In Agile, ethical decisions are made by the empowered teams made up of five to nine people. A group of this size gives a good base for ethical decisions as most of the members can guide one or two confused Agile practitioners. Several of the Agile methodologies are based upon values like the PMI code of conduct. Extreme Programming has the core values of respect and courage, which are closely related to the PMI view on responsibility.

Respect

The second value is respect. The fact that it is second on the list does not imply that respect is second to responsibility. All four core values are equally important. Respect is perhaps one of the four that is the most integral to Agile DNA.

Respect includes negotiating in good faith. Part of the Agile manifesto our commitment to seek customer collaboration over contract negotiation. This certainly implies that we negotiate in good faith and will go a long way to find a proper solution rather than resort to a legal solution.

Negotiations are also an integrated part of working Agile. We talk or negotiate all the time whether it is with the product owner or in the team when we make estimates. Respect also means that we do not use our position to gain favor. This is a misuse of leadership. In Agile, we favor servant leadership. Leaders who serve the team will not use an opportunity to use their position over those lower in the hierarchy. The team is empowered and consists of individuals who can make it difficult for one or two team members to use their positions in self-serving ways.

Respect also applies to how we relate to other cultures or people who are different. In Agile, we work in a global environment, whether the teams are collocated or distributed. We put great effort into creating high-performing teams where cultural differences and diversity are strengths rather than weaknesses. Agile is global born. Ideas and concepts flow globally and are established in respect for the work being done. If a team struggles with the proper level of respect, we have in place methods for conflict resolution, coaches, and monthly retrospectives that give the team a range of opportunities to tackle the issue.

Mandatory standards

- We negotiate in good faith.
- We do not exercise the power of our expertise or position to influence the decisions or actions of others to benefit personally at their expense.
- We do not act in an abusive manner toward others.
- We respect the property rights of others.

Aspirational standards

- We inform ourselves about the norms and customs of others and avoid engaging in behaviors they might consider disrespectful.
- We listen to others' points of view, seeking to understand them.
- We directly approach those persons with whom we have a conflict or disagreement.
- We conduct ourselves in a professional manner, even when it is not reciprocated.

Fairness

The value of fairness includes an aspirational standard of transparency. This is very much in line with Agile thinking as we go to great lengths to demonstrate transparency. In Agile, we communicate frequently and maintain a high level of information within the team. Information is posted on information radiators and boards for various purposes, not the least of which is the need for transparency.

Fairness also deals with resolving conflicts. Agile has the tools and procedures in place to deal with them quickly and in a fair manner. Conflicts are part of working Agile, so it is not a big deal. People in teams are experienced in handling them effectively. Fairness also contains an element of nondiscrimination, which can be an issue with distributed teams who might work under different conditions. Agile cannot prevent unfair events because Agile is like a human being, who can be by nature unfair. But Agile techniques and concepts offer tools and techniques that address unfairness.

Mandatory standards

- We proactively and fully disclose any real or potential conflicts of interest to the appropriate stakeholders.
- When we realize that we have a real or potential conflict of interest, we refrain from engaging in the decision-making process or otherwise attempting to influence outcomes, unless or until: we have made full disclosure to the affected stakeholders, we have an approved mitigation plan, and we have obtained the consent of the stakeholders to proceed.
- We do not hire or fire, reward or punish, or award or deny contracts based on personal considerations, including but not limited to, favoritism, nepotism, or bribery.
- We do not discriminate against others based on, but not limited to gender, race, age, religion, disability, nationality, or sexual orientation.
- We apply the rules of the organization (employer, Project Management Institute, or other group) without favoritism or prejudice.

Aspirational standards

- We demonstrate transparency in our decision-making process.
- We constantly re-examine our impartiality and objectivity, taking corrective action as appropriate.

- We provide equal access to information to those who are authorized to have that information.
- We make opportunities equally available to qualified candidates.

Honesty

The fourth value is honesty, and one might wonder why such a basic ethical behavior is highlighted. Still, consider that the concept of honesty might vary quite a lot between people, nationalities, or cultures. Transparency is part of being honest about what we are doing. This works well with Agile practices with public truthful communications and accurate information. In addition, we use techniques like value-driven development to understand the truth to deliver value to our customers.

Mandatory standards

- We do not engage in or condone behavior that is designed to deceive others, including but not limited to, making misleading or false statements, stating half-truths, providing information out of context, or withholding information that, if known, would render our statements as misleading or incomplete.
- We do not engage in dishonest behavior with the intention of personal gain or at the expense of another.

Aspirational standards

- We earnestly seek to understand the truth.
- We are truthful in our communications and in our conduct.
- We provide accurate information in a timely manner.
- We make commitments and promises, implied or explicit, in good faith.
- We strive to create an environment in which others feel safe to tell the truth.

E.1 Sample test questions on Code of Ethics and Professional Conduct

This section contains five short exam questions in the CAPM® format for you to check your knowledge of the content presented in this chapter and to check your readiness for the CAPM® exam. The answers will be provided in the next section. If you make mistakes, you should go back and learn why mistakes were made. Do not learn the questions and answers, learn the content.

Question 1
What is the difference between aspirational and mandatory standards, as referred to in the PMI Code?

A. Aspirational standards are not mandatory but good practice and encouraged
B. Aspirational standards are backed by federal law and mandatory backed by state and local law
C. Aspirational standards are enforced by state law and mandatory standards are backed by federal law
D. Both are compulsory standards and backed by law

Question 2
While leading a risk workshop, a subject matter expert disagrees with a decision you have made and makes it a point to be very vocal about it. He uses the meeting to express his doubts of your skills and even goes so far as to suggest that your race plays a part in the way you make decisions. How should you react?

A. Do nothing. File a complaint with the manager's boss after the meeting
B. Use your authority as the meeting leader to take control of the discussion and present your rebuttal
C. Suggest an immediate meeting between the two of you to discuss your differences
D. Bring the manager's boss into the meeting and ask for assistance in addressing his comments

Question 3
A team member is stealing from the company – Which value is violated?

A. Responsibility
B. Respect
C. Fairness
D. Honesty

Question 4

You work for a European-based company hired to perform risk management services in a foreign country. Other companies who have done business in this country inform you that gifts must be made to the government to obtain the necessary approvals. What do you do?

    A. Offer the recommended gifts to obtain project approvals
    B. Do not offer gifts to obtain project approvals
    C. Ignore the need for project approvals
    D. Both B and C

Question 5

You are responsible for developing a cost estimate to bid on a government contract. The scope was set by the government. Your supervisor says the cost estimate is too expensive and should be reduced by one-third to assure your company wins the contract. Your analysis shows that any reduction to the proposed cost estimate makes the project unable to meet the specified scope. What do you do?

    A. Reduce the cost estimate and submit the proposal
    B. Submit your initial cost estimate without reducing the cost
    C. Explain to your supervisor in writing that your analysis shows a reduction in the cost estimate makes the project unable to meet the specified scope
    D. Both A and C

Answer to Question 1: The correct answer is A.
Aspirational standards are standards that every professional should strive to uphold but are not compulsory. Mandatory standards are required and often backed by law.

Answer to Question 2: The correct answer is C.
The PMI Code of Ethics and Professional Conduct requires that you act in a professional manner even when others do not. Answer A is incorrect because doing nothing solves nothing. Going to the manager's boss is likely to make the situation worse, not better. Answer B is incorrect because it is an emotional response, not a professional one. Answer D is incorrect because you should always first attempt to solve differences one-on-one.

Answer to Question 3: The correct answer is A.
Stealing is a case of many broken values; however, it is considered part of Responsibility, which is probably the best answer, while B, C, and D to some degrees also are violated.

Answer to Question 4: The correct answer is B.
Answer A is not correct because you have a responsibility to refrain from offering inappropriate gifts for personal gain. The exemption regarding conformity with applicable laws or customs of the country where project management services are being performed does not apply because you are working for a European-based company and are subject to EU law. Answers C and D are incorrect because you have a responsibility to comply with laws and regulations in the country where providing project management services requires project approvals.

Answer to Question 5: The correct answer is C.
You have a responsibility to provide accurate and truthful representations in the preparation of estimates concerning costs, services, and expected results. This responsibility makes Answers A and D inappropriate. You have accountability to your management and Answer B is not appropriate because you are usurping your manager's authority and undermining your own professional conduct by doing so.

Appendix F: Project Management Ready

The PMI Project Management Ready™ certification is for practitioners new to projects with 0–3 years of experience. The same applies for the CAPM® exam.

The PMI Project Management Ready certification is a way for students to immerse themselves in the project management industry and connect with this passionate community of professionals including tools needed to apply this knowledge to a wide range of career paths and to the student's day-to-day activities.

The PMI Project Management Ready introduces learners to Project Management Fundamentals and Core Concepts, Traditional Plan-Based Methodologies, Agile Frameworks/Methodologies, and Business Analyst Frameworks.

The Examination Content Outline of the Project Management Ready certification is described. The content is very similar to the CAPM® exam. We completed both exams, so we know you can use this book if you want to prepare for the CAPM® or the Project Management Ready exam. Topic 1 matches Chapter 3 of this book, topic 2 matches chapter of this book, and so on.

Project Management Fundamentals and Core Concepts (Read Chapter 4 for details)

    1.1 Recognize core terminology

        1.1.1 Define a project, product, program, portfolio, etc.

        1.1.2 Define project management

        1.1.3 Define a business case

        1.1.4 Define project scope

1.1.5 Define deliverables

1.1.6 Define a milestone and task

1.1.7 List components of a project

1.1.8 List components of a business case

1.1.9 Define issues, risks, assumptions, and constraints

1.1.10 Identify features of traditional plan-based delivery

1.1.11 Identify features of agile delivery

1.1.12 Identify project management ethics (refer to PMI code of ethics)

1.2 Identify concepts and terminology of project management planning

1.2.1 Identify concepts of a project management plan (e.g., cost, quality, risk, schedule, etc.)

1.2.2 Define the different types of resources (e.g., human and material)

1.2.3 Identify common terminology in business concepts related to project management (e.g., change management, culture, strategy, governance, trade-off, performance metrics, prioritization, categorization, work breakdown, reporting, conflict, accuracy vs. precision, leadership, and motivation, etc.)

1.2.4 Identify the features of different organizational environments (e.g., co-location and virtual teams, decentralized and centralized organization, and organizational structures (functional, matrix, projectized))

1.2.5 Describe organizational structures (e.g., co-location and virtual teams, decentralized and centralized organization, and organizational structures (functional, matrix, projectized))

1.2.6 Identify benefits and concepts associated with the risk register

1.2.7 Identify benefits and concepts associated with the stakeholder register

1.3 Identify project roles and responsibilities

1.3.1 Define the key stakeholder roles such as project managers, sponsors, team leaders, team members, project clients, etc.

1.3.2 Define the key stakeholder responsibilities such as project managers, sponsors, team leaders, team members, project clients, etc.

1.3.3 Identify leadership and management

1.4 Identify tools and systems used for or associated with project management

1.4.1 Identify the typical tools used for creating a project schedule

1.4.2 Define the characteristics and benefits of various project management tools

1.5 Identify common problem-solving tools and techniques

1.5.1 Define common information-gathering tools or techniques

1.5.2 Describe the components of an effective meeting

Traditional Plan-Based Methodologies (Read Chapter 5 for details)

2.1 Recognize when a traditional plan-based approach is appropriate

2.1.1 Identify the primary rationale for traditional plan-based projects

2.1.2 Identify the process groups and knowledge areas (e.g., cost, quality, risk, schedule, etc.)

2.1.3 Identify project phases and the correct order of the phases

2.1.4 Define a typical project structure for a traditional plan-based approach

2.2 Identify attributes of a project management plan schedule

2.2.1 Identify the steps to create a schedule

2.2.2 Define a work breakdown structure

2.2.3 List the types of dependencies (e.g., sequence, start to start, finish to start, etc.)

2.2.4 Define a critical path

2.3 Identify attributes of executing and controlling traditional plan-based projects

2.3.1 Describe the project controls in traditional plan-based projects (e.g., earned value, baselines, etc.)

2.3.2 Identify monitoring and controlling techniques in traditional plan-based projects

3 Agile Frameworks/Methodologies (Read Chapter 6 for details)

3.1 Recognize when agile project management is appropriate

3.1.1 Identify the primary rationale for agile and traditional plan-based projects

3.1.2 Identify the key tenants/principles of agile

3.1.3 Recognize hybridization

3.1.4 Define the use of transparency in Agile projects

3.1.5 Describe the principle of Servant Leadership

3.1.6 Describe the process of engaging customers

3.1.7 Identify common Agile methodologies

3.2 Identify attributes of plan iterations of a project

3.2.1 State the components of Agile sequencing

3.2.2 Identify the factors/inputs for determining the framework (e.g., time, scope, etc.)

3.2.3 Identify Agile project progress metrics

3.2.4 State the importance of Agile project tracking

3.3 Identify Agile roles and responsibilities

3.3.1 Define the role of the Agile project lead

3.3.2 Define the role of the Agile project member

3.3.3 Identify good team principles in Agile project management

3.3.4 Identify examples of team collaboration in Agile project management

3.4 Identify attributes of document project controls of an Agile project

3.4.1 Describe the project controls in Agile projects

3.4.2 Identify monitor and controlling techniques in Agile project Identify components of an Agile plan

3.5 Identify components of an Agile plan

3.5.1 Identify the components of a specific agile plan (e.g., Scrum, XP, Scaled Agile Framework, Kanban, etc.)

3.6 Describe task management steps (e.g., decomposition, prioritize, etc.)

3.6.1 Describe the task decomposition process in an agile project management

3.6.2 Describe the task prioritization process in an agile project management

3.6.3 Identify stakeholders of the final product

Business Analysis Frameworks (Read Chapter 7 for details)

4.1 Identify business analysis roles and responsibilities

4.1.1 List critical/core stakeholder roles and responsibilities (e.g., business analysts, business sponsor, process owner, product manager, product owner, etc.)

4.1.2 Define types of roles (internal vs external)

4.2 Identify attributes of stakeholder communication

    4.2.1 List elements in a communication plan

    4.2.2 Identify communication channels/tools

4.3 Identify attributes related to gathering requirements

    4.3.1 List types of requirements (e.g., functional, nonfunctional, stakeholder, security, solution, business, migrating, market research, benchmarking, etc.)

    4.3.2 List ways of gathering requirements

    4.3.3 List tools used for capturing requirements (e.g., use case, user stories, process diagrams, etc.)

    4.3.4 Define requirements traceability matrix/product backlog

4.4 Identify product roadmap attributes

    4.4.1 Define what a product roadmap is

    4.4.2 List product roadmap components

    4.4.3 Define a release plan

4.5 Identify components of product delivery

    4.5.1 Define components of project/product acceptance (e.g., requirements traceability matrix/product backlog, transition plan, etc.)

Glossary of terms and acronyms

A

Acceptance criteria: The criteria that a system or component must satisfy in order to be accepted by a user, customer, or other authorized entity.

Affinity diagram: A group creativity technique that allows a large number of ideas to be classified into groups for review and analysis.

Adaptive approach: A development approach focused on the discovery and progressive refinement of user needs all along the project.

Agile: An iterative and incremental approach to the project that emphasizes collaboration, adaptability, and delivering value to customers.

Assumption: a form of hypothesis considered to be true to enable project planning.

B

Backlog: A prioritized list of requirements, tasks, or user stories that are yet to be addressed or completed in a project or agile development.

Baseline: A formal approved version of the scope, schedule, and cost plan of a project. It serves as a benchmark for measuring project performance.

Benchmarking: The comparison of actual or planned practices, such as processes and operations, to those of comparable organizations to identify best practices, generate ideas for improvements, and provide a basis for measuring performance.

Benefits: See business value.

Burn-down Chart: A visual representation of the work remaining versus time during a sprint or project, showing the progress made toward completing the planned work.

Brainstorming: Rapid technique to gather ideas.

Burn-down Chart: A visual representation of the work remaining versus time during a sprint or project, showing the progress made toward completing the planned work.

Business Case: A document that justifies the need for a project, outlining its expected benefits, costs, risks, and potential return on investment. This documented economic feasibility study is used as a basis for the authorization of further project management activities.

Business value: A concept that is unique to each organization and includes tangible and intangible elements, through the effective use of project, program, and portfolio management disciplines, organizations will possess the ability to employ reliable, established processes to meet enterprise objectives and obtain greater business value from their investment.

Business need: The impetus for a change in an organization, based on an existing problem or opportunity. The business need provides the rationale for initiating a project or program.

C

Capability: The ability to add value or achieve objectives in an organization through a function, process, service, or other proficiency.

Cause and effect diagram: See root cause analysis.

Change Control: A formal process to evaluate, approve, and manage change requests to project scope, schedule, and budget to ensure they align with project objectives.

Change Management: The process of preparing, equipping, and supporting individuals and teams to effectively adopt and adapt to project-related changes. Or the process to enable the organization to receive and use the deliverables of the project.

Constraint: an element that limits the range of possibilities for executing a project (e.g. schedule, cost).

Context Diagram: A visual depiction of the project scope showing a business system (process, equipment, computer system, etc.) and how people and other systems (Actors) interact with it.

Continuous Integration: The practice of frequently integrating code changes from multiple developers into a shared repository, allowing for early detection of integration issues.

Compliance standard: Adherence to standards or regulations.

Control Chart: A statistical tool used to monitor and display process variation over time, helping identify and address anomalies or out-of-control situations.

Cost-Benefit Analysis: A financial analysis tool used to determine the benefits provided by a project against its costs.

Creative thinking: The ability to come up with unique, original solutions.

D

Daily Stand-up: A brief daily meeting where team members discuss their progress, plans, and any potential obstacles, fostering transparency and alignment within the team.

Decision Tree: A graphical representation of different possible decisions, their potential outcomes, and associated probabilities, aiding in decision-making processes.

Definition of Done: A shared understanding and agreement within the team on the criteria that must be met for a user story, feature, or increment of product to be considered complete and ready for release.

Deliverable: A tangible or intangible output produced because of completing a project or a phase or an activity.

Dependency: A relationship between project tasks or activities.

Document Analysis: An elicitation technique that analyzes existing documentation and identifies information relevant to the requirements.

E

Earned Value Management (EVM): A technique used to measure project performance by comparing planned value, earned value, and actual costs.

Epic: Large body of work, with size not fitting in one iteration, that can be broken down into smaller features, providing a high-level view of product requirements.

Estimation: The process of determining the approximate effort, time, resources, and cost required to complete project activities or deliverables.

Expert Judgment: Judgment provided based upon expertise in an application area, knowledge area, discipline, industry, etc., as appropriate for the activity being performed. Such expertise may be provided by any group or person with specialized education, knowledge, skill, experience, or training.

F

Feature: A distinct functionality or capability, with size fitting in one iteration, that delivers value to users or customers. Features are often decomposed in User Stories.

Five Whys technique: A form for root cause analysis.

Float: The amount of time an activity or task can be delayed without impacting the project's critical path or overall project duration.

Force Field Analysis: Decision-making technique.

G

Gantt Chart: A visual representation of a project schedule that shows tasks, milestones, and dependencies over time, allowing for better planning and tracking.

Gate Review: A formal review conducted at specific project milestones or decision points to assess the project's progress, risks, and readiness for the next phase.

Governance: The framework and processes established to ensure effective decision-making, accountability, and control throughout the project lifecycle.

H

Hybrid approach: A development approach that combines elements of different other approaches, such as adaptive and predictive, tailored to specific project needs.

I

Impact Analysis: An assessment of the potential consequences or effects of a proposed change or risk event on project objectives, scope, schedule, or resources.

Increment: A visible, working product functionality that is produced at the end of each iteration, showcasing progress toward the final product.

Initiation: A Process Group name of the Process Group model, where the project is defined, and stakeholders are identified.

Interviews: A formal or informal approach to elicit information from a group of stakeholders by asking questions and documenting the responses provided by the interviewees.

Issue: A problem that arises during the project execution, requiring attention, analysis, and resolution.

Issue Log: A document or tool used to record, track, and manage project issues or problems, including their status, priority, and resolution actions.

Iteration: The work done in a fixed time, usually one to four weeks, by the development team to complete a set of tasks and deliver a potentially shippable increment of the product.

J

Just-in-Time (JIT): A project management approach that aims to minimize waste, reduce inventory, and deliver necessary resources or materials precisely when needed.

K

Kanban: A visual project management method that focuses on optimizing the flow of work, using a Kanban board to visualize tasks and their progress.

Kano classification: Technique using dissatisfiers, satisfiers, and delighters to prioritize requirements.

Key Performance Indicator (KPI): A quantifiable metric used to measure and evaluate the success of a project or specific objectives within the project.

Kickoff Meeting: An initial meeting held at the start of a project to communicate project objectives, roles, responsibilities, and expectations to the project team and stakeholders.

L

Lean: A philosophy and methodology that aims to eliminate waste and maximize customer value by continuously improving processes and reducing unnecessary work.

Lessons Learned: Insights, knowledge, and practices gained from past projects or project phases, used to improve future project performance.

Life cycle: all the sequential phases a project goes through from start to finish.

M

Milestone: A significant event or achievement in a project that marks the completion of a phase, deliverable, or important objective.

Minimum Viable Product (MVP): The most basic version of a product that contains enough features to provide value to early users and gather feedback for further iterations and enhancements.

Multivoting process: A technique used to facilitate decision-making among a group of stakeholders. Participants are provided with a limited number of votes and are asked to apply those votes to a list of possible options. The option with the most votes is determined to be the most favorable option. Multivoting processes can be used to prioritize requirements, determine the most favorable solution, or to identify the most favorable response to a problem.

MoSCoW prioritization: Technique to prioritize requirements.

O

Operations: Ongoing activities carried out to run a company or execute a business process, with no specified start or end date.

Outcome: The observable result obtained at the end of a project or iteration.

Outsourcing: The practice of delegating project tasks, activities, or processes to external vendors or contractors, leveraging their expertise or resources.

P

Persona: Make up pretend users.

Planning Poker: A collaborative estimation technique used in Agile projects, where team members assign relative effort or complexity points to user stories or tasks using a deck of cards.

Portfolio: Set of projects, programs, portfolios and operations coherently grouped around a strategic objective.

Predictive approach: A development approach that details a project as much as possible right from its start (scope, schedule, etc.).

Problem solving: The process of finding solutions to difficult or complex issues.

Product: A measurable artifact resulting from the end of a project or an intermediate stage.

Procurement: The process of acquiring goods, services, or resources from external sources to support project needs, often involving contracts or agreements.

Product Backlog: A prioritized list of user stories, and features, that need to be realized in an Adaptive project.

Product management: All activities carried out using resources during a product's life cycle, from the idea to its retirement.

Product Owner: The person responsible for representing the interests of the stakeholders and prioritizing the product backlog.

Product roadmap: An overview that shows an overall plan with each planned release and the relevant features associated with those releases.

Program: A set of projects and programs that have a common objective and whose coordination makes it possible to obtain overall benefits that cannot be achieved individually by its components.

Project management: Discipline applied to project activities to achieve project objectives

Project manager: The individual responsible for driving the team to reach project goals.

Project Charter: A document that formally authorizes the existence of a project, defines its high-level objectives, scope, and stakeholders, establishes initial constraints, and formally identifies the project manager.

Project Schedule Network Diagram: A visual representation of project activities and their dependencies, typically shown using nodes (activities) and arrows (dependencies).

Project team: The people who carry out the project's activities in order to reach its goals.

Proof of Concept: Evidence, typically deriving from an experiment or pilot project, which demonstrates that a design concept, business proposal, etc. is feasible.

Prototype: A method of obtaining early feedback on requirements by providing a working model or the expected product before actually building it.

Q

Quality Assurance (QA): The process of defining the quality processes to adopt to verify that project deliverables meet specified requirements and standards through planned activities and audits.

Quality Control: The set of activities and techniques used to monitor and verify that project deliverables meet specified quality standards.

R

RACI model: A common type of responsibility assignment matrix that uses responsible, accountable, consult, and inform statuses to define the involvement of stakeholders in project activities.

Resource: Any person or material element necessary for the project's work.

Resource Leveling: A technique used to adjust project schedules and resource assignments to optimize resource utilization and balance workloads.

Retrospective: A team meeting held at the end of an iteration to reflect on what went well in the processes, what could be improved, and to identify actionable steps for future iterations.

Requirement: A condition or capability to which a system must conform.

Requirements documentation: A description of how individual requirements meet the business need for the project.

Requirements Elicitation: The activity of drawing out information from stakeholders and other sources for the purpose of further understanding the needs of the business, to address a problem or opportunity, and the stakeholders' preferences and conditions for the solution that will address those needs.

Requirement Management Plan: A component of the project or program management plan that describes how requirements will be analyzed, documented, and managed.

Requirement Traceability Matrix: A grid that links product requirements from their origin to the deliverables that satisfy them.

Risk: An event that may happen, the realization of which may have negative or positive consequences for the achievement of the project's objectives.

Risk Assessment: The process of identifying, analyzing, and evaluating risks and their impacts on project objectives, followed by appropriate risk response planning.

S

Scope: The sum of the products, services, and results to be provided as a project. In business analysis, scope is defined as the boundary for the product, services, or results. Scope can be split into product and project scope.

Scope Creep: The gradual not controlled expansion of a project's scope beyond its original boundaries, often resulting in increased costs and timeline delays.

Scrum: An Agile framework that divides work into time-boxed iterations called sprints, with specific roles (Scrum Master, Product Owner, Development Team) and ceremonies (Sprint Planning, Daily Stand-up, Sprint Review, Sprint Retrospective).

Scrum Master: The facilitator and servant-leader of the Scrum team, responsible for ensuring that Scrum principles and practices are followed, removing impediments, and fostering a productive environment.

Sprint: A time-boxed iteration, typically lasting one to four weeks, during which the development team works to complete a set of user stories or tasks. Sprint is the term used in Scrum instead of the term Iteration

Sprint Planning: A collaborative meeting held at the beginning of each sprint to determine the work to be done, select user stories from the product backlog, and create a sprint backlog.

Sprint Review: A meeting held at the end of a sprint to demonstrate the completed work to stakeholders, gather feedback, and identify any adjustments or changes needed for future sprints.

Sponsor: For a project, a sponsor is a person or group, often from the top management of the performing organization, who is responsible for supporting the project, providing resources and strategic decisions when needed.

Stakeholder: An individual, group, or organization that has an interest in or is affected by the project and can influence its outcomes or be influenced by them.

Stakeholder Analysis: A technique of systematically gathering and analyzing quantitative and qualitative information to determine whose interests should be taken into account throughout the project.

Story Points: A relative measure of effort or complexity assigned to user stories or tasks during estimation, helping the team gauge the amount of work.

SWOT analysis: Analysis of strengths, weaknesses, opportunities, and threats of an organization, project, or option.

T

Test-Driven Development (TDD): A development practice where tests are written before the code, driving the development process and ensuring that the code meets the specified requirements.

Timeboxing: Setting fixed time periods, known as timeboxes, for completing specific project activities, phases, or iterations promoting focus and timely decision-making.

Traceability: The ability to interrelate any uniquely identifiable software engineering artifact to any other, maintain required links over time, and use the resulting network to answer questions of both the software product and its development process.

Trend Analysis: A technique used to track and analyze the progress and performance of a process over time, identifying trends and potential issues (risks).

U

Use case: An analysis model that describes a flow of actor–system interactions and boundaries for those interactions including trigger, initiating, and participating actors, and preconditions and postconditions.

User Acceptance Testing (UAT): A phase in the project lifecycle where end-users test the system or product to ensure it meets their requirements and expectations.

User Story: Specifying software requirements in a brief statement.

V

Validation: Ensures that software being developed or changed satisfies functional and all other requirements.

Value Stream Mapping: Method adopted by Agile to analyze an entire chain of processes with goals of eliminating waste.

Variance: The difference between planned and actual values, such as cost variance (CV) or schedule variance (SV), used to assess project performance.

Velocity: A metric that measures the amount of work completed by the development team in a sprint or iteration, providing insights into the team's productivity and forecasting capabilities.

Verification: Ensures that every step in the process of building the software delivers the correct product.

W

Wireframes: Lightweight non-functional user interface design.

Work Breakdown Structure (WBS): A hierarchical decomposition of project deliverables into smaller, manageable work packages, facilitating planning and control.

Reference list

Furman, J. (2014) *The Project Management Answer Book*. Second edition. Berrett-Koehler Publishers.

Project Management Institute. (2015) *Business Analysis for Practitioners: A Practice Guide*. PMI.

Project Management Institute. (2017a) *Agile Practice Guide*. PMI.

Project Management Institute. (2017b) *The PMI Guide to Business Analysis*. PMI.

Project Management Institute. (2021) *A Guide to the Project Management Body of Knowledge PMBOK® Guide* 7th Edition. PMI.

Project Management Institute. (2022) *Process Groups: A Practice Guide*. PMI.

Wysocki, R. K. (2019) *Effective Project Management: Traditional, Agile, Extreme and Hybrid*. Eighth edition. Wiley.

Index

For Product Safety Concerns and Information please contact our
EU representative GPSR@taylorandfrancis.com Taylor & Francis
Verlag GmbH, Kaufingerstraße 24, 80331 München, Germany